[handwritten note at top] Xididio 231 — rethinkingw

8 *rejres class — colub working classes*

9 *gendered exist, Ren writers*

11 *how to date Harlem Ren*

12 *Ren as origin for vernacular — bont this quickly undermined —*
9 thorns, chesnutt — so not a
transition g who can modernism on

Women of the Harlem Renaissance *[cut as dff w/ periodization]*

14 *rhymes, 9 sexuality — cite this —*
+k/c blues tra a future more accomodating
space carved out for 9 — w/ let speell — 20

[margin left] + the blues singers

24 *Hurston Lt Bessie Smith?*

25 *+ home/racial identity*

28 *+ Harlem primitivism*

140 *cult richness orient against matterial poverty*

142 *vernacular as let art + & a mere attempt to render speech*
authnty of the word

145 *material legacy as origin for critique*

[margin left]
144-7
bio
plas, grin
o swats,
fieldwork w/ Boas
originates
stereotypes

Women of Letters

SANDRA M. GILBERT AND SUSAN GUBAR
General Editors

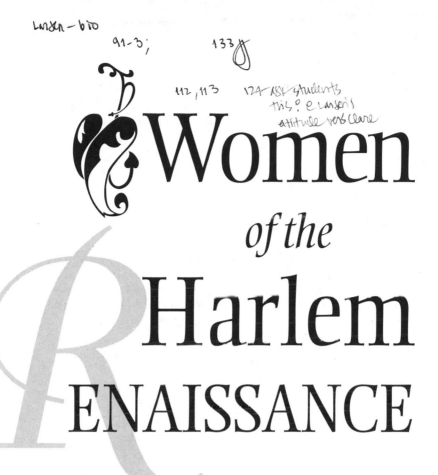

Women

of the

Harlem

ENAISSANCE

Cheryl A. Wall

Indiana University Press

Bloomington & Indianapolis

The paper used in this publication meets the minimum requirements
of American National Standard for Information Sciences—Permanence of Paper for
Printed Library Materials, ANSI Z39.48-1984.
⊛™
Manufactured in the United States of America

Library of Congress Cataloging-in-Publication Data

Wall, Cheryl A.
    Women of the Harlem renaissance /
    Cheryl A. Wall.
        p.   cm. — (Women of letters)
    Includes bibliographical references and index.
    ISBN 0-253-32908-6 (alk. paper). —
    ISBN 0-253-20980-3 (pbk. : alk. paper)
        1. American literature—Afro-American authors—
History and criticism.   2. Women and literature—
United States—History—20th century.
3. American literature—Women authors—History
and criticism.   4. American literature—20th century—
History and criticism.   5. Afro-American women—
New York (N.Y.)—Intellectual life.   6. Fauset,
Jessie Redmon—Criticism and interpretation.
7. Hurston, Zora Neale—Criticism and interpretation.
8. Larsen, Nella—Criticism and interpretation.
9. Harlem (New York, N.Y.)—Intellectual life.
10. Afro-Americans in literature.   11. Harlem
Renaissance.   I. Title.   II. Series: Women of letters
(Bloomington, Ind.)
PS153.N5W33   1995
810'.9'896073—dc20   95-3132

2 3 4 5 00 99 98 97 96

In Loving Memory of
My Parents

Rennie Strayhorn Wall
Reverend Monroe Wall

Contents

FOREWORD

"ON THE FIELD OF LETTERS"

Then Lady Reason . . . said, "Get up, daughter! Without waiting any longer, let us go to the Field of Letters. There the City of Ladies will be founded on a flat and fertile plain, where all fruits and fresh-water rivers are found and where the earth abounds in all good things. Take the pick of your understanding and dig and clear out a great ditch wherever you see the marks of my ruler, and I will help you carry away the earth on my own shoulders."

I immediately stood up to obey her commands and . . . I felt stronger and lighter than before. She went ahead, and I followed behind, and after we had arrived at this field I began to excavate and dig, following her marks with the pick of cross-examination.

So wrote Christine de Pizan at the beginning of the fifteenth century in *The Book of the City of Ladies*, the first feminist utopia. She was imagining a "strongly constructed and well founded" community which would be inhabited by "ladies of fame and women worthy of praise," and one of her speakers prophesied, "as a true sybil, that this City . . . will never be destroyed, nor will it ever fall, but will remain prosperous forever, regardless of all its jealous enemies. Although it will be stormed by numerous assaults, it will never be taken or conquered."

Founded on the "Field of Letters," the female literary tradition *is*, at least metaphorically speaking, the City of which Christine dreamed. Yet despite the optimism of this Renaissance woman's vision, most of its walls and towers disappeared from view for centuries. Even when its individual inhabitants gained recognition as "ladies of fame and women worthy of praise," the avenues they strolled and the cafes

where they conversed were largely forgotten. Louise Labé, Aphra Behn, Jane Austen, Charlotte Brontë, George Eliot, Emily Dickinson, Gertrude Stein, Virginia Woolf—all these figures were duly recorded in literary histories, but their membership in a "strongly constructed and well founded" community—a *female* literary community—went, until recently, unremarked. Only in the last two decades, in fact, have feminist critics established thematic and stylistic links between women from very different places and periods. Moreover, only in recent years have scholars begun "to excavate and dig" in a general effort to recover the lives and works of forgotten or neglected "women worthy of praise." Mary Wroth, Mary Astell, Charlotte Smith, Kate Chopin, Charlotte Perkins Gilman, Mary Elizabeth Coleridge, H.D., Zora Neale Hurston—all these figures had been relegated to the margins of literary history despite the fact that they too deserved places on the "fertile plain" where Christine's utopia was founded.

Our "Women of Letters" series is designed to introduce general as well as academic readers to the historical situations and aesthetic achievements of many of the citizens of Christine's City. The national, chronological, racial, ethnic, economic, and social circumstances of these women vary widely: the contours of the female literary community are complex, its highways and byways labyrinthine and often unfamiliar. Thus each volume in this series will pay close attention to what is in effect a single neighborhood. At the same time, precisely because the subject matter is complex, no volume in the series is intended as an encyclopedic guide to women writers in a particular place or period. Rather, each book will have a distinctive argument of its own, framed independently by its author; we should stress that we have not provided blueprints or even construction codes to the surveyors of our City, all of whom have used their own methodologies and developed their own critical perspectives. We do, however, expect that every volume will explore the individual situations of literary women in their specific cultural contexts.

Finally, we should emphasize that we see this series as part of an ongoing project in which a range of feminist critics, scholars, essayists, novelists, and poets have increasingly participated in recent years, one that seeks to understand the strictures and structures that

may have affected (or will affect) the lives and works of, in Christine's words, "ladies from the past as well as from the present and future." Such a project can by its nature come to no definitive conclusion, offer no single last word, because the City of Ladies, along with our vision of the Field of Letters, is growing and changing all the time. Furthermore, the heightened awareness on the part of current feminist theorists that such a City has always existed, and that it is ever evolving, has itself transformed our general sense of history, putting in question received modes of periodization, traditional genre hierarchies, and what once seemed to be universal evaluative criteria. Yet, diverse as may be the solutions posed by different thinkers to theoretical problems presented by contemporary literary study, we hope that in their various ways the volumes in this series will confirm Christine's faith that the City she helped found might be a "refuge" as well as a "defense and guard" against enemies and that it would be "so resplendant that you may see yourselves mirrored in it."

Composed c. 1405, Christine's utopia went unpublished and virtually untranslated for more than five centuries, a fact that gives special urgency to the admonitions with which she concluded her text. Indeed, her advice should still be taken to heart by those who study the field of women's letters: ". . . my dear ladies," Christine counseled, "do not misuse this new inheritance" but instead "increase and multiply our City." And as she herself knew, such a resettlement of the old grounds can best be accomplished by following "the marks" of Reason with "the pick of cross-examination."

Sandra M. Gilbert and Susan Gubar

A NOTE ON THE JOURNEY

"I sailed in my dreams to the Land of Night" begins a poem Gwendolyn Bennett published in 1927. Entitled "Fantasy," the poem depicts a dreamscape lit by "moon-veiled light," which reveals "the loveliest things," among them a peacock, "a garden of lavender hues," and most incredibly, a "dusk-eyed queen." The vision of this dark woman inspires the speaker's song. Ruler of the realm, the queen sits in the garden in an "amethyst chair," with her feet in "hyacinth shoes." But, even as she directs her song to the queen, the speaker hides herself behind a bush.

The concealed speaker may be read as a metaphor for the woman writer of the Harlem Renaissance: a woman "half in shadow," as Mary Helen Washington once described Zora Neale Hurston, a woman whose life and work had or have vanished from literary history. Many factors ranging from shifting literary tastes to changing notions of value to racism and sexism may account for the writer's neglect. Most puzzling are those instances where the writer, like Bennett's speaker, has collaborated in her disappearance. But her song lingers and testifies to her existence.

Inverting the symbolism of light and dark was a favorite strategy of Harlem Renaissance poets, notably Countee Cullen in whose anthology, *Caroling Dusk*, "Fantasy" was published. Rather than evoking ignorance or terror, the Land of Night is a place of magical beauty. One assumes the "dusk-eyed," "dark-haired" queen is also dark skinned, but since she commands a realm where racial designations are not required, the speaker need not say. The poet recognizes that

but a)
chapter
better no?
a while

such a realm is the stuff of fantasy, but the Land of Night remains the destination of the speaker's dreams. In the process of the journey, she achieves her voice.

Metaphors of travel recur in writing by Harlem Renaissance women. Despite the restrictions against it, they traveled widely in fact and in imagination. Bennett is an apt example. Born in Giddings, Texas, in 1902, she grew up in Washington, D.C.; Harrisburg, Pennsylvania; and Brooklyn, New York. After graduating from Pratt Institute in 1924, she joined the fine arts faculty of Howard University in Washington and then spent a year studying painting in Paris. Her letters home relate her encounters with George Antheil, Ernest Hemingway, and Henri Matisse. She allows that "this year in Paris has been a revelation to me so far as modern work is concerned," yet recognizes that in her own work she might not be a modernist. In one letter she promises a friend that she will make a camouflage cover so she can spirit his copy of *Ulysses* through the mails. In another she reports on the sensation made by the show *La Revue Nègre*, which starred Josephine Baker and which she had not seen. Despite her being in the vortex of modernist culture, the tone of her letters is more often melancholy than not. Young, black, and female, she finds Paris a cold and lonely place. She is relieved to get back to "the center of things," to New York and the Harlem Renaissance in June 1926.[1] The imaginary journey depicted in "Fantasy" seems altogether happier. But it was perhaps the product of her travels abroad. Certainly the palette of lavenders from which she painted the metaphors of the poem owes something to her study of art.

Back in the United States, Bennett joined African-American writers Countee Cullen, Langston Hughes, Zora Neale Hurston, Bruce Nugent, and Wallace Thurman, several of whom were modernists, to edit the now legendary little magazine *Fire!!* Her story "Wedding Day" was set in Montmartre and explored the persistence of U.S. racism among Americans abroad. Bennett took on numerous projects. She initiated what she dubbed a literary gossip column, "The Ebony Flute," in *Opportunity* magazine, a leading black journal, and penned reviews of major Harlem Renaissance novels, including Nella Larsen's *Quicksand* and Claude McKay's *Home to Harlem* for various publica-

tions. She continued to work as a visual artist as well, studying at the Barnes Foundation, teaching at Howard, and designing magazine covers. By decade's end, Bennett was married to a physician, and her travels were in support of his efforts to establish a practice, first in Florida and then in the New York suburbs.

Reflecting on her decisions ten years later, she lamented her failure to combine marriage and vocation. The failure was all the more painful because while she felt that she had given up her work "in order to assist my husband in having his chance," the sacrifice had been in vain. He was unable to achieve professional success in the depression. By 1938, she was widowed, left "out of touch with my own world and penniless."[2] She was undefeated, nevertheless, and quickly determined to re-create her world. But times had changed. Bennett could not resume her career as a poet or a painter. She became instead a respected art teacher and activist whose students and admirers included Jacob Lawrence, Charles White, and Romare Bearden.[3]

Gwendolyn Bennett's literary output was slender, and few of her paintings and drawings, save for the magazine covers, are extant, but her journeys reflect the sense of possibility, disappointment, and perseverance that characterize the lives of many of her sisters. Unlike Bennett, the three central figures of this study—Jessie Fauset, Nella Larsen, and Zora Neale Hurston—left substantial legacies. But their life journeys reflect a similar trajectory.

One goal of this book is to chart the journeys of the women of the Harlem Renaissance, those who succeeded in their artistic quests and some of those who did not. It examines both the journeys they traveled to create their literary texts and the journeys those texts depict. Although part of a series of books published under the rubric "Women of Letters," the subjects of this study are women of words and music. To be sure, the focus is more on novelists than performers, sonneteers rather than blues singers, but an underlying premise is that the journeys of literary women can be better understood in the context of the lives of African-American women artists, more broadly defined. A second goal is to locate their writing in multiple contexts. Not only does this study read their texts alongside each other's; it situates them in the traditions of African-American and American writing.

Writing this book has been a long journey for me, one that I could not have completed without the assistance of many generous colleagues and friends. I am fortunate beyond measure to have a community of colleagues at Rutgers University. For their endless encouragement and their willingness to read drafts of the manuscript, I thank Adrianne Baytop, Wesley Brown, Abena Busia, Donald Gibson, and Judylynn Ryan; I am grateful to Whitney Bolton, Gerald Davis, Marianne DeKoven, Elin Diamond, Francine Essien, Cora Kaplan, Renee Larrier, Carol Smith, Thomas Van Laan, and Deborah White as well. I owe a special debt to Barry V. Qualls, English Department Chair.

I have been gratified to meet, share ideas, and be inspired by an ever widening community of scholars and colleagues who are making journeys similar to my own. I thank first Mae Henderson and Deborah McDowell, who are always willing to take time from their own work to read and encourage mine. My ideas are in dialogue with theirs, as well as with those of Joanne Braxton, Hazel Carby, Barbara Christian, Thadious Davis, Frances Smith Foster, Paula Giddings, Sandra Govan, Daphne Duval Harrison, Karla Holloway, bell hooks, Lillie Howard, Gloria Hull, Nellie McKay, Valerie Smith, Hortense Spillers, Claudia Tate, and Mary Helen Washington. Like all Hurston scholars, I am indebted to Robert Hemenway for his pioneering research and his intellectual generosity. I thank Houston Baker for his careful reading of an early draft of this book. As the notes to this volume attest, I have learned much from my former Rutgers colleague, Arnold Rampersad. For his encouragement, I thank Joel Porte. Inevitably, I have omitted some whom I should mention; I can only hope they will read my oversight as a failure of memory rather than of gratitude.

A special note of thanks goes to those who shared with me their personal reminiscences of the women of the Harlem Renaissance: Sadie T. M. Alexander, C. C. Benton, C. E. Bolen, Ida Cullen Cooper, Arthur Huff Fauset, Pearl Fisher, Jean Hutson, Edith Peacock McDougald, Henry Lee Moon, Edward Murrow, Mathilda Clarke Moseley, Richard Bruce Nugent, Louise Thompson Patterson, Marjorie Silver, and Mazie O. Tyson. I am particularly grateful to the poet

Helene Johnson, who consented in 1987 to answer in writing my questions about her 1920s literary career.

For their invaluable assistance in locating correspondence, manuscripts, and other sources, I thank the staffs of the Amistad Research Center, New Orleans, Louisiana; the Trevor Arnett Library at Atlanta University; Ann Allen Schockley at the Fisk University Library Special Collections; Esme Bhan of the Moorland-Spingarn Research Center at Howard University; the James Weldon Johnson Collection, the Beinecke Rare Book Library at Yale University; the Carl Van Vechten Collection at the New York Public Library; the Harry Ransom Center for the Humanities at the University of Texas; the Zora Neale Hurston Collection, Rare Books and Manuscripts, the University of Florida; the Rollins College Archives, and the Schomburg Center for Research in Black Culture.

Finally, for being there at the beginning and the end of this journey, I am indebted to my family: my parents, to whose memory this book is dedicated; my late brother, Henry; my beloved sister, Gatsie; my niece, Monique; and my daughter, Camara Rose Epps, who remains my sweet inspiration.

ACKNOWLEDGMENTS

Grateful acknowledgment is made to the following: The Howard University Gallery of Art, Howard University, for permission to reproduce "Rise, Shine for Thy Light Has Come" by Aaron Douglas; the Moorland-Spingarn Research Center, Howard University, for permission to quote correspondence of Jessie Fauset and Zora Neale Hurston from the Alain A. Locke Papers; the Hal Leonard Corporation for permission to reprint the lyrics to "Young Woman's Blues" and "Dixie Flyer Blues" by Bessie Smith; the Joel E. Spingarn Papers, Rare Books and Manuscripts Division, The New York Public Library, Astor, Lenox and Tilden Foundations for permission to quote from letter of Jessie Fauset; the Carl Van Vechten Papers, Rare Books and Manuscripts Division, The New York Public Library, Astor, Lenox and Tilden Foundations for permission to quote from letters of Nella Larsen; Rutgers University Press for permission to reprint "Wishes" (Georgia Douglas Johnson), "Sonnet to a Negro in Harlem" (Helene Johnson), and "Oriflamme" (Jessie Fauset) from *Shadowed Dreams: Women's Poetry of the Harlem Renaissance*, Maureen Honey, ed., copyright © 1989 by Rutgers, The State University, reprinted by permission of Rutgers University Press; the Schomburg Center for Research in Black Culture for permission to quote from a letter of Zora Neale Hurston; the Schomburg Center for Research in Black Culture, The New York Public Library, Astor, Lenox and Tilden Foundations for permission to reproduce photographs of Regina Anderson Andrews et al., Gwendolyn Bennett, Jessie Fauset, Zora Neale Hurston, and Georgia Douglas Johnson; Mr. Chauncey

Spencer and the Anne Spencer Foundation for permission to reproduce the photograph of Anne Spencer; the University of Florida, Rare Books and Manuscripts Collection, for permission to quote from correspondence of Zora Neale Hurston; and the Yale Collection of American Literature, Beinecke Rare Book and Manuscript Library, Yale University, for permission to quote from letters in the James Weldon Johnson and Carl Van Vechten Collections, and for permission to reproduce the photograph of Nella Larsen from the Carl Van Vechten Collection and the photograph of Jessie Fauset, Langston Hughes, and Zora Neale Hurston from the Langston Hughes Papers.

One

On Being Young
–A Woman
–and Colored

When Harlem Was in Vogue[1]

Harlem, the fabled cultural capital of the black world, gave its name to the awakening among African-American artists during the 1920s and 1930s. The Harlem Renaissance with its outpouring of literature, art, and music defined a new age in African-American cultural history. To a degree, the difference was formal; artists' explorations of vernacular culture yielded new genres of poetry and music. The transformation was, however, larger than that. Proclaiming the advent of the "New Negro" in 1925, Alain Locke argued for a revised racial identity. The migration of thousands of blacks from the rural South to northern cities reflected and produced a renewed race consciousness and pride. As his lead essay in the landmark anthology *The New Negro* announced, African-Americans had achieved at long last a

+ Alain
Locke

spiritual emancipation, "shaking off the psychology of imitation and implied inferiority" that were slavery's legacy. Locke's essay, also titled "The New Negro," defined the terms in which the Harlem Renaissance has been discussed ever since.[2]

Writing that "the day of 'aunties,' 'uncles' and 'mammies' is equally gone" (5), Locke argued that the imposed and anonymous identities these appellations denoted belonged to the "Old Negro," a term that had always signified more myth than man, more formula than human being. As such, the Old Negro was properly the concern of the sociologist, the philanthropist, and the race leader. To see beyond the formula and to grasp the transformations that were occurring within the race required the insights of psychology. Locke's analysis shifted uneasily between individual and group characteristics.[3]

The New Negro was self-defined; indeed, "self" appears as a hyphenated prefix in the essay eleven times in thirteen pages. Self-understanding, self-direction, self-respect, self-dependence, and self-expression supplanted the self-pity that is the sole emotion to which the Old Negro seems to have been entitled. Ironically, the new positive sense of self was motivated by a "deep feeling of race," not altogether unlike the one that had inspired the self-hatred it replaced. But heretofore only a common condition and the fears and shame it produced had bound blacks to each other; now a common consciousness became "the mainspring of Negro life." To a degree only tacitly acknowledged in reality and in Locke's analysis, New Negro consciousness resulted from "an attempt, fairly successful on the whole, to convert a defensive into an offensive position, a handicap into an incentive" (11).

Perhaps more paradoxically, only by reclaiming a positive racial identity would the New Negro be empowered to struggle for his rights as an American. In this revision of Du Bois's famous formulation of African-American identity ("one ever feels his twoness,—an American, a Negro . . ."), Locke looks forward first to a suspension, then to a release, of the tension in which the terms of racial identity and deferred citizenship are held. The "forced attempt to build his Americanism on race values is a unique social experiment," Locke

conceded, and "its ultimate success is impossible except through the fullest sharing of American culture and institutions" (12). Having raised the question, Locke broached no answer regarding the dominant society's willingness to permit such participation.

To have done so would have undercut the optimism that defines Locke's tone in "The New Negro." However qualified his assertions and cautious his predictions for success, Locke was persuaded that the "New Negro" was indisputably a sign of progress. Evidence of progress was everywhere. The Great Migration was itself "a deliberate flight not only from countryside to city, but from medieval America to modern" (6). This interpretation was echoed elsewhere in Locke's volume in essays by Charles S. Johnson and James Weldon Johnson, although the former emphasized the economic motive rather than the "new vision" that Locke avers inspired black people's flight. Having escaped southern feudalism, blacks needed no longer to be preoccupied with racial problems; rather, in the process of their acculturation to urban life, they would wrestle with "the large industrial and social problems of our present-day democracy" (5).[4]

A symbol of their fitness for the task was Harlem, the physical embodiment of New Negro consciousness. Nothing symbolized better the black's entrance into the modern age.[5] Harlem was, or would be, the race capital, drawing blacks from throughout the African diaspora: from the American North and South, the West Indies, and even Africa itself. Not yet typical, Harlem was the augury of the future. It was the home alike of the cosmopolite and the peasant, the worker and the professional, the artisan and the artist, the preacher and the criminal. For the first time since the advent of slavery had ruptured the ancestral community, people of African descent could through their group expression—and the art it generated—forge a new unity.

Art inscribes the transformation from the Old Negro to the New. Like the migrant masses, "shifting from countryside to city," the young black artists "hurdle several generations of experience at a leap." The result was the "Negro Renaissance" that the volume named and proclaimed. Thinking perhaps of Countee Cullen's poem "Heritage," or Aaron Douglas's drawings and decorative designs, among other contributions to the volume, Locke considered New

Negro art reflective of the New Negro's "consciousness of acting as the advance-guard of the African peoples in their contact with Twentieth Century civilization" (14). But as important as the African re-connection was, and as necessary in Locke's view for the eventual rehabilitation of the image of the race, the immediate benefit of New Negro art did not depend on its content, but derived simply from the fact that it existed. The new generation of artists would be seen and cause the race to be seen not as society's wards, but as "collaborator[s]" and "participant[s]" in American civilization. With far more optimism than prescience, Locke concluded that "the especially cultural recognition [artists] win should in turn prove the key to that revaluation of the Negro which must precede or accompany any considerable further betterment of race relationships" (15).

Locke does not directly contemplate issues of gender in his essay, but with its imagery drawn from industry, technology, and war, and the extended citations of poems by Langston Hughes, Claude McKay, and James Weldon Johnson, the essay takes on a masculinist cast. Consider, for example, the terms in which Locke couches his analysis of the Negro's "racialism": "it is only a constructive effort to build the obstructions in the steam of his progress into an efficient dam of social energy and power" (12). Whatever had become of the "aunties" and "mammies," the New Negro seemed to be gendered male.[6]

In 1925, the same year that Locke published *The New Negro*, Marita Bonner published the essay "On Being Young—A Woman—and Colored"; her perspective was far less sanguine. Preponderant images in Bonner's essay evoke stasis and claustrophobia, not change and movement. Bonner addresses a female reader, presumably as well educated and refined as she, who cannot plan even an excursion from Washington to New York. To travel alone would offend propriety. "You decide that something is wrong with a world that stifles and chokes; that cuts off and stunts; hedging in, pressing down on eyes, ears and throat." This pressure is applied by blacks. Its intensity is explained by their sensitivity to whites' perception of black women as "only a gross collection of desires, all uncontrolled." The essay concludes with the speaker's comparing herself to a Buddha, "motionless on the outside. But on the inside?"[7]

Alain Locke, Harvard, Ph.D., Rhodes Scholar, and professor of philosophy at Howard University was a major figure in the Harlem Renaissance and beyond. He edited a special issue of *Survey Graphic* magazine, which in expanded form became the anthology *The New Negro*, widely accepted as the manifesto of the period. Shuttling regularly between Washington and New York, he was both a cultural critic and an intermediary between the community of black artists and the white patrons on whom several were dependent for financial support.

Marita Bonner, Radcliffe, B.A., short story writer and playwright, published her work regularly in black journals during the 1920s and 1930s. Her early stories were about "passing," but her more memorable pieces, written after she moved to Chicago in 1930, explored the dislocation southern blacks experienced in northern cities and the consequent disruption in family life, as well as the concomitant social, economic, and cultural conflicts between black migrants and European immigrants. Despite publishing more than a score of stories and several plays, Marita Bonner remained almost unknown until 1987, when her writing, including several never-before-published pieces, was first collected in book form under the title *Frye Street & Environs*. The publication was posthumous. Marita Bonner died in 1971. Bonner's notebooks had been kept by her daughter, who wrote the introduction to the volume.[8]

The contrast I want to develop is not between the careers of Alain Locke and Marita Bonner, two gifted individuals, but rather between the sense of the Renaissance that their two essays convey. The paradigm set forth in "The New Negro" overstates the case for male writers, but it contradicts the experience of many women. Although Harlem was "a magnet" for Negro intellectuals, as Langston Hughes put it, few of them were migrants from the rural South. Zora Neale Hurston is the outstanding exception. Unlike Hurston, the literary women were mostly northern born and bred; they knew little of rural southern black culture, and what they did know they had been trained to deny. Despite being born in Atlanta and rural Virginia respectively, Georgia Douglas Johnson and Anne Spencer wrote poetry that neither spoke in the accents of the region nor represented its social reality.

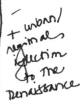

Marita O. Bonner, about 1928.
The Crisis.

Less innovative in form and less race conscious in theme, black women's writing generally does not seem to "hurdle several generations of experience in a leap."

Moreover, much of it, like Bonner's essay, reflects a strong sense that the stereotypes Locke dismissed continued to haunt. Many of these stereotypes, of course, were sexist as well as racist. But the heightened race consciousness of the period made issues of sexism

more difficult to raise. Paula Giddings points to "the rise and subsequent decline of Black militancy, and the decline of feminist consciousness after passage of the Nineteenth Amendment" as factors that made black women in the twenties subordinate their concerns about sexism.[9] Amid the effort to forge a revised racial identity, a woman who persisted in raising such concerns might see them dismissed as irrelevant or trivial; she might herself be perceived as disloyal to the race.

In her title, Bonner makes it plain, nevertheless, that she wants to claim a racial *and* a gendered identity. Writing from a position of privilege—the opening line of the essay reads "You start out after you have gone from kindergarten to sheepskin covered with sundry Latin phrases"—Bonner leaves no doubt that she knows exactly what she desires. First is a career, then time, (in her phrase the one real thing that money buys) and of course "a husband you can look up to without looking down on yourself." But only youth, Bonner quickly adds, makes things appear so simple. Race is the first problematic. Gender is the second. "All your life you have heard of the debt you owe 'Your People' because you have managed to have the things they have not largely had." The effort to discharge that debt entraps her in a doubled ghetto—the ghetto of race and the ghetto within the ghetto that is the gilded cage of the middle class. Bonner writes acidly of the endless rounds of parties and cards and poignantly of the metaphorical bars that prevent escape. The price of escape is the loss of respectability, which for the black woman Bonner apostrophizes carries a racial as well as an individual cost.

Bonner's attack on bourgeois vacuity might be considered in the context of another well-known essay of the Harlem Renaissance: Langston Hughes's often reprinted "The Negro Artist and the Racial Mountain." Published in 1926, just four months after his first volume, *The Weary Blues* appeared to mainly admiring reviews, Hughes's essay brims with the brio of youth and the authority of authorship. He chides his fellow poets and African-Americans in general for "their desire to pour racial individuality into the mold of American standardization." If, for Hughes, the empty and imitative culture of the black middle class represented "a very high mountain indeed for the would-

be racial artist to climb in order to discover himself and his people," there was a definite alternative.

> But then there are the low-down folks, the so-called common element, and they are the majority—may the Lord be praised! The people who have their hip of gin on Saturday nights and are not too important to themselves or the community, or too well wed, or too learned to watch the lazy world go round. They live on Seventh Street in Washington or State Street in Chicago and they do not particularly care whether they are like white folks or anybody else. Their joy runs, bang! into ecstasy. Their religion soars to a shout. Work maybe a little today, rest a little tomorrow. Play awhile. Sing awhile. O, let's dance![10]

Hughes leaves a term as problematic as "racial individuality" undefined. And, his representation of the poor veers close to familiar stereotypes. But however much he romanticizes the lives of the urban masses, Hughes as an artist is clearly revitalized by their example. Not only is he inspired by the specific vernacular forms—spirituals, blues, and jazz, which he goes on to cite and which become essential elements in his poetry—but by the broader example of an autonomous self-concept. He ends his essay with one of the most stirring declarations of artistic autonomy in African-American letters:

> We younger Negro artists who create now intend to express our individual dark-skinned selves without fear or shame. If white people are pleased we are glad. If they are not, it doesn't matter. We know we are beautiful. And ugly too. The tom-tom cries and the tom-tom laughs. If colored people are pleased we are glad. If they are not, their displeasure doesn't matter either. We build our temples for tomorrow, strong as we know how, and we stand on top of the mountain, free within ourselves. (309)

What a sharp contrast Bonner presents. Never referring to herself as an artist, but more and more often toward the end of her essay referring to women, Bonner concludes with a cluster of images of silence, entrapment, and paralysis. Rather than building a temple, she images herself a god, a Buddha, who, in an aside, she thinks perhaps is a woman. Like Buddha, she sits "still; quiet; with a smile, ever so slight, at the eyes so that Life will flow into and not by you. And you can gather as it passes, the essences, the overtones, the tints, the shadows; draw understanding to yourself" (7).

To a notable degree, Bonner's essay anticipates themes and metaphors that inform much of the fiction written by women during the Renaissance. Like several of the texts discussed in this study, particularly the novels of Jessie Fauset and Nella Larsen, Bonner's essay images the consequences of racial prejudice, gender bias, and class stratification in metaphors of confinement and self-division. It provides therefore a useful context in which to read black women's fiction. Moreover, "On Being Young—A Woman—and Colored" defines as well major contrasts between the Harlem Renaissance memorialized by male writers and that remembered by women.

The Harlem Renaissance was not a male phenomenon. A substantial number of literary women played significant roles: Jessie Fauset and Zora Neale Hurston were among the most prolific writers of the era; Nella Larsen's two novels, published in successive years, were widely read and reviewed; and a host of lesser-known poets published regularly in journals and magazines. Long ignored, their work is now being rescured from obscurity. Alongside such men as Langston Hughes, Sterling Brown, Countee Cullen, and Jean Toomer, black women writers struggled to claim their own voices. The voice of novelist and folklorist Zora Neale Hurston is by far the most distinctive; belatedly, she has become the first woman to be added to the list of "major" writers of the period.[11]

Hurston's recuperation intensifies the need to examine the lives and works of her female contemporaries: to identify common themes and metaphors in their writings, to determine who they were and where and how they lived, and to study the level of interaction among them. Hurston's achievement in *Their Eyes Were Watching God* and other books was the end result of a struggle enjoined by a generation of literary women to depict the lives of black people generally and of black women in particular, honestly and artfully.

As these facts are filled in, new questions are raised about the history of the Harlem Renaissance we have at hand. "Harlem Renaissance" is, of course, a contested term, with some scholars arguing that no renaissance occurred and others asserting that one did, but Harlem was not its principal setting.[12] Although some have sought to substitute labels such as "New Negro Renaissance" or "New Negro

Movement," which are in fact more accurate historically, no term has come close to displacing "Harlem Renaissance." When one focuses on the participation of women writers, the limitations of the term are clear. Few of the women lived in Harlem for any length of time. Jessie Fauset and Nella Larsen did. But Anne Spencer lived in Lynchburg, Virginia; for much of her life, Alice Dunbar-Nelson called Wilmington, Delaware, home. Indeed, Washington, D.C., where Georgia Douglas Johnson hosted her Saturday Nighters in her S Street home, rivals Harlem as a center for the female literary community. Marita Bonner, Alice Dunbar-Nelson, Jessie Fauset, Angelina Grimké, and Zora Neale Hurston (who spent much of the Renaissance on the road) all frequented Johnson's salon at one time or another.

When one considers women central to the movement, a more expansive definition is clearly preferable. Jessie Fauset and several other female poets wrote and published well before World War I. All of Hurston's novels and one of Fauset's were published after the start of the Great Depression. As a consequence, neither Huggins nor Lewis in their studies of the Harlem Renaissance considers Hurston's major fiction. With good reason, Gloria Hull has written that "women writers are tyrannized by periodization."[14] In an effort to undo that tyranny, this study will draw flexible perimeters.

Literary and cultural historians have debated the dates of the Harlem Renaissance as vigorously as its name. As Huggins observes, periodization is always a fiction of sorts; the moment a movement begins or ends can never be absolutely identified. So while some scholars apply the term strictly to the decade of the twenties, Huggins's dates are somewhat elastic: he refers to a "decade of change—roughly between World War I and the Great Depression." Rejecting the Harlem label, Arthur P. Davis and Michael Peplow date the New Negro Renaissance from 1910, the year in which the National Association for the Advancement of Colored People and its journal *The Crisis* were founded, to 1940, the year that saw the publication of Richard Wright's *Native Son* and preparation for World War II. Following David Lewis, Bruce Kellner marks the rise and fall of the Renaissance in terms of political events: the silent protest march through Harlem in 1917 and the Harlem riot of 1935.[13]

Convenient, if arbitrary, literary markers of the Harlem Renaissance are the publication of two significant anthologies: James Weldon Johnson's pioneering *The Book of American Negro Poetry*, first published in 1922, and the massive anthology *The Negro Caravan*, edited by Sterling Brown, Arthur P. Davis, and Ulysses Lee, issued in 1941. They are also useful measurements of the shifts in the critical status of women writers. Johnson presented the work of Jessie Fauset, Anne Spencer, and Georgia Douglas Johnson alongside that of their male peers, including Claude McKay, the poet whose lyrics seemed to the editor to break most dramatically with the past. Johnson's assessments of the women's poetry were measured but laudatory. Two decades later, *The Negro Caravan* included most of the women writers of the Harlem Renaissance, but the editors' introductory essays and headnotes often devalued their work. For example, after asserting that during and after World War I, "poetry by Negroes was a fairly sensitive barometer of [social] changes," the editors declare that "delicate lyricism was still present in the works of such poets as Georgia Douglass [*sic*] Johnson and Angelina Grimké, but in general a more vigorous, socially aware poetry was produced." Similarly, the paragraph that follows the description of Fauset's and Larsen's novels begins: "During the New Negro movement, many young artists stepped free from the 'problem,' or rendered it implicitly rather than explicitly. That is, they tried to be novelists rather than lecturers."[15] More comprehensive than any anthology of African-American literature before or since, *The Negro Caravan* not only offered an influential version of the canon of African-American literature, it set the tone for much of its criticism.

Despite the emphasis on novelty, the art of the Harlem Renaissance was not as new as its press agents claimed. Necessarily, much of the writing echoed precursor texts in both the African-American and Anglo-American traditions. What those echoes register is open to debate. Too often critics, like the editors of *The Negro Caravan*, have used them to relegate women writers to the "Rear Guard" of the movement, or to the so-called "Best Foot Forward" or "genteel" schools. I would suggest instead that black women's writing, like African-American writing generally, exists on a continuum.

Albeit in more subdued tones than their turn-of-the-century fore-mothers, the women of the Harlem Renaissance continued to explore creatively the implications of what Anna Julia Cooper called the "colored woman's" unique position. "She is confronted by both a woman question and a race problem," Cooper wrote in 1904, "and is as yet an unknown or an unacknowledged factor in both."[16] The same situation obtained two decades later, although the social climate was less congenial to feminism and more preoccupied with racial politics. As the vogue for Harlem subsided, black women writers probed the social and psychological meanings of their positionality in ever increasing depth. In so doing, they reappropriated "old" definitions of the race, "colored" for example, and figured new definitions of a racial "home."

Understandably, as the most visible promoter of the New Negro Renaissance, Alain Locke stressed the discontinuities between the race's past and present cultural contributions. Although the value of African-American folk art had too long been unacknowledged, Locke argued, it was important in ways that would be recognized eventually. More vital, however, was "a second crop of the Negro's gifts" (15). These gifts were the harvest of the younger generation. For Locke, the "New Negro" was synonymous with youth. He dedicated the volume to the "younger generation" and chose as its epigraph several bars of a spiritual: "O, rise, shine for Thy Light is a'coming." "Youth speaks," he wrote in another essay in the volume, "and the voice of the New Negro is heard" (47). Despite the emphasis on youth, however, many of the New Negroes were not young. Yet no man felt compelled to take years off his age. Several of the women did. Fauset, Georgia Johnson, and Larsen all invented later birth dates. Hurston, as usual, was the most dramatic; she was a full decade older than her contemporaries believed her to be.

Even those general conclusions that remain persuasive are complicated when the experience of women writers is added to the evidence. For example, the exploration of the vernacular—the incorporation of folk speech and folk forms such as spirituals, gospel, and blues—is a hallmark of the Harlem Renaissance. These forms are indeed the building blocks of African-American modernism. The hesitation of women to experiment with these forms is certainly a major reason so

many women have been consigned to the "Rear Guard" of the period. But, significantly, even when women writers like Hurston embrace these forms, they modify and extend them in what I consider to be gender-inflected ways.

Strikingly, even in *The New Negro* anthology, Elise Johnson McDougald offers a perspective not wholly congruent with editor Locke's. A social worker and educator, McDougald was one of eight female contributors and the only one to address gender issues.[17] Her essay, entitled "The Task of Negro Womanhood," is both a survey of black women's employment in the New York City labor force and a charge to successful black women to take up the cause of racial uplift. In both these aspects, the essay requires the reader to differentiate among black women, to see them and their problems individually, rather than en masse. McDougald delineated four groups of black women: a leisure group made up of the wives and daughters of successful men, the women in business and professions, the women in trades and industry, and the preponderance of black women "struggling on in domestic service"; the second, "a most active and progressive group," garnered most of her attention. To some degree, this emphasis mirrored McDougald's own class identity, but in keeping with the volume's theme, she used it to mark racial advancement as well.

Whatever progress life in New York afforded blacks, however, McDougald concluded that the race was free "neither economically, socially, or spiritually." One passage responds tellingly to Locke's declaration that two generations after slavery the New Negro could finally proclaim his spiritual emancipation. Demurely, McDougald recounts what she felt the African-American woman had to be emancipated from:

> She is conscious that what is left of chivalry is not directed toward her. She realizes that the ideals of beauty, built up in the fine arts, have excluded her almost entirely. Instead the grotesque Aunt Jemimas of the street-car advertisements proclaim only an ability to serve without grace or loveliness. Nor does the drama catch her finest spirit. She is most often used to provoke the mirthless laugh of ridicule; or to portray feminine viciousness or vulgarity not peculiar to Negroes. This is the shadow over her. (369–70)

Although McDougald was not a writer, her concerns were shared by some black women who were. As a group, the female poets bore the burdens of the past most visibly. Not only does their work project a version of the feminine ideal glorified in the dominant society's literature and culture, it reveals more than a little of the defensiveness that underlay the words of race women like Elise Johnson McDougald. What strikes many as their conservatism reflects in part a determination not to conform in even the slightest manner to hateful stereotypes. In a society reluctant to recognize sexuality in most women, black women were burdened with an almost exclusively sexual identity. Not surprisingly, then, in their poetry certain subjects, particularly sex, were taboo, and the language was mostly genteel.[18] Perhaps reflecting the restrictions on their mobility in life, these women took imaginative journeys in their verse.

Consider, for example, the poem "Wishes," first published in *The Crisis* in April 1927, by Georgia Douglas Johnson (1880–1966):

> I'm tired of pacing the petty round of the ring of the thing I
>   know—
> I want to stand on the daylight's edge and see where the sunsets go.
>
> I want to sail on a swallow's tail and peep through the sky's blue
>   glass.
> I want to see if the dreams in me shall perish or come to pass.
>
> I want to look through the moon's pale crook and gaze on the
>   moon-man's face.
> I want to keep all the tears I weep and sail to some unknown
>   place.[19]

After its brief opening reference to the world of social reality, "Wishes" transports the reader on a journey through a dreamscape. In contrast to the constraint and tedium of a life represented by "the petty round of the ring," the poem introduces images of physical and psychological freedom. Sailing through the limitless expanse of the sky, in flight as graceful as a bird, the speaker transcends time as well as space. From the point at which she stands "on the daylight's edge," she visualizes the night sky and her future. The desire simply to look seems as strong as the yearning to sail; it seems to underscore the extent of the speaker's current confinement. The nature of that con-

Georgia Douglas Johnson.
Schomburg Center for Research in
Black Culture, New York Public
Library.

finement is left undefined of course, as is the cause of her tears. Defined or not, the forces that confine her will keep the speaker earthbound. Her wishes will remain dreams deferred.

Like most of Johnson's poems, "Wishes" is written in a pattern of meter and rhyme that aspires to be as regular as the swallow's flight. Typical too are the use of the first person pronoun and the absence of racial references. The images please; they do not startle. "Wishes"

might be read as a pretty lyric expressing a speaker's longing to escape from some personal anguish. In the 1920s, Johnson's admirers eagerly compared her poems to those of Sara Teasdale, a then fashionable poet. That comparison is significant, if only to show how completely Johnson relied on the safest, least controversial models.

Yet the knowledge that Johnson is an African-American woman writing in 1927 invites alternative interpretations of "Wishes." For example, "the thing I know" and "all the tears I weep" might allude to the burdens of racism that are unceasing and inescapable except through flights of the imagination and the spirit. Johnson's journeys of the imagination, like the images of stasis and deferral in poems by Alice Dunbar-Nelson and Angelina Grimké might be read as statements of protest.[20]

The desire to invent another world in poetry is the topic of the aptly titled sonnet "Substitution," by Anne Spencer (1882–1975). In the sestet of the poem, as the speaker and auditor wrestle with philosophical imponderables, the addressee is lifted clear "Of brick and frame to moonlit garden bloom,—/ Absurdly easy now our walking, dear, / Talking, my leaning close to touch your face. / His All-Mind bids us keep this sacred place."[21] Neither racism nor any other problem will invade this idealized world where beauty and love flourish. The principle of substitution is central to Spencer's aesthetic.

In most of her poems, her speakers and subjects find at least momentary release from the real world of ugliness, impurity, and hate. For example, one of her freshest and most striking poems, "At the Carnival," offers a finely hued, evocative description of a tawdry street fair. Onlookers like "the limousine lady" and the "bull-necked man," "the unholy incense" of the sausage and garlic booth, the dancing tent where the "quivering female-thing gestured assignations," and the crooked games of chance combine to produce an atmosphere of unrelieved ugliness and depravity. Yet the possibility of beauty exists even here, in the person of a young, female diver, the "Naiad of the Carnival tank." Her presence transforms the scene.

Despite her work as a civil rights activist in Lynchburg, Virginia, Anne Spencer makes few references to race or racism in her poetry.[22] Gardens, by comparison, are a frequent setting and metaphor. (Along

Anne Spencer, age twenty-three.
Courtesy of Chauncey E. Spencer.

with her civil rights activism, the garden she cultivated was the chief source of her local fame.) In an autobiographical statement composed for Cullen's anthology, *Caroling Dusk*, Spencer proposes this artistic credo: "I write about the things I love. But have not civilized articulation for the things I hate. I proudly love being a Negro woman—it's so involved and interesting. *We* are the problem—the great national game of TABOO."[23] In fact, however, very few of Spencer's poems present black women as speakers or subjects. The juxtaposition of "Negro woman" and "TABOO" in her statement suggests a tension that Spencer never reconciles in her art.

An important exception is "Lady, Lady." Here Spencer subverts the class connotations of the title by applying it to a washerwoman. Investing her subject with a dignity the world denies, Spencer addresses the poem to her. The poem protests the exploitation of black women's labor, but in the final quatrain it does more: "Lady, Lady, I saw your heart, / And altared there in its darksome place / Were the tongues of flames the ancients knew, / Where the good God sits to spangle through."[24] Anticipating the impulse of present-day black women writers, Spencer not only claims nobility for her subject, she attributes the gift of poetry to her as well. That gift is stated; however, it is not represented in the poem. The subject, unlike Paule Marshall's "poets in the kitchen," does not speak. Indeed, Spencer's language and her allusions serve to hold both the subject's condition and her voice at a distance.

When one thinks of the women of the Harlem Renaissance, one does not think of Bessie Smith, Alberta Hunter, Ida Cox, or Ma Rainey. Yet these women achieved artistic maturity and enjoyed tremendous popular success during the same years that their literary sisters published their books, short stories, and poems. They too grappled with issues of identity, sought forms that could encompass the reality of their experience as black women, and struggled to control their own voices. Unlike the literary women, however, the blueswomen worked within an aesthetic tradition that recognized their right to speak. Free of the burdens of an alien tradition, a Bessie Smith could establish the standard of her art; in the process she would compose a more honest poetry than any of her literary sisters. Consider, for example:

Bessie Smith. Courtesy of the
Michael Ochs Archive.

"Young Woman's Blues"
Woke up this mornin' when chickens was crowin' for days
And on the right side of my pilla my man had gone away
By the pilla he left a note reading I'm sorry Jane you got my goat
No time to marry, no time to settle down
I'm a young woman and ain't done runnin' round
I'm a young woman and ain't done runnin' round.

Some people call me a hobo, some call me a bum
Nobody knows my name, nobody knows what I've done
I'm as good as any woman in your town
I ain't high yeller, I'm a deep killa brown
I ain't gonna marry, ain't gonna settle down
I'm gonna drink good moonshine and run these browns down.

See that long lonesome road
Lord, you know it's gotta end
I'm a good woman and I can get plenty men.[25]

The poem's language and references immediately define the speaker and her setting as black and southern. Her tone expresses a complex mixture of bravado and vulnerability. She is a woman who, though resigned to life's broken promises and disappointments, refuses to let them defeat her ("I'm a young woman and ain't done runnin' round"). Still, she is painfully aware of the judgement the ✓ world assigns: "hobo" is most assuredly a euphemism. In the end, she draws strength only from an implicit faith that the future is not as bleak as it appears—the "long lonesome road" must only *seem* endless. In the meantime, she boasts of her ability to attract new lovers; it is the only boast she has to make. She pledges to take joy where she can find it, and her words condemn a world that offers so little.

Musicologist Ortiz Walton has written that "the blues as lyric/sung poetry is a medium through which passes the essence of the life experience, both its travails and its ecstasies."[26] The truth of this statement is verified when one listens to Bessie Smith's recording of "Young Woman's Blues," which despite its lyric is anything but despairing. When she sings, "I'm gonna drink good moonshine and run these browns down," the listener recognizes that life's pleasures, though transitory, are nonetheless real.

According to one historian of the Great Migration, "migrants, though harsh in their criticism of the South and its peculiar form of 'justice,' nonetheless retained an attachment to and a longing for the region."[27] To Alain Locke, Charles Johnson, and James Weldon Johnson, the South represented political oppression, economic exploitation, and social degradation; to the blues singers and to the masses of black people who heard in their songs a reflection of their lives, the South was also home.[28]

In the year of the New Negro, Bessie Smith wrote and recorded a blues that registered the disillusionment with Harlem and other northern cities that many migrants had already begun to feel. "Dixie Flyer Blues" began in the imperative mood. In a spoken introduction, Smith commands the conductor to "hold that train." Then she sings:

> Hold that engine, let sweet mama get on board,
> Hold that engine, let sweet mama get on board,
> Cause my home ain't here, it's a long ways down the road.
>
> On that choo choo, mama's gonna find a berth,
> On that choo choo, mama's gonna find a berth,
> Goin' to Dixie land, it's the greatest place on earth.
>
> Dixie Flyer, come on and let your drivers roll
> Dixie Flyer, come on and let your drivers roll
> Wouldn't stay up North to save nobody's doggone soul.
>
> Blow your whistle, tell 'em Mama's coming too,
> Blow your whistle, tell 'em Mama's coming too,
> Take it up a little bit, cause I'm feelin' mighty blue.
>
> Here's my ticket, take it please conductor man,
> Here's my ticket, take it please conductor man,
> Goin' to my mammy, way down in Dixie land.[29]

Smith allows her listeners to fill in their own reasons for wanting to leave: low wages, poor working conditions, lack of opportunity, higher cost of living, or family problems.[30] But, whatever the specific complaint, the disenchantment with northern urban life was sufficiently widespread that Smith counted on an audience who would empathize with her lyrics. To be sure, the event the song depicted, the actual return to the South, was at best a fantasy for most of her northern listeners; at worst, it was a nightmare. But many of them,

like the singer's persona, were linked to the South by family and communal ties. Claude McKay's title *Home to Harlem* notwithstanding, when asked where "home" was, black New Yorkers were more likely to name a southern town than give a street address in Harlem.

In "Sonnet to a Negro in Harlem," Helene Johnson (1907–) expresses this sense of emotional displacement. She writes in the octave:

> You are disdainful and magnificent —
> Your perfect body and your pompous gait,
> Your dark eyes flashing solemnly with hate;
> Small wonder that you are incompetent
> To imitate those whom you so despise —
> Your shoulders towering high above the throng,
> Your head thrown back in rich, barbaric song,
> Palm trees and mangoes stretched before your eyes.[31]

Rather than blaming the migrant for his failure to adapt to the requirements of urban life and granting him the right to his anger as well as his pride, the speaker concludes exultantly, "You are too splendid for this city street!" The home the Boston-born poet evokes through her references to palm trees and mangoes is more likely Africa than the American South, however. In this respect, the sonnet belongs to a cluster of poems including Cullen's "Heritage," Waring Cuney's "No Images," Claude McKay's "Africa," and Gwendolyn Bennett's "To a Dark Girl." Yet in other poems, Helene Johnson is more likely than any of these poets to treat the African re-connection with an irony that problematizes, even as it affirms, it.

Born in Harlem to southern migrants in 1924, James Baldwin once told an interviewer, "I am, in all but in technical fact, a Southerner. My father was born in the South—my mother was born in the South, and if they had waited two more seconds I might have been born in the South. But that means I was raised by families whose roots were essentially southern rural. . . ."[32] Members of Baldwin's parents' generation established social organizations in the North that maintained relationships among migrants premised on links to communities in the South. They founded new chapters of the lodges, fraternal and sororal organizations that had flourished "down home." In their churches, they preserved the ceremonies and rituals, the ideals, and the vision

Gwendolyn Bennett.
Schomburg Center for Research in
Black Culture, New York Public
Library.

that had sustained them in the past. On a more practical note, they exploited their nostalgia to raise funds for building churches; one common gambit was a rally of the states in which, for example, the Virginia club and the Georgia club might vie for first place. Entrepreneurs—from chefs to morticians—attempted to capitalize on the migrants' nostalgia for their southern homes. Not only did cafes specialize in southern "barbeque," one Harlem undertaker advertised his establishment as "the Carolina Chapel."

To claim a southern home without enumerating the factors that mitigated against the claim could be problematic, however, even in a three-minute blues record. Not even Bessie Smith can quite pull off the line about Dixie land being "the greatest place on earth." Yet, despite the strong overlay of commercialism in the spoken introduction, the trite sound effects imitating the train whistle and roar, and the untroubled references to the stereotypes of "Mammy" and "Dixie" within a single line, "Dixie Flyer Blues" might have connected with its audience on a more profound level.[33] Its most resonant line— "Cause my home ain't here, it's a long ways down the road"—comes directly from the storehouse of blues and spiritual lyrics. Its theme, that in leaving the South blacks might have left the closest thing to a home they would know in the United States, looks forward to the writing of Zora Neale Hurston.

The raw material from which Bessie Smith refined her art was alien to most of the women of the Harlem Renaissance. Almost to a woman, they abhorred the raunchiness so much a part of Bessie's public persona and, unlike her audiences, could hear nothing of the spirituality or the art in her work. Hurston was the one literary woman who was free to embrace Bessie's art and who was also heir to the legacy she evoked.

Hurston's meditation on racial identity, "How It Feels to Be Colored Me," was published in May 1928. The title, with its colloquial tone and emphasis on the personal, differentiates it from the formal essays Locke anthologized in *The New Negro*. The contrast is reinforced when Hurston opens her essay with a joke: "I am colored but I offer nothing in the way of extenuating circumstances except the fact that I am the only Negro in the United States whose grandfather on the mother's side was *not* an Indian Chief."[34] The joke is aimed both at those whites who would assume that blackness is a condition requiring some apology or explanation and at those blacks, almost certainly including race-conscious New Negroes, who want it understood that they are not *merely* black. Hurston claims her color gladly.

The essay's next paragraph, with its striking assertion—"I remember the very day that I became colored"—reveals Hurston's understanding that racial identity is not grounded in biology; it is socially constructed. Racial identity for African-Americans might be constructed in response to the harsh racism of the deep South, manifested in the system of legal segregation, or it might be shaped by the more benign racism expressed through and stimulated by the vogue for the Negro, a climate that was both supportive of and crippling to artistic expression by blacks. "How It Feels to Be Colored Me" explores a third possibility.

Hurston's often-cited declaration not to be embittered by either form of racism—her refusal to be "tragically colored"—is premised on her assertion of a prior identity that was constituted before she encountered racism, an identity she achieved at "home." Out of this prior identity, Hurston drew the strength to acknowledge, even to celebrate, racial and cultural differences, while affirming the commonalities that underlay them.

Home for Hurston was Eatonville, Florida, the all-black town that became the privileged site of her fiction. According to the essay, the only white people in Eatonville were those passing through, and of these only the Northerners were worth watching. The townspeople, Hurston asserts, "got just as much pleasure out of the tourists as the tourists got out of the village." The townspeople and their chronicler, Hurston, derive the confidence that makes this reciprocity possible from their sense of being "at home."

For herself, Hurston affirms the identity of "Everybody's Zora"—an identity that makes her one with the community. Yet she asserts some distance from it as well. For example, she acknowledges a certain uneasiness with the community's values—the townspeople, she charges, "deplored any joyful tendencies in me"—but she was "their Zora nevertheless" (153). In her adult recollection, the "everybody" who

claimed her extends to include white tourists motoring through, guests in the nearby hotels, and "the county." While the blacks listened for free, she recalls whites giving her "small silver" for "speaking pieces," singing, and dancing. The offer of money is a gesture that strikes the child Zora as strange as well as generous, because performing made her so happy that she needed "bribing to stop." Retrospectively, her uneasiness with her black neighbors stemmed perhaps in part from their failure to share her joy in performances that partook of a communal cultural heritage—the heritage to which Hurston was to devote her subsequent career to reclaiming.[35] Almost certainly, the joy she remembers here is an impetus to that reclamation.

Describing as a "sea change" her relocation from Eatonville to Jacksonville, Florida, Hurston defines its most traumatic aspect: "I was not Zora of Orange County any more, I was now a little colored girl. I found it out in certain ways. In my heart as well as in the mirror, I became a fast brown—warranted not to rub nor run" (153). A fixed racial identity imposed from outside becomes stigmatized inwardly as well. The persona who reveled in the possibility inscribed by the adjective "colored" becomes vulnerable to the kind of negative self-definition that the New Negro movement was striving to displace.

Tellingly, this recognition of a diminished sense of self in racial terms also occasions the first explicitly gendered reference in the essay. "Zora of Orange County" becomes a "little colored girl" after changes occurred in her family when she was thirteen. In her autobiography, *Dust Tracks on a Road*, Hurston identifies those changes, unspecified here, as the death of her mother and the dissolution of her family home. Although the essay emphasizes the impact of her delayed racial awareness, Hurston's sense of constricted possibilities may have derived as well from the experience of puberty and the recognition of the limitations and dangers to which her emergent womanhood made her vulnerable. Indeed, especially given the unmentionability of "the certain ways" through which she became aware of her gender identity, the reference to "fast brown" might be heard as a muted echo of Bessie Smith's phrase in "Young Woman's Blues."

[handwritten annotation at top:] but how is this told given the wall points nt, it's not emphasis on Eatonville as an historical fre cation

What makes the tone and texture of Hurston's meditation on identity so different from the others considered here is the sense of home
that gives rise to an identity that is not constructed in response to
racism and sexism. Her term for it is the "unconscious Zora of Eatonville before the Hegira." In his article "The Trope of a New Negro
and the Reconstruction of the Image of the Black," Henry Louis
Gates argues that "the register of a New Negro was an irresistible,
spontaneously generated black and sufficient self. A rhetorical figure
and a utopian construct, the term New Negro signified 'a black
person who lives at no place and at no time.'"[36] I would argue that
partly in response to this term, Hurston invents a mythic autobiographical self that she derives from her ability to claim a very specific
place, her "home," Eatonville.[37] Moreover, unlike even those unre-
constructed black people who claimed their homes in the South with
a deep-rooted ambivalence, Hurston seemed to claim hers with an
uncomplicated pride. Eatonville was, as she never tired of pointing
out, the first all-black town incorporated in the United States, "the
first attempt at organized self-government on the part of Negroes in
America" (*Dust Tracks*, 3). Hurston roots her literary persona in this
historical anomaly.

Wherever she journeyed, the essay implies, Hurston was able to
draw on this heritage and find the strength to remain herself. At least
on occasion, she could reclaim or, as she prefers, "*achieve* the unconscious Zora of Eatonville before the Hegira" (my emphasis). Her
flight takes her eventually to New York—to Barnard, to "Harlem
City," and to the site that becomes the essay's symbolic antithesis of
home, the New World Cabaret. The cabaret is a basement speakeasy,
complete with a jazz orchestra and jazz waiters, perhaps like those
who made Smalls' Paradise a favorite twenties haunt. There, sitting
with a white companion and listening to the music's "narcotic harmo-
nies," Hurston's "color comes."

This passage depicts a second moment of cultural performance
and cultural exchange in the essay. This time Hurston is spectator,
rather than performer, and African-American music and dance have
become commodities in the cultural marketplace of New York. The
description of the jazz performance relies on jungle metaphors, as

does the description of the writer's response: "I dance wildly inside myself; I yell within, I whoop; I shake my assegai above my head, I hurl it true to the mark *yeeeeooww!*" (154). When the song ends, she "creeps back slowly to the veneer we call civilization," and her white friend, whose race has made her sharply aware of her own, sits "motionless in his seat, smoking calmly" (154).[38]

The scene Hurston draws is a staple in the literature of the Harlem Renaissance and in the popular mythology of the 1920s, the Jazz Age. For those white Americans with the time, money, and sophistication to make the trip, Harlem at night seemed a world apart. In contrast to their own world, discipline, hard work, and frugality were counterfeit coin in the realm of imaginary Harlem. Nothing symbolized its otherness more than the cabaret.

Fiction writer and physician Rudolph Fisher satirized the vogue for Harlem night life in a 1927 essay, "The Caucasian Storms Harlem." Tongue in cheek, he describes his return to his old stomping ground after a five-year absence, and finding no familiar faces, he concludes: "The best of Harlem's black cabarets have changed their names and turned white." He notes the popularity of black art on Broadway, on the concert stage, and even in the galleries of the Metropolitan Museum: "Negro stock is going up, and everybody's buying." The fad for the cabaret remains peculiar. Reflecting on the spectacle of whites doing black dances in Harlem nightclubs while blacks watch, he concludes: "This interest in the Negro is an active and participating interest. It is almost as if a traveler from the North stood watching an African tribe-dance, then suddenly found himself swept wildly into it, caught in its tidal rhythm."[39]

Metaphors of travel and exploration, primitivism and civilization were intrinsic to the mythology. Commenting sardonically on its convenience, Nathan Huggins describes Harlem night life as "merely a taxi trip to the exotic for most white New Yorkers." Once there they listened to "jazz, that almost forbidden music," in cabarets decorated in tropical and jungle motifs or in establishments, like the Cotton Club, that evoked the old plantation. For these Harlem night visitors, "it was a cheap trip. No safari! Daylight and a taxi ride rediscovered New York City, no tropic jungle. There had been thrill without danger. . . ."[40]

As Hurston's description makes clear, blacks could take the same trip, although the price of the ticket was higher. The psychic journey required a denial of the reality they could not escape when the music ended. Familiar as they were with actual Harlem, they recognized that survival there depended on work and sacrifice. Indeed, according to inveterate Harlem booster James Weldon Johnson, "of a necessity the vast majority of [Harlemites] are ordinary, hard-working people. . . . Most of them have never seen the inside of a nightclub."[41] Whether they had or had not, most knew that the poshest cabarets earned big money for gangsters, who lived far from Harlem. They knew no tourist would trade his position of privilege for the supposed license of the Harlem dandy. They knew as well that black women on or off the chorus line might become objects of exchange between the tourist and the dandy. Most important, they knew that New York was no more exotic or primitive uptown than it was down.[42]

On one level, Hurston seems, through her exaggerated metaphors, to parody the myth of exotic primitivism. On another, she insists that the power of the music, so often expropriated to propel the myth, is genuine. But its power is undefinable and unspeakable—at least in the context in which it is heard. Extravagant as her response to the music is, it is wholly internalized. In fact, the key to survival in the mecca of the New Negro seemed to be to play the part the cultural script assigned and keep one's feelings safely hidden.

But, in contrast to Marita Bonner's persona, Hurston's does not lose access to the feelings she suppresses. Instead of imaging herself a Buddha, she can "set [her] hat at a certain angle and saunter down Seventh Avenue, Harlem City. . . . The cosmic Zora emerges" (154–55). At these moments, she contends, she has no race. Rather than the Du Boisian conflict between one's identity as an American and a Negro, she draws the distinction between a racial or "colored" identity and "me." "Me" is at one point associated with the "eternal feminine," but its definition is never fixed.

Racial identity, expressed through the metaphor of a brown bag, becomes merely the container that holds a multiplicity of elements out of which an individual identity is constituted. Instead of a divided self, Hurston images an inner space filled with such disparate pieces as

"a first-water diamond, an empty spool, bits of broken string, a key to a door long since crumbled away . . ." (155). This jumble of elements, "both priceless and worthless," both unique and interchangeable, constitutes a self that is at once individual and transcendent. Thus, "cosmic Zora" shares a bond with humanity ("other bags, white, red and yellow"), yet remains unmistakably herself.

In "How It Feels to Be Colored Me," Hurston demonstrates the utility of the biomythography she continued to elaborate throughout her life. What Claudine Raynaud writes of Audre Lorde's "biomythography," *Zami: A New Spelling of My Name*—"the reflexiveness and the individualism of the autobiographical gesture give way to the construction of a mythic self"—is also true of several of Hurston's texts, including the volume of folklore, *Mules and Men*, and *Dust Tracks on a Road*.[43] Like Lorde, Hurston fuses the three modes of consciousness that critic Chinosole discerns in *Zami*: collective memory rendered through myth and legend (for Hurston, read "folklore"), the memory of personal experience, and the memory accessible through dream (for Hurston, read "spiritual experience").[44] Unlike Lorde, Hurston does not develop her biomythography in a single text, but produces it in fragments throughout her oeuvre; it informs her fiction as well.

Its earliest expression was "How It Feels to Be Colored Me." Even as Hurston wrote the essay for a white periodical in 1928—re-creating the situation that obtained in her girlhood—being paid by whites for her words, her sense of her mythic self, the "cosmic Zora," was strong enough that she believed she could dictate the terms of exchange. It was out of this self-authorizing posture that she could proclaim:

> BUT I AM NOT tragically colored. There is no great sorrow dammed up in my soul, nor lurking behind my eyes. I do not mind at all. I do not belong to the sobbing school of Negrohood who hold that nature somehow gave them a lowdown dirty deal and whose feelings are all hurt about it. . . . No, I do not weep at the world—I am too busy sharpening my oyster knife."[45]

Despite the earlier references to sauntering down Seventh Avenue, by the time this essay was published, Hurston was shucking oysters in rural Florida, where she had begun to collect the folk tales, songs, and sermons that would eventually constitute the volume *Mules and Men*. It was as if she heeded the lyrics of "Florida Bound Blues," a song recorded by Bessie Smith that began, "Goodbye North, Hello South, / Goodbye North, Hello South, / It's so cold up here that the words freeze in your mouth."[46] Although she would return to New York intermittently over the next two decades, she wrote and lived most of her life in her native state. There she was, figuratively and literally, at home.

The idea of "home" has a particular resonance in African-American expressive tradition, a resonance that reflects the experience of dispossession that initiates it.[47] In the spirituals, blacks had sung of themselves as motherless children "a long way from home." Images of homelessness—souls lost in the storm or the wilderness—abound. In the absence of an earthly home, the slaves envisioned a spiritual one, a home over Jordan, for example; or they laid claim defiantly to "a home in dat rock." As Melvin Dixon observes, the images of home, self, and freedom in the spirituals reflect a manipulation of language that "thwarts the dehumanizing effects of slavery by depicting alternative spaces and personae slaves could assume" (14). "This reconstruction of self and space" through language is a hallmark of twentieth-century secular traditions as well. Hurston's contemporary, Jamaican expatriate Claude McKay entitled his memoir *A Long Way from Home*. The efforts to claim Harlem as home found voice in texts such as James Weldon Johnson's *Black Manhattan* and McKay's *Harlem: Negro Metropolis*. In the political realm, Marcus Garvey sought through his visionary rhetoric to inspire a New Negro who would fight to redeem Africa, the ancestral home.

Hurston was well aware of this legacy, as her manipulations of the Eatonville setting in her nonfiction and novels make clear.[48] But her relationship to "home" is problematic. Whether in the process of documenting the expressive traditions of her people or considering the usefulness and implications of those traditions for her own writing, or in the physical reencounter with the landscape of her childhood, Zora Neale Hurston confronted anew the ways in which women were silenced in the performances she recorded, the ways in which sexism in the African-American community stunted female (and male) poten-

tial, and perhaps the ways in which she had herself first become aware she was a little colored girl. She did not deny the impact of racism on the community, but she was iconoclast enough to find it most cruelly manifested in African-Americans' adoption of the inferior values of the dominant culture.

For women, feminist theorists Biddy Martin and Chandra Mohanty argue, home often offers only "an illusion of coherence and safety, based on the exclusion of specific histories of oppression and resistance, the repression of differences even within oneself."[49] But for cultural and personal reasons, home was too valuable an illusion for Hurston to relinquish. What she attempted to do instead was to reconstruct a home in language that acknowledged but did not dwell on the history of racial oppression, counted African-American creative expression as a powerful mode of resistance, and fostered the recognition of differences without and within oneself. Hers was an effective solution to the literary dilemma posed by being young, a woman, and colored when Harlem was in vogue.

Two

Jessie Redmon Fauset

Traveling in Place

In January 1925, Jessie Fauset, who had traveled extensively throughout Europe, broadened the circuit of her travel to include northern Africa. Reporting in *The Crisis*, she wrote with passion about the thrill of being, even if for only a few days, resident in "Dark Algiers the White," a dweller in Africa itself. As Fauset explained, "White Algiers," the epithet given the city by the French, refers to its topography: "the city rises white on tiers up the side of a hill, many hills"; one might take "Dark Algiers" to be a reference to its people.[1] Describing her arrival, Fauset wrote that from its harbor, the city offered a vista of brown and black faces, red fezzes, white turbans, white burnouses, and red blanket robes. "All the strangeness and difference of that life, which starting far, far in the interior of Africa yet breaks off so abruptly at the southern edge of the Mediterranean, rose instantly to meet us" (255). In an age when the idea of Africa enthralled the imaginations of many black American intellectuals, Jessie Fauset was one of a handful (along with W. E. B. Du Bois, Langston

Hughes, and Claude McKay) who actually saw the continent face to face.[2]

To Fauset, the images Algiers created were unforgettable, though their meanings were difficult to decipher. Skillfully developing her cinematic metaphor, Fauset freezes a series of scenes. At one moment a group of men reminds her of Old Testament patriarchs. A couple comes into view and Fauset thinks the silent woman is "like an automaton besides her lord." An old woman looks out above her veil and seems to Fauset "the very savor of the East." Though her descriptions of people can be condescending and even racist, Fauset most often maintains the perspective of respectful outsider.[3] At the least, she is sensitive enough to recognize that to the Algerians she is "equally exotic."

The climax of the trip and of the essay is Fauset's solitary exploration of the city's most fabled quarter, the Kasbah. Vividly, Fauset describes first her ascent to "The Court of Miracles," where beauty and suffering, the "farthest possibilities of mankind," meet and then her descent to the quarter with its pattern that an "inexperienced eye can glimpse but cannot follow." Unable to find her way, she grows increasingly fearful but restrains "an impulse to run," walking "very erectly instead." When she returns the next day with her two traveling companions (one of whom, Laura Wheeler, illustrated *The Crisis* article), they meet a French woman who warns them that the quarters are too dangerous to visit without an escort. Fauset's courage is totally undermined. She will not enter the Kasbah again except under the French woman's guidance. The experience of difference, now carefully mediated, is safe. Indeed, in the home of the guide's Algerian friend, they "exchange polite and admirable banalities after the fashion of ladies calling the world over" (18). Fauset's title, "Dark Algiers the White," takes on a painfully ironic meaning.

Analogically, Jessie Fauset was an unusually gifted, intellectually curious woman who was bound by cultural dictates. Frequently drawn to new territory, in art as in life, she was occasionally brave enough to enter it. But she was unlikely to remain once she realized where she was. The potential risk was too great, as much to the image she reflected as a proper Negro woman as to herself. The lessons of the Methodist parsonage of her childhood and those of the elite universities in which she studied made her a reluctant explorer. From this distance, it is perhaps too easy to see those instances where Jessie Fauset's courage failed her. It is important to acknowledge the ways it did not. After all, how many other American women of her generation had even the desire to traverse the Kasbah? How many fewer still could have found the means to make the journey?

If Fauset's spirit of adventure was circumscribed by the demands of propriety, if her freedom of expression was checked by restraint, she was eager to encourage exploration and innovation in others. In his popular memoir, *The Big Sea*, Langston Hughes praised Jessie Fauset at *The Crisis*, along with Charles Johnson at *Opportunity* and Alain Locke in Washington, as the three people "who midwifed the so-called New Negro literature into being. Kind and critical—but not too critical for the young—they nursed us along until our books were born." David Lewis adds Walter White, James Weldon Johnson, and Casper Holstein to the list of essential mentors, then concludes that "for honesty and precocity," Jessie Fauset's influence upon the Harlem Renaissance "was probably unequalled. . . . There is no telling what she would have done had she been a man, given her first-rate mind and formidable efficiency at any task."[4]

A woman, Fauset occupied a much less powerful position than any of her male counterparts. From 1919 to 1926, she was literary editor of *The Crisis*. She assumed that position after fourteen years of high school teaching in Baltimore and Washington, and when she left the journal she returned to the classroom. Even with her degrees from Cornell and the University of Pennsylvania, she had no other options. By contrast, several of the men who shaped the Renaissance held the most influential posts then available to black men in the United States; the others had money or access to it.

For most of the century, W. E. B. Du Bois had been recognized as perhaps the preeminent black American intellectual; only racism kept him from being regarded as the eminent *American* intellectual he was. Du Bois had founded *The Crisis*, the official journal of the NAACP and the most widely read black periodical of the era, in 1910. Like Du Bois, a pioneering sociologist, Charles Johnson edited

Opportunity, the house organ of the Urban League; *Opportunity* would surpass *The Crisis* in literary influence only after Fauset resigned. Walter White and James Weldon Johnson were high-ranking officials in the NAACP. Ironically, Fauset had once been considered for the post of chief administrator ("Secretary" was the organization's title) White held in the 1920s.[5] Alain Locke, despite a modest salary as a university professor, wielded influence through the access he provided to Charlotte Mason, a patron to many black writers including Hughes and Zora Hurston. Holstein provided money too; the Harlem numbers boss bankrolled the *Opportunity* literary awards.

Fauset had no money of her own; neither did she have a wealthy benefactor. Unlike White and the two Johnsons, she had no entree to prestigious publishing houses. As literary editor of *The Crisis*, however, she could put a writer in print. As he gratefully remembered, Jessie Fauset was the first to publish Langston Hughes; at her behest, he became "virtually the house poet of the most important journal in black America." Nella Larsen made her first appearance with an article, "Scandinavian Games," under Fauset's auspices. Even before joining *The Crisis* staff, Fauset had acted as a mentor. In *Caroling Dusk*, Georgia Douglas Johnson recounted that Fauset "very generously helped her to gather together material for her first book." Later, Fauset quoted Johnson's poem "The Supplicant" in her novel *Plum Bun*. Fauset encouraged the careers of numerous writers, including Countee Cullen, Anne Spencer, and Jean Toomer. She was particularly supportive of women, both literary and visual artists. Indeed, she was at the center of a network of black women cultural workers.[6]

During the heyday of the Harlem Renaissance, Jessie Fauset was herself the most prominent black woman writer. She published poems, reportage, reviews, short stories, and translations. In the early twenties, it was a rare issue of *The Crisis* that did not carry the Fauset byline. More impressively still, she published four novels in less than ten years. In so doing, Jessie Fauset became one of the most prolific writers of the Renaissance, male or female. She is now among the least respected.[7] Fauset's critics are correct when they identify such weaknesses in her novels as melodramatic plots, flat characterizations, and stilted prose. But these flaws exist in varying degrees.

Jessie Fauset.
Schomburg Center for Research in
Black Culture, New York Public
Library.

At their best, Fauset's fictions illuminate the ways in which race, gender, and class construct and constrain identity. As she explained in the foreword to *The Chinaberry Tree*, she represented in her fiction those "breathing-spells, in-between spaces where colored men and women work and love." At home, "colored" people are "not so vastly different from any other American, just distinctive."[8] These "breathing-spells" are in some ways comparable to Hurston's renderings of the lying sessions on the store porch in Eatonville. In *Their Eyes Were Watching God*, Hurston refers to those porch sitters who "had been tongueless, earless, eyeless conveniences all day long" but in the evening cease to be mules and become men and women (1). For Hurston, "in-between" spaces like the store porch are inscribed by cultural difference; Fauset emphasizes commonality. Like her essay "Dark Algiers the White," Fauset's fiction often works to deny the difference that is its most promising subject. In the end, the novels' too-easy universalism is the clearest evidence of the constraints that constructions of race and gender impose upon Fauset's work.

Although she is often identified as the child of an old Philadelphia family, Jessie Fauset was born on 27 April 1882, in Fredericksville, New Jersey, then a hamlet in rural Camden County, now incorporated into the town of Lawnside. Perhaps because she left it so early in life, Jessie Fauset never spoke of her birthplace, preferring to foster the belief that she was a Philadelphian. Had she remained in Fredericksville, she might have been nurtured in the all-black settlement of Snow Hill, where her father, Reverend Redmon Fauset, pastored the Mt. Pisgah African Methodist Episcopal Church. Also known as Free Haven, Snow Hill was founded by Quakers to provide refuge for escaped slaves. The family moved back to Philadelphia when Jessie was a young child, and it was left to Zora Hurston to celebrate in literature the psychic freedom a black child growing up in an all-black environment could enjoy. Jessie grew up instead in what she termed "a distinctly white neighborhood," and the loneliness racism imposed from without was intensified by the series of losses within the Fauset home.

The early deaths of her mother, Anna Seamon Fauset, and four of her seven siblings strengthened the bonds between Fauset and her father and Fauset and her sister, Helen, the only other child of this marriage to live to adulthood.[9] Redmon Fauset was almost fifty years old when Jessie was born. To his adoring daughter, he cut a noble figure as he ministered to isolated enclaves of blacks in New Jersey backwaters. Not only did she attribute her literary talent to him, but throughout her life Fauset remained true to the ideals of service and uplift her father instilled. She remained likewise bound by his ethical precepts.[10]

According to her stepbrother Arthur, Jessie would listen enthralled to the stories her father told, stories that outlined an unusual personal and family history.[11] Whereas most blacks had been slaves up until 1865, the Fausets had been free for several generations. Whereas most blacks were rural and southern, the Fausets were primarily urban and northern. Indeed, the family Bible traced their residence in Philadelphia to the late eighteenth century. If theirs was a relatively privileged position among black Americans, the Fausets did not flaunt or abuse it. To the contrary, they internalized the biblical tenet "to whom much is given, much is required."

The legacy Redmon Fauset bequeathed his children inhered in the values he imparted; the family had little money. Perhaps due to stubbornness of principle, as Arthur Fauset believed, Redmon Fauset did not rise far in the hierarchy of the African Methodist Episcopal Church. For much of his career, he rode the circuit, and his congregations were never much larger or more prosperous than that in Snow Hill. But his calling ensured respectability, if not prosperity, and Jessie looked back on her childhood with pride.

Inevitably, the values of the Methodist parsonage were conservative. In the essay "Sunday Afternoon," Fauset remembered the "inhibitions" placed on a small child after the obligatory church attendance. "I might not sing songs, I might not play, I didn't know how to write letters, it was wrong to read even fairy-tales." Only the Bible and a richly illustrated edition of Dante's *Inferno* were permissible reading. The melancholy lifted with evening when "after supper there was music—hymns, played on the organ; in summer-time a gathering on the front steps, a general sense of good-fellowship and reunion in which I joined gladly."[12]

Above all, her father prized education. Jessie, who won admission to the academically competitive Philadelphia High School for Girls, met or surpassed his expectations. Although she later explained that she was raised to be a teacher, gaining the necessary training was no easy task. Reflecting on her childhood in a 1929 interview, Fauset recalled: "I happened to be the only colored girl in my classes at high school and I'll never forget the agony I endured on entrance day when the white girls with whom I had played and studied through the graded schools, refused to acknowledge my greeting." Even more embittering, upon graduation, she "found the training schools barred to me because of my color. Philadelphia, birthplace of Independence and City of Brotherly Love—I have never quite been able to reconcile theory with fact."[13]

In various aspects, her account suggests enduring patterns in Fauset's personal history. A dutiful daughter, she was raised to assume the only "safe" occupation available to black women; teaching offered both job security and protection from the sexual exploitation to which uneducated women in domestic service were often prey. Secondly, at an early age, Fauset became aware that her experience was exceptional, but she declined to draw any conclusions from that fact. (She *"happened* to be the only colored girl.") Finally, though she was always hurt and angered by racial prejudice, Fauset often managed, as in this instance, to overcome it. Denied admission to Bryn Mawr, the elite women's college, as well as to local teachers colleges, Fauset went on to enter Cornell University and receive instruction superior to any her hometown institutions offered.[14] However, the frequency with which she referred to this episode and to other encounters with racism in Philadelphia suggests that these experiences left lasting scars.

At Cornell, Jessie Fauset embarked on a "chiefly classical" curriculum. She studied four years of Latin, German, and English, along with two years of Greek and French as well as courses in bibliography, psychology, logic, ethics, archaeology and political science. More than meeting the challenge this course of study presented, Fauset was elected to Phi Beta Kappa in 1905. Official documents do not record race, so it is impossible to confirm whether Fauset was the first black woman to achieve this honor. She probably was. Similarly, Fauset, who wrote in 1905 that she had been "for the past four years . . . the only colored girl in a college community of over 3,000 students," was probably the first black woman to matriculate at Cornell.[15] In any event, the quality of her instruction and the excellence of her performance combined to ensure that Jessie Fauset was one of the best-educated Americans of her generation.

She recognized nevertheless that the education Cornell provided was incomplete. She yearned to know something of her people. In 1903, she wrote Du Bois, then a professor at Atlanta University, requesting his aid in securing summer employment. "I want to work in the South," she explained. "I know only one class of my people well, and I want to become acquainted with the rest." She succeeded in gaining a place teaching English at Fisk the following year. In expressing her gratitude to Du Bois, she exclaimed: "I liked the work—frankly I suppose no work will ever have about it again for me the glamor which this summer's work wore. It was my first attempt at being useful you see—that is a wonderful feeling is it not?" Having passed this first test, she was looking forward to her teaching days "with much pleasure."

These letters initiated one of the most important relationships of Fauset's life. Teacher, mentor, and friend, Du Bois in some respects became a surrogate for Redmon Fauset, who died the year the correspondence commenced. Certainly, he represented an intellectual and personal ideal, and Fauset thanked him for *The Souls of Black Folk* "as though it had been a personal favor. . . . I am glad, glad you wrote it." But if Fauset sometimes wrote to flatter ("the man of fine sensibilities has to suffer exquisitely, just simply because his feeling is so fine"), she also wrote to reason and debate. If in the first instance, she came across as the undergraduate she was, in the second she reflected a remarkable self-possession and sense of her own destiny. Responding to his essay "Credo," she averred that at the time she read it:

> . . . I meant to write you to tell you how glad I was to realise that that
> was your belief, and to ask you if you did not believe it to be worth-
> while to teach our colored men and woman [*sic*] *race* pride, *self*-pride,
> self-sufficiency (the right kind) and the necessity of living our lives as
> nearly as possible, *absolutely*, instead of comparing them always with

white standards. Don't you believe that we should lead them to understand that the reason we adopt such and such criteria which are also adopted by the Anglo Saxon is because these criteria are the *best* and not essentially because they are white?[16]

Clearly, Fauset was claiming the leadership role for which she had been trained. Her ideas were congruent with those Du Bois had expressed: she shared the sense that race pride was essential for the group's progress and indeed survival, the view that the wrong kind of self-sufficiency (as promoted by Booker T. Washington) led to disrespect and defeat, and the belief that certain values and ideals transcended race. These "absolute" standards eluded definition, however, particularly with respect to art. When Fauset attempted later to write according to the "best" criteria, she was in the position of writing race and gender without acknowledging that these had aesthetic consequences; she declined even to contemplate the possibility that race and gender might in fact shape the form as well as the content of one's expression.

Whether or not Fauset had aspirations to become a writer immediately after college is unknown. So many of the young female characters in her fiction express the ambition to be great artists, however, that it seems likely their creator might have as well. In any case, like most of those characters, Fauset left the campus for the classroom. She had first to endure yet another insult from her hometown. Her credentials were not deemed good enough for her to teach in the integrated high schools of Philadelphia. She went instead to segregated Douglass High School in Baltimore and then to the M Street High School in Washington, D.C., where she taught French and Latin for more than a decade.

Renamed for the poet Paul Laurence Dunbar in 1916, M Street was the jewel of black public secondary schools. It trained the sons and daughters of Washington's sizable black middle class, numbering poet and scholar Sterling Brown, historian Rayford Logan, and writer Jean Toomer among its graduates. Until the year Fauset joined the faculty, the formidable Anna Julia Cooper, author of *A Voice from the South*, had been its principal. Cooper had fought to preserve an academic curriculum and to gain admission for her graduates into the

most prestigious universities in the country. The standards she set for
the faculty were sustained after her departure. In 1921, when the first
three black women in the United States to earn doctorates received
their degrees, two were on the staff of Dunbar High School. This fact
of course says as much about the options then available to educated
black women as it does about the quality of the Dunbar faculty.[17]
Whatever the reasons, for Jessie Fauset, teaching at Dunbar meant
membership in a community of her peers.

Living in a strictly segregated city heightened Fauset's commitment to the black political struggle. Behind the scenes, she worked
with the NAACP on several cases. One, an effort in 1913 to gain
housing for a young black student at Smith College, must have
brought back memories. During her undergraduate years at Cornell,
Fauset had not been welcomed in the dormitories; she boarded with a
professor's family. The NAACP case involved Carrie Lee, whose request for regular accommodations was denied by Smith officials, due
to the objections they anticipated from Lee's Southern classmates and
their parents. Instead of a dormitory room, Lee was offered a place in
the servants' quarters. Fauset's work on this case may have led to her
being considered for NAACP Secretary in 1916.[18]

Despite segregation, the city of Washington offered a young black
intellectual meaningful social outlets. Angelina Grimké, a poet and
playwright, was Fauset's colleague at Dunbar. Grimké was also a
member of the literary circle that had begun to form around Georgia
Douglas Johnson. Fauset and Johnson quickly struck up what
became an extended friendship. At a point early in her Washington
sojourn, Fauset evidently met the long admired Du Bois as well. In
1912, she began to contribute to his still fledgling journal, *The Crisis*.

Among her earliest pieces for *The Crisis* is a series of seven co-
lumns, "What to Read," in which Fauset annotated the titles of
books relating to race issues, articles on educational subjects (in the
July 1912 number was her very favorable report on the "Montessori
method"), short fiction, personal essays, and the poem "Rondeau."
The sketch "My House and a Glimpse of My Life Therein" limns a
fictive mansion in Spain with a library that probably reflects some of
Fauset's real life taste. Prominent among the volumes noted are the

Bible, the *Rubaiyat*, Walter Pater's essays, Mrs. Humphrey Ward's most popular novel *Robert Elsmere*, and Elizabeth Barrett Browning's "Aurora Leigh."

Fauset's first short story, "Emmy," published in two installments in the December 1912 and January 1913 issues, reflects most of the weaknesses of her later fiction, but none of its strengths. The title character exists mainly as the prize whose worth the male protagonist must eventually recognize; Emmy has very little to say and less to do in the story. The persona Fauset projected in her essays offered a welcome contrast.

A good example is "Tracing Shadows," which reports on an eventful stay in Paris during the summer of 1914; the "shadows" of the title were the portents of war. But the essay's subject is the rite of passage experienced by the author's persona. Traveling with a group of women and men identified only by type (the Musician, Our Lady of Leisure, the Artist), the "I" of the essay has come to Paris to study. So enamored of the city is she ("Paris was for us and we were for Paris!") that she is oblivious to the warnings imbedded in the conversations of the Europeans, mainly working class, whom she meets.[19] Consequently, when the mobilization begins she and her friends have neither the cash nor the documents required for immediate departure. For two weeks, she lives through a "nightmare of sorrow and grief and pain" that will "mark" her forever. The tales of heroism she records celebrate the courage of men on their way to war as well as the courage of women who stay behind and add the work of the absent men to their usual labor. The persona earns a measure of the reader's admiration for her self-criticism, empathy, and fortitude. Overall, the essay is carefully constructed. Drawing on the example of Du Bois in *The Souls of Black Folk*, Fauset uses several bars of music as an epigraph. Only at the end of the essay are they identified as a folk song played by a schoolgirl who lived in a neighborhood the Americans visited. The bars become another trace of the now shattered world they left behind.

Travel was one means through which Fauset broadened her experience and perspective. Graduate study was another. During the summer of 1914, she had taken courses at the Sorbonne, just as in

previous summers she had enrolled for classes at the University of Pennsylvania. On a sabbatical in 1918–19, she completed work for the M.A. degree in Romance Languages at the University of Pennsylvania. By this time, Fauset had decided to change careers. In 1918, she formalized her relationship with *The Crisis*, agreeing among other assignments to write a regular column, "The Looking Glass," a digest of new items and literary miscellanea culled from international journals, for a salary of $50 a month. Her salary was doubled when she arrived in New York to assume the position of literary editor.[20]

The Crisis, with its resonant subtitle, "A Record of the Darker Races," was by then a powerful presence in African-American intellectual and political life. The inaugural issue had attributed its name to the editor's belief that the present was "a critical time in the history of the advancement of men," and subsequent events had confirmed the judgment. Initially designed as a national newspaper for African-Americans, it aimed to report on matters concerning race, particularly those facts and arguments that demonstrated the danger of the prejudice manifested toward blacks in the United States. It would also review articles, books, and other pieces published on the "race problem" and publish a small number of original articles. On its editorial pages it would "defend the rights of all men irrespective of color or race, for the highest ideals of American democracy." Its overarching goal was utopian: to realize "the world-old dream of human brotherhood."[21] The rhetorical flourishes were a Du Bois trademark, and his editorials were unquestionably the journal's major drawing card. Readers were stirred by his eloquent praise for the "gifts of black folk," his impassioned denunciation of racial injustice, his advocacy of self-defense in the face of mob violence, his proselytizing for Pan-Africanism, and his insistent celebration of black achievement.

Testimony to the reception of Du Bois's message and to the importance of *The Crisis* abounds. Langston Hughes once recalled that his "earliest memories of written words [were] Du Bois and the Bible." Though the operation was ideologically and, for a time, financially independent of the NAACP, trustee Joel Spingarn asserted rightly that without *The Crisis*, "there would be no Association." The journal was the association's primary vehicle for recruiting members,

most of whom surely believed it spoke for the NAACP. Literary scholar Saunders Redding wrote of the reverence in which *The Crisis* was held in his family's home. Though he and his siblings could "child-handle and mistreat" other magazines, Redding remembered: "The *Crisis* was strictly inviolate until my father himself had unwrapped and read it—often, as I have said, aloud." Surely, the most moving evidence preserved in the NAACP archives are the crudely composed letters from readers who could not afford the modest subscription price. Some enclosed fifty cents and promised to send the balance in installments; in the meantime they pleaded that Dr. Du Bois send *The Crisis* right away.[22]

No wonder Jessie Fauset was pleased to join this enterprise. She arrived at an auspicious time. Kindled by the peace achieved in Europe and the apparent prospect for liberation in Africa, Du Bois's rhetoric burned at a new intensity. Echoing the Victorian poet Alfred, Lord Tennyson, the January 1919 cover proclaimed, "Ring in the Thousand Years of Peace." Inside, Du Bois editorialized that while all Europe "rejoices in its new gifts"—a liberal labor program for British workers, nationalism for Czechoslovakians, a free France, and a recovering Belgium—"*our* men, who have helped mightily to awaken and preserve the spirit which makes these things possible, are returning to what?" A February article proclaimed, "Africa must ultimately be returned to the Africans. They are the best custodians of their lives and ideals."[23] Readers' responses matched the fervor of the rhetoric. The June 1919 number was the best-selling issue in *Crisis* history; over 104,000 copies were sold.

In September, the journal announced that it was raising its price from 10 to 15 cents a copy or $1.50 annually. In exchange, it promised a substantial increase in its size to include "more illustrations, more poetry and fiction as a permanent feature, and above all, one or two solid articles monthly on historical or sociological subjects affecting the Negro."[24] Fauset was well prepared to oversee literary matters— much more so than her boss—and she soon demonstrated an informed appreciation for his progressive political agenda.

Auspicious too was the fact that Fauset's arrival coincided with the first stirrings of the Renaissance. Boston journalist and critic William S.

Braithwaite had reported on "Some Contemporary Poets of the Negro Race" in the April *Crisis*. He heaped praise upon Georgia Douglas Johnson's *The Heart of a Woman* (1918) and James Weldon Johnson's *Fifty Years and Other Poems* (1917). He foresaw a "new movement in racial poetic achievement."[25] Its "keystone" was likely to be one "Eli Edwards," whose two sonnets Braithwaite had read in the magazine *The Seven Arts*; he had subsequently learned that Edwards was the pseudonym for Claude McKay. The July 1919 issue of the *Liberator* proved Braithwaite's prescience. The white, leftist journal published seven of McKay's most searing poems, including his signature sonnet "If We Must Die." These poems heralded a new militancy in black American poetry. In the "new day a-coming," Jessie Fauset would see to it that the best-known poems of McKay's most distinguished contemporaries were first published in *The Crisis*.

An important bridge to the new era was Du Bois's *Darkwater: Voices from within the Veil*. Among other pieces, it reprinted "Credo," the essay Fauset had admired when she read it at Cornell. In "New Literature on the Negro," a review essay in *The Crisis*, she singled out "The Souls of White Folk," "Litany of Atlanta," and "The Damnation of Women" as the "favorites for colored readers." This last essay, perhaps Du Bois's strongest feminist statement, celebrates the history of black women and advances a progressive vision in which "the future woman must have a life work and economic independence. She must have knowledge. She must have the right of motherhood at her own discretion. The present mincing horror at free womanhood must pass if we are ever to be rid of the bestiality of free manhood; not by guarding the weak in weakness do we gain strength, but by making weakness free and strong."[26] To a remarkable degree, Fauset achieved in the twenties this ideal of the future woman.

For seven years *The Crisis* became the focus of Fauset's professional life. Not only did she take charge of literary matters for the journal; in Du Bois's absence, and he traveled frequently, she acted as its managing editor. At the same time, she determined to hone her skills as a writer. During the twenties, she submitted a variety of pieces to the *Crisis*: essays and articles, book reviews, translations, poetry, and short stories. In 1924, while still a full-time editor, she

published her first novel, *There Is Confusion*. Although the fiction and poetry are better known, in my view Fauset achieved more distinction as a journalist and essayist.

Fauset's articles reveal her willingness to grapple with new cultural and political concepts. Through these one can chart the process by which a woman conditioned by background and training to accept a very conservative social ethic assimilated a good many progressive ideas. Her personal essays contain her best writing. Fauset's rhetorical skills far outshine her fictional inventiveness. Like "Tracing Shadows," many of the essays appeal to sentiment without turning sentimental as Fauset's fiction is prone to do. Moreover, she enlivens her essays with the kind of telling detail that rarely turns up in her fiction.

Fauset's essays cover a wide array of subjects; the earliest and least successful ones are on educational themes. In keeping with the Pan-African politics of *The Crisis*, Fauset profiled outstanding men of African descent across the world. "The Emancipator of Brazil" (co-authored with Cezar Pinto) told the story of José Do Patrocinio, a journalist and the son of a Catholic priest and a black woman. "A terrible agitator, . . . for whom there was only one cause—abolition," Patrocinio spoke, wrote, and traveled abroad in its interest. His zeal was rewarded when the slaves of Brazil were liberated in 1888. Less political but no less noble in Fauset's eyes were the exploits of Joseph Boulogne Saint-George, "Chevalier of France." Born in Guadeloupe, Saint-George made his fame in France as a composer, violinist, and swordsman. In "Looking Backward," an essay on Reconstruction, "the single finest instance of the effort of a nation to set immediately right an ancient wrong," Fauset offers her evidence that nobility could be found even among "thwarted and despised" black Americans. Robert Brown Elliott, a congressman from South Carolina, is in this instance the avatar of nobility. Like all these men, Elliott presented, in Fauset's phrase, a "model . . . of the possibilities of our race."[27]

Some years would pass before Fauset wrote about her boss, but clearly Du Bois was another model of possibilities for the race. Indeed, in 1921, the similarities between his career and the Brazilian emancipator's must have struck at least some of the journal's readers. A "terrible agitator" himself, Du Bois devoted increasing amounts of time to the cause of Pan-Africanism. The titular secretary of the Second Pan-African Congress, he was in fact its guiding light; Du Bois planned and orchestrated all four meetings of the congress in 1919, 1921, 1923, and 1927. The mission was at one with that of *The Crisis*: to realize "the world-old dream of human brotherhood." The political goal was to free African people from the shackles of colonialism. Representatives from throughout the African diaspora as well as sympathetic whites met to plan long-range strategies and to mount an immediate propaganda campaign toward this end. These activities naturally received heavy coverage in *The Crisis*.

Not only did Du Bois write extensive commentary on the meeting himself, the impact of his tutelage can be clearly discerned in Fauset's less-formal "Impressions of the Second Pan-African Congress." In this piece, she responded with enthusiasm to an experience rich in history and drama and one in which very few women took part. The Congress had met in three European capitals—London, Brussels, and Paris, after which a delegation was sent to the League of Nations in Geneva. In her account, Fauset attempted to convey the flavor of these cities while reminding her readers that the wealth and the children of Africa had made much of the Old World charm possible. She described the conditions in various parts of Africa and drew broad parallels between the problems of colonialism in Africa and segregation in the United States. Without meaning to, Fauset reflected the false simplicity of those parallels when she expressed dissatisfaction with the lack of militancy on the part of some African delegates. She wrote, "Already we had realized that the black colonial's problem while the same intrinsically, wore on the face of it a different aspect from that of the black Americans. Or was it that we had learned more quickly and better than they the value of organization, frankness, of freedom of speech? We wondered then and we wonder still though Heaven knows in all humility."[28]

Such a comment, despite the disclaimer of humility, is fraught with an arrogance as terrible as it is naive. Noting that arrogance and naivete were endemic in most efforts at building alliances among

Africans and African-Americans does not excuse Fauset's hubris.[29] Yet, there is a sense of reaching out, of honestly groping for a better understanding that is admirable. Fauset's assessments of the Congress's accomplishments were measured and reasonable. She observed that out of this conference and the earlier one held in 1919, a permanent organization had evolved. She acknowledged that enormous stumbling blocks lay ahead and compared the Congress's future to that of the League of Nations, a comparison that proved more accurate than either she or Du Bois were wont to imagine. Finally, Fauset ended her article on a note often sounded by her mentor:

> All the possibilities of all black men are needed to weld together the black men of the world against the day when black and white meet in battle.
> God grant that when that day comes we shall be so powerful that the enemy will say, "But behold! these men are our brothers." (17–18)

Perhaps in consequence of the masculinist perspective encoded in these words, Fauset never directly reported her own activities at the Congress. In "What Europe Thought of the Pan-African Congress," she quoted from an article *The Glasgow Herald* had done on the meeting. It noted that Fauset spoke on the subject of black American women who had been a great force behind all the movements for emancipation in the United States. She emphasized the activities of women in social work, the professions, and business. She also "asked the African delegates to carry a message of friendship and encouragement to African women from the colored women of America."[30]

The following year, Fauset expanded her contacts with black women activists in the United States by attending and reporting on the thirteenth biennial convention of the National Association of Colored Women. This group, under the leadership of Hallie Quinn Brown and Mary McLeod Bethune, was committed to upgrading the Negro woman's image, offering recreational activities for women and providing social services for the black community. At a time when few public welfare agencies existed, the N.A.C.W. sponsored orphanages, reformatories, community centers, and homes for the elderly. Chapters sponsored high school and college scholarships;

they raised funds for the restoration of the home of Frederick Douglass as a historical shrine. Because so few organizations existed, the agenda of the N.A.C.W. was manifold. In Fauset's words, it was "a great and far-reaching organization with immense possibilities."

Delegates to the 1922 convention heard speeches on topics ranging from home hygiene and organized charity to the development of modern Negro poetry and the need for passage of an anti-lynching bill. "Miss Jessie Fauset," the article noted in passing, "spoke of Africa" and "interpreted the meaning" of the Pan-African Congress. The article's emphasis was on the scope of the N.A.C.W.'s mission. While Fauset felt compelled to list the organization's faults—too much bickering, "too many personal, petty, needless jealousies"— they detracted little from what in the main was a glowing tribute. "The sincerity, the determination, the forthrightness of womanhood are in this N.A.C.W. and that quality which makes women so much more so than men realize that the practical good is in the last analysis the thing to be secured. These women have proved that they are determined, above all else, to secure it."[51]

Fauset was a more than competent reporter, but her greater talent was for the personal essay. "Nostalgia," published in August 1921, is an example of the growing skill with which she manipulated the genre. Two anecdotes open the essay. In one, Fauset recounts a conversation with her grocer, a Greek whose homesickness is palpable; "his tongue linger[s] with love" on the name of his native land. She asks him where he lives, and he answers in a lyrical phrase: "I live in the islands of the sea." In the second anecdote, an Italian cobbler tells tales of his World War I battle days to ease his loneliness as he works to save enough money to return home. Then with shrewd rhetorical economy, Fauset introduces the essay's theme. Defining nostalgia in several languages, she asserts that yearning to return home is "as universal a phenomenon as that of possessing a mother."

Asserting its universality allows Fauset to make all the more dramatic the absence of nostalgia on the part of the young Jewish girl and young black man who are the subjects of the next two anecdotes. Twelve-year-old Rachel worries that her Zionist father's longing for a home in a Jerusalem he has never seen will overpower his devotion

to his family in America. Newly returned from France, the black student is eager to go back; home, he decides, is not necessarily where one has lived all his life, but home is "where mentally and spiritually he is recognized and taken for what he is." For African-Americans generally, there is no place to call home. New under the sun, according to Fauset, the black American is left to wonder: "shall he ever realize the land where he would be?" Fauset's essay is a moving and skillfully rendered formulation of this often-posed question in African-American literature and cultural expression.

Fauset's longstanding interest in various modes of cultural expression gave rise to some of her best work, although her perspective is by turns enlightening and reactionary. "The Symbolism of Bert Williams," an essay occasioned by the death of the celebrated vaudeville comedian and mime, goes beyond an appreciation of the individual performer to an analysis of race prejudice in the cultural life of the United States. The meaning of the title is two-fold: if Williams's stage persona symbolized the black man as fool to whites, to blacks Williams's confinement in the role of stage "darky" symbolized the constraints of racism. Images of dualism recur throughout the essay.

To Fauset, Williams's performances revealed "that deep, ineluctable strain of melancholy, which no Negro in a mixed civilization ever lacks." For a comedian in blackface to convey such melancholy was a "strange and amazing contradiction." What explains it is Williams's artistry. He elicited laughter not by playing himself and revelling in "his own spontaneous subjective joy" but by assuming a role through which he conveyed the "humorously objective presentation of his personal joys and sorrows."

The essay next sketches Williams's life, emphasizing at every turn the contrasts between the actor and his role. West Indian-born, intelligent and ambitious (Fauset notes that he once hoped to attend Stanford University), and aspiring to a career on the legitimate stage, Egbert Austin Williams had to invent the only kind of persona white audiences would accept. His was a strange and amazing education: studying phonetics in order to master southern black vernacular and practicing until he perfected a shuffling gait. To Fauset the speech and the shuffle had similar value. She was forever deaf to the poetry of the folk.[32] Fauset's regressive views are also evident in the attention she draws to Williams's "golden skin, his silken hair, his beautiful, sensitive hands" hidden "under the hideousness of the eternal black make-up." That it was humiliating and absurd for any black person, regardless of complexion or hair texture, to be forced to wear blackface goes unsaid. Accompanying the essay were photographs of the private Williams as a child and a man, which provided a more telling contrast. The child in the studio photograph and the dignified man with the pensive expression and tailored clothes gainsay the reality of the public persona.

What Williams could never understand was the relentless race prejudice he encountered in the United States. Prejudice is the ultimate enigma for both the author and her subject:

> Why should he and we obscure our talents forever under the bushel of prejudice, jealousy, stupidity—whatever it is that makes the white world say: "No genuine colored artist; coons, clowns, end-men, clap-trap, but no undisguisedly beautiful presentation of Negro ability."[33]

In 1920 and 1921, Fauset divided her energies between *The Crisis* and a new publication for children, *The Brownies' Book*. By any measure *The Brownies' Book* was an extraordinary effort. Du Bois and Augustus G. Dill, the business manager of *The Crisis*, were its publishers; Jessie Fauset was the managing editor. The magazine was, in its editors' words, "designed for all children but especially for ours." In a poem in the first issue, Fauset wrote:

> To Children, who with eager look
> Scanned vainly library shelf and nook,
> For History or Song or Story
> That told of Colored Peoples' glory, —
> We dedicate *The Brownies' Book*. (32)

To this end, the magazine published short stories and poetry, African folk tales, games, puzzles, and monthly historical features. Among the figures profiled were Alexander Dumas, Harriet Tubman, Alexander Pushkin, Benjamin Banneker, and Phillis Wheatley. A column by Du Bois, "As the Crow Flies," covered current events on

a level incredibly sophisticated for a children's magazine. But what other children's magazine can boast an editor of Du Bois's erudition and perspicacity, or one who so steadfastly refuses to condescend to his readers? "The Judge" was Fauset's column; if no match for Du Bois, Fauset offered her own political commentary, advice, and recommendations for further reading. A feature, "Little People of the Month," highlighted the achievements of children, who were sometimes but far from always, the offspring of well-known parents. As in *The Crisis*, there was an annual salute to graduates. Finally, "The Jury" was a letters-to-the-editor column that printed correspondence from the juvenile readers; its counterpart was "The Grown-Ups Corner."

As managing editor, Fauset solicited manuscripts from a list of contributors that reads like a who's who of the Harlem Renaissance. James Weldon Johnson published poetry; Willis Richardson, whose folk drama *Compromise* appeared in *The New Negro*, contributed two plays; folklorist/biographer Arthur Huff Fauset offered an essay on Blanche K. Bruce, a political leader during Reconstruction. Frequent contributor Langston Hughes was represented not only by his poems, but by an early play, *The Gold Piece*, and his offering to the playtime feature, *Mexican Games*.

As she would in *The Crisis*, Fauset championed the work of women writers in *The Brownies' Book*. Poems came from Georgia Douglas Johnson and Mary Effie Lee (later Effie Lee Newsome), a longtime contributor to *The Crisis* who eventually published a volume of children's verse, *Gladiola Gardens* (1940). NAACP colleague and sometime antagonist Mary White Ovington offered games. Fauset also promoted women illustrators, including Laura Wheeler, Hilda Wilkinson, and Louise Latimer. As was true of Nella Larsen, several of these writers and illustrators launched their careers in *The Brownies' Book*.[34]

As short-lived as it was remarkable, *The Brownies' Book* ceased publication with the December 1921 issue, its twenty-fourth. For the vast majority of black families, a subscription to a children's magazine was an unthinkable luxury. A "valedictory" signed by Du Bois and Dill, but not Fauset, expressed regret and this consolation: "The fault has not been with our readers. We have had an unusually enthusiastic set of subscribers. But the magazine was begun just at the time of industrial depression following the war, and the fault of our suspension therefore is rather in the times which are so out of joint, than in our constituency." At a time when black children were totally ignored in juvenile literature, *The Brownies' Book* offered them a superb and diverse collection of features. The magazine remains a testament to the vision of Du Bois, Dill, and Fauset.

Although the demise of *The Brownies' Book* did not mean a decline in Fauset's editorial responsibilities—Du Bois continued to travel extensively, and Fauset assumed responsibility for editing *The Crisis* during his absence—she continued to write prolifically. Over her years as literary editor of *The Crisis*, Fauset penned numerous book reviews. Because her tenure at the journal began before the Harlem Renaissance was in full flower, she devoted much of her attention early on to books of negligible literary interest. These included historical monographs such as *The Negro Trailblazers of California* and biographies of "race men" like L. J. Coppin, an African-American who became bishop of the A.M.E. church in South Africa. To Fauset, the bishop's *Unwritten History* was "more wonderful than any fairy tale." For the most part, such books were published privately or through church-owned presses like the A.M.E. Book Concern. Although she was rarely harsh in her criticism of such works, Fauset did point out their defects. Not surprising, given their sponsorship, a frequent flaw was the tendency of the authors to write "in the vein of the Sunday School Teacher."[35]

Another response to such works was Fauset's longing for novels and poetry that aspired to be recognized as "art." Reviewing two now deservedly forgotten novels, which she acknowledged were inferior works of fiction, Fauset asserted that their significance was "the launching of an essay by Negro writers into the realm of pure romantic fiction. This is a relief when one considers that nearly all writing on the part of colored Americans seeks to set forth propaganda" ("New Literature of the Negro," 80). To whatever extent this was true, romantic fiction was hardly where the future lay; in other reviews, Fauset read the literary future more clearly.

In a review of Claude McKay's first volume published in the United States, she proclaimed: "The first thought that will rush into

the reader's mind with *Harlem Shadows* will be *This is poetry*." She praised his "fiery, impassioned language" and argued that the poems were free of propaganda. To modern readers, McKay's poetry, particularly the sonnets like "America," which Fauset used to illustrate her point, is explicitly ideological; she responded to the formal skill that distinguished McKay's work from that of his predecessors.

In the same article, she wrote that *The Book of American Negro Poetry* "has the value of an arrow pointing the direction of Negro genius." Fauset singled out only four of the thirty-two poets anthologized by name; two were women, Georgia Douglas Johnson and Anne Spencer. Not allowing friendship to overcome critical judgment, she commented that Johnson's "power however is checked by the narrowness of her medium of expression." Fauset's praise for Spencer was unqualified; she called Spencer's art "true and fine; she blends a delicate mysticism with a diamond clearness of exposition."[36]

One of Fauset's most significant reviews, appearing under the inconspicuous heading "Our Book Shelf," considers the first books by Countee Cullen and Langston Hughes. By any reckoning, these are two of the major poets of the Harlem Renaissance. They are also strikingly dissimilar in their approach to their craft. Fauset's critical acumen enabled her to identify the strengths in each man's work, though she was clearly more comfortable with the traditional poetics to which Cullen adhered. Cullen had "the feeling and the gift to express colored-ness in a world of whiteness." Indeed, the poems on racial themes "are not only the most beautifully done but they are by far the most significant in the book." Expressing a more acute understanding of the lure of false universalism than her own work demonstrated, she added, "I hope that no one crying down 'special treatment' will turn him from his native and valuable genre. There *is* no 'universal treatment'; it is all specialized."

Writing about Hughes's *The Weary Blues*, Fauset was careful to state that she was "no great lover of dialect," and she was rather too eager to place Hughes's work in the context of western literary tradition. Certainly, her assertion that Hughes was not preoccupied with form is mistaken; Hughes's experiments with vernacular forms such as spirituals, blues, and jazz are now regarded as building blocks of

African-American modernism. Yet, with all her temporizing, Jessie Fauset reached a conclusion from which few of Hughes's many subsequent critics would demur: "I doubt if any one will ever write more tenderly, more understandingly, more humorously of the life of Harlem shot through as it is with mirth, abandon and pain."[37]

Although, stylistically, her criticism is badly dated, most of Fauset's judgments are similarly sound. Impressionist by design, Fauset's mode was subjective rather than analytical. Despite the polemical aims of *The Crisis*, her approach was not ideological. For Fauset, art was to serve a moral and spiritual purpose, not a narrowly political one. As a critic, her probable model was Walter Pater, although the realities of black life in the United States limited the applicability of his aestheticism. Given these predilections, even her limited appreciation of the literary innovation Hughes's poetry exemplified is admirable.

In other reviews as well as in a series of translations, Fauset introduced *Crisis* readers to writing in French by African and Caribbean authors. Here, as was true generally, the journal's literary perspective complemented its political viewpoint. For example, Fauset twice reviewed René Maran's pioneering *Batouala*, one of the first novels to make Africans its central characters. The Caribbean-born author had served as a colonial official in Africa, and his book became a cause célèbre in France; in 1923, it won the prestigious Prix Goncourt. In her first review, Fauset judged it "a great novel. It is artistic, overwhelming in its almost cinema-like sharpness of picturization. And there lies its strength. No propaganda, no preachments, just an actual portrayal of life." Six months later, Fauset reviewed the English translation. She pointed out several errors in the translation, but adjudged them to be minor. Arguing that the strength of the novel is the depiction of traditional as well as colonial Africa, Fauset concluded that for black Americans its most arresting aspect "is the excoriation by Maran in the preface and by his characters in the novel proper of the white colonial who has entered Africa and changed it so sadly."

Unbeknown to *Crisis* readers, Jessie Fauset had turned down the opportunity to translate the novel she regarded so highly. Conceivably, the representations of customs such as polygamy and bride price

put Fauset off the project. Then, too, fewer pages of the novel were devoted to anticolonialist sentiment than to sensationalist depictions of putative rituals like the "dance of love." While *Batouala* was less condescending in its treatment than earlier fictions, it compromised its credibility with such descriptions of rituals as "intoxication. It was the immense joy of brutes loosed from all control."[38] One can only surmise that these were the faults Fauset found in the novel; she never specified them. Instead, she confided to Joel Spingarn: "Alas, alack, I know my own milieu too well. If I should translate that book over my name, I'd never be considered 'respectable' again."[39]

No objection could be raised to the verse she translated. A passionate admirer of Haitian literature, she wrote of the first four Haitian books she reviewed that they "open up to me an undiscovered country." She was tempted to claim it. Quite apart from its historical importance as the first black republic, Haiti had an impressive literary history. Fauset argued that eighteenth-century Haitian poetry was marked by a stylistic maturity not found in colonial American writing. In her highest praise, she asserted that some Haitian writers had achieved a charm in their work "ranking with the charm of the poetry of France." While some Haitian poets propagandized against the color line and in defense of Haitian culture, particularly of "voodooism," others wrote poetry for its own sake. Fauset preferred to translate the latter. Her translation of "Oblivion," by Massilon Coicou, a writer better known for his patriotic verse, was published in Johnson's *Book of American Negro Poetry*. Coicou's speaker expresses the hope that when dead he shall lie in a deserted grave and thereby achieve "oblivion—the shroud and envelope of happiness." Perhaps the poem is memorable in French; Fauset's translation is not.[40]

Fauset's own verse reflects a similar pull toward a vague universalism. Most of her poems are forgettable lyrics written to honor seasons, places, and heroes. Somewhat more interesting is "Oriflamme," the first poem Fauset published after joining the *Crisis* staff:

> *I can remember when I was a little, young girl, how my old mammy would sit out of doors in the evenings and look up at the stars and groan, and I would say, "Mammy, what makes you groan so?" And she would say, "I*

am groaning to think of my poor children; they do not know where I be and
I don't know where they be. I look up at the stars and they look up at the
stars."——— SOJOURNER TRUTH

> I think I see her sitting bowed and black,
>   Stricken and seared with slavery's
>   mortal scars,
> Reft of her children, lonely, anguished, yet
>   Still looking at the stars.
> Symbolic mother, we thy myriad sons,
>   Pounding our stubborn hearts on Free-
>   dom's bars,
> Clutching our birthright, fight with faces
>   set,
>   Still visioning the stars![41]

However inspiring the sentiment, "Oriflamme" is dreary poetry. The epigraph is more "poetic" than the poem with its stilted diction and clichés. The incongruous title lends credence to charges by Fauset's detractors that she used French titles merely to show off.

That charge is, however, overstated. "La Vie C'est La Vie," Fauset's most-often anthologized poem, is nothing if not aptly titled:

> On summer afternoons I sit
> Quiescent by you in the park,
> And idly watch the sunbeams gild
> And tint the ash-trees' bark.
>
> Or else I watch the squirrels frisk
> And chaffer in the grassy lane;
> And all the while I mark your voice
> Breaking with love and pain.
>
> I know a woman who would give
> Her chance of heaven to take my place;
> To see the love-light in your eyes,
> The love-glow on your face!
>
> And there's a man whose lightest word
> Can set my chilly blood afire;
> Fulfillment of his least behest
> Defines my life's desire.
>
> But he will none of me, nor I
> Of you. Nor you of her. 'Tis said

> The world is full of jests like these, —
> I wish that I were dead.[42]

This poem moves carefully from the serenity of the first stanza to the agony and frustration of the last. The concluding line is melodramatic but affecting at least on first reading; the poem's sentiments have obvious popular appeal. Yet "La Vie C'est La Vie" has serious flaws. Its language shifts uneasily from the overly literary ("chaffer," "behest") to the mundanely popular ("love-light in your eyes," "love-glow on your face," and "set my chilly blood afire"). Consequently, Fauset's speaker seems to exist in a cultural limbo.

Fauset herself did not. When she moved to Harlem in 1919, Jessie Fauset was youthful if not young at thirty-seven, idealistic, independent, and single. Decorous though she was, she was also a charming conversationalist and a "superb dancer" (Lewis, 123). She was sufficiently attuned to the contemporary mood in 1921 to sign on as an usher and patron for a benefit performance of *Shuffle Along*, the most famous musical of the era, at Harlem's Lafayette Theater. More characteristically, she enlisted as a volunteer at the 135th Street Library, where she helped host the readings and lectures that became the heart of Harlem's literary life. She made her home in an apartment on West 142nd Street, which she shared with her sister, Helen Lanning. It soon became a gathering place for the writers and artists who would arrive in New York in ever increasing numbers over the next few years.

Claude McKay met Fauset during the twenties and remembered her as being "prim, pretty and well dressed." He did allow, in slightly less patronizing terms, that she "talked fluently and intelligently." Most impressive to McKay, "all the radicals liked her, although in her social viewpoint she was away over on the other side of the fence."[43] In part because of their political differences, McKay emphatically did not like Fauset's boss. Working for Du Bois, whose hauteur was as legendary as his brilliance, Jessie Fauset frequently sought out and was sought out by young writers whom he intimidated.

For example, in a series of letters she exchanged with Jean Toomer in 1922 and 1923, she offered encouragement and incisive criticism. Undoubtedly more important to him, she agreed to publish his poems in *The Crisis*. Payment for two poems published in 1922,

From left to right: Regina Andrews,
Esther Popel, Helen Lanning,
Louella Tucker, Jessie Fauset, Marie
Johnson, Ethel Ray, Clarissa Scott,
and Pearl Fisher. Taken at a party for
Langston Hughes in Harlem. Regina
Andrews Collection. Schomburg
Center for Research in Black Culture,
New York Public Library.

one of which was the classic "Song of the Son," was five dollars.
Fauset's praise was less parsimonious: "I cannot tell you how vividly
your work has renewed my interest in you. When I see you I feel as
though I should like to assist you in putting the world at [your?]
feet." She added the well-considered cautionary note, that he was "a
little inclined to achieve style at the expense of clearness," but she
emphasized that he avoided this tendency in his best work. In their

subsequent correspondence, Fauset solicited more material for *The Crisis* and noted that she had shown the poetry to James Weldon Johnson, who expressed regret that it had not been received in time to be included in the first edition of *The Book of American Negro Poetry*, which was published in 1922. For his part, Toomer made reference to a variety of works in progress (the manuscript of *Cane* was already in the hands of a publisher). Fauset's efforts to meet with the elusive author failed; her invitations to lunch were either not received or ignored.

This inattention did not change Fauset's high opinion of Toomer's work. She sent samples of it to Arthur B. Spingarn, NAACP vice president and legal counsel, and wrote: "I consider the lines which I have marked proof of an art and a contribution to literature which will be distinctly negroid and without propaganda. It will have in it an element of universality too, in that it shows the individual's reaction to his own tradition."[44]

Countee Cullen accepted Fauset's encouragement more graciously. Cullen had first published in *The Crisis* in 1922, the year he graduated from high school. A local prodigy, Cullen could not escape the attention of the *Crisis* staff. Fauset wrote in May 1923 to congratulate Cullen on a speech he delivered at Town Hall for an organization called the League of Youth. At her request, he sent her a copy, which she published in the August *Crisis*. Cullen kept in touch. When he wrote to ask the status of his article, he was polite and politic enough to inquire about the progress Fauset was making on her novel. She asked in turn that Cullen, a minister's son, pray for her success in placing her first book. Fauset was a generous friend. Several years later, when Cullen invited Fauset to contribute to *Caroling Dusk*, she was flattered to be asked and offered him the benefit of her editorial expertise: "I'll be glad to contribute—and if you'd like to collaborate in work not in name."[45]

Early in 1924, Fauset's keen eye fixed upon a poem submitted to *The Crisis* by a twenty-one-year-old college graduate working the night shift for the post office in Los Angeles. Her response changed Arna Bontemps's life. Word of it got out on the job, and Bontemps learned he was not the only fledgling author sorting mail. Wallace

Thurman also spent his days writing and hoping. By July, Bontemps recorded in his memoir, he had "a) received a copy of the August issue, which carried my poem, b) resigned my job in the post office, and c) packed my suitcase and bought a ticket to New York City." Meeting fellow poets Cullen and Hughes, reencountering Thurman, and taking the opportunity to thank Fauset in person for her encouragement, Bontemps joined "the Awakening," as he called the Renaissance.[46]

The friendship Fauset offered Langston Hughes was special. Fauset had accepted the first poem he submitted for publication, "The Negro Speaks of Rivers." As she later recalled, she took "the beautiful dignified creation to Dr. Du Bois and said: 'What colored person is there, do you suppose, in the United States who writes like that and yet is unknown to us?'" She determined to find out and thereby initiated a longstanding personal and professional relationship.[47]

Soon after Hughes arrived in New York to attend Columbia University in the fall of 1921, Fauset invited him to lunch at the Civic Club to meet her and Du Bois and commented that Hughes had been "so generous to us and our work." Filled with fear and trepidation at the prospect of meeting Du Bois, Hughes brought along his mother. Fauset's charm helped to ease his fears. "A gracious tan-brown lady, a little plump, with a fine smile and gentle eyes," as he recalled, Fauset thrilled him by repeating compliments *Crisis* readers had paid his poems. He was "interested, too, to hear" that she herself was writing poems and planning a novel.[48]

The most important thing Fauset did for Hughes was to publish his poems, but it was far from the only service she rendered. From the start, she expressed absolute confidence in his talent. In May 1923, she wrote, "You assuredly have the true poetic touch, the divine afflatus, which will some day carry you far." Her faith went beyond words to deeds. She offered critiques of his writing, which, at least initially, he appreciated. She advised him on his educational plans: disappointed that he had dropped out of Columbia, she recommended that he apply to Harvard; he chose instead Lincoln University, the black college in Pennsylvania, which he entered in February 1926. An un-

selfish mentor, she helped Hughes meet people who had the where-withal that she did not to advance his career. For example, she insisted Hughes attend the dinner at which he met Carl Van Vechten, who submitted Hughes's first manuscript to his own publisher, Alfred A. Knopf. Helping to build an audience for his work, she discussed and recited his poems in the lectures on "modern Negro poetry," which she delivered at libraries, high schools, and civic organizations.[49]

Fauset also invited Hughes to social gatherings in her home. His oft-quoted account in *The Big Sea* of one of these occasions helped seal the image of Fauset as a woman utterly removed from ordinary life. "At Miss Fauset's, a good time was shared by talking literature and reading poetry aloud and perhaps enjoying some conversation in French." Rarely were white guests present, "unless they were very distinguished white people, because Jessie Fauset did not feel like opening her home to mere sightseers, or faddists momentarily in love with Negro life" (247).

Fauset's guests were serious black people—editors and students, writers and social workers—"people who liked books and the British Museum, and had perhaps been to Florence. (Italy, not Alabama.)" Not surprisingly, this atmosphere could grow too rarefied, particularly from the perspective of a young man in his twenties. Hughes reports that after one of Fauset's at-homes, he and Charles Johnson took the guest of honor, a Spanish diplomat and savant, to unwind at the famed Harlem nightspot Smalls' Paradise.

By the time this incident occurred in February 1928, the Fauset-Hughes friendship was strained by tensions that had nothing to do with their different ideas of a good time and much to do with differ-ences in their aesthetic philosophies. Both Hughes's essay "The Negro Artist and the Racial Mountain" and his second volume of poems, *Fine Clothes to the Jew*, had signaled how divergent their views on the content and form of African-American art had become. Not only did the essay announce Hughes's intention to depict the lives of the urban masses in his writing, it celebrated those ways of the "low-down folk" most likely to gall Jessie Fauset. She could hardly have missed the point that he did not care whether "colored people" liked his work, when she was prominent among those from whom he was declaring his independence.

The book was an even stronger declaration. In poems like "Po' Boy Blues," "Hard Daddy," "Red Silk Stockings," and "Hey!" Hughes experimented with the rhythms of blues and jazz. Apart from the blues poetry, free verse predominated. Fauset, who was still deaf to the poetry of the folk and certain that formal poetry should have rhyme, could not have been pleased. She was probably pained by the epithet the volume earned her protégé: "Poet Low-Rate of Harlem."[50]

Her viewpoint was adumbrated in her responses to the *Crisis* symposium on "The Negro in Art: How Shall He Be Portrayed." Like Hughes, she asserted that the artist was under no obligation to portray any particular type of black character. However, when asked if there were a danger that young writers of the race would be "tempted to follow" the fashionable trend of portraying black underworld characters "rather than seeking to paint the truth about themselves and their own social class," she replied, "Emphatically. This is a grave danger making for a literary insincerity both insidious and abominable" (*The Crisis*, June 1926: 71–73). Hughes might well have imagined she had him in mind.

Despite their disagreements, Hughes and Fauset remained steadfast in their loyalty to each other. Nevertheless, the image of her that he preserved in *The Big Sea* suggests the tensions underlying their friendship, tensions that remained submerged beneath a surface both were too gracious to disturb.

Fauset credited the 1922 publication of T. S. Stribling's novel *Birthright* with inspiring her own career as a novelist. As she recalled in an interview, "a number of us started writing at that time. Nella Larsen and Walter White, for instance, were affected just as I was. We reasoned, 'Here is an audience waiting to hear the truth about us. Let us, who are better qualified to present that truth than any white writer, try to do so.'"[51] Well intentioned, but crudely written, *Birthright* depicts the return of a black man, newly graduated from Harvard, to his southern hometown and a predictably tragic end; the town has no place for him. Other versions of this story had been told, notably by Du Bois in *The Souls of Black Folk*. But, in Stribling's text, the tragedy inheres in the hero's black ancestry, which prevents him from achieving the noble ambition to which his "white blood" causes him to aspire. Reviewing the book for *The Crisis*, Fauset called it "a drastic, most

unpleasant but valuable commentary on American life," but she was disturbed by the "fallacies" about black American life it conveyed. She determined in her novels to tell "the truth" about the race.[52]

In fiction as in poetry, Fauset was drawn to traditional forms. The literary allusions that recur throughout her prose make that plain. Though she read the modernists, her heart belonged to the Victorians. Following the example of earlier black women writers, Fauset attempted to adapt the conventions of the sentimental novel to her own purposes. Chief among these was her effort to explore the impact of racism and sexism on black Americans' lives and represent the means by which black Americans overcame these oppressions and got on with the business of living. But the content and the form of her novels are at odds. Their plots often strain credulity, and their resolutions are uniformly happy: the still courageous but chastened heroine finds happiness with a protective yet more understanding hero. The more progressive issues that Fauset explored in her essays are relegated to subplots. While to an extent, as Deborah McDowell argues in "The Neglected Dimension of Jessie Fauset," Fauset uses literary and social conventions as a "deflecting mask for her more challenging concerns," more often these concerns are eclipsed by her reliance on convention.[53]

This is surely true of her first novel, *There Is Confusion*. Its title has long been an irresistible target for critics wearied by the effort of deciphering the novel's several plots. Central is the marriage plot that traces the unsteady courtship of Joanna Marshall and Peter Bye. Talented, disciplined, and ambitious to a fault, Joanna has from childhood aspired to greatness. Her goal is a career in the theater, but her ambition is not entirely self-seeking. Inspired by the stories of Harriet Tubman, Phillis Wheatley, and Sojourner Truth her father has told her as a child, Joanna's ambition is grounded in the belief "that if there's anything that will break down prejudice it will be equality or perhaps even superiority on the part of colored people in the arts."[54] Confident that "colored people can do everything that anybody else can do," Joanna is determined that race will not interfere with her reaching her goal. Peter Bye is not so sure about his own goal. He hopes to be a doctor, but his ambition is often overcome by his rage and despair at

the "damned petty injustice" meted out to him because of his race. Before they can marry, he must transcend his bitterness and seize control of his own life; she must in effect surrender her ambition and yield control of her life to him. "It was Peter now whom she wished to see succeed. . . . In a thousand little ways she deferred to him, and showed him that as a matter of course he was the arbiter of her own and her child's destiny, the *fons et origo* of authority" (292).

The ending seems all the more reactionary given the protagonist's quest for personal and artistic autonomy earlier in the novel. Though flawed by class snobbery, Joanna is clearly the novel's heroine. She works hard and refuses to be dissuaded by prejudice. Denied a place in a famous teacher's dance class, she organizes a separate class for her friends, which the teacher agrees to instruct; hers is a self-conscious, deliberate compromise. When despite her acknowledged talent she cannot find a job, she holds to her determination to "show them we can stick to our last as well as anybody else" (157). Finally, her performance of a Negro folk dance attracts a producer's attention and she secures a role in a production called "The Dance of Nations." With her success comes exposure to the world of her white counterparts. She meets "girls not as old as she who had already 'arrived' in their chosen profession"—young editors, artists, teachers, and activists whose causes included birth control, single tax, and psychiatry. Although she sees common cause in the struggle to overcome "disabilities of sex and of tradition," she sees dissimilarity as well. As she reflects, "sometimes she felt like a battle-scarred veteran among all these happy, chattering people, who, no matter how seriously, how deeply they took their success, yet never regarded it with the same degree of wonder, almost of awe with which she regarded hers" (235).

To meet the demands of the marriage plot, Joanna quickly grows disillusioned with her success. To be just a dancer seems hardly worthwhile; she sees herself more vaudevillian than artist. Her father encourages this view: "his voice half glad, half sorry, told her that he, too, had hoped for something different" (236). If, on the level of cultural commentary, Joanna's situation echoes that of Bert Williams and critiques the way racism and the marketplace distort black artistic expression, its narrative function is to offer a rationale for Joanna

to renounce her quest and marry. Through marriage and motherhood, she redefines her self: "her desire for greatness had been a sort of superimposed structure which, having been taken off, left her her true self" (291).

The novel's subplots provide more varied representations of women and the lives they can create for themselves, but the more venturesome characters are those whose romantic aspirations have been thwarted. Maggie Ellersley, a poor girl whom the Marshalls befriend, is taught bookkeeping by the father. After Joanna destroys Maggie's hope of marrying her brother and the man Maggie marries on the rebound turns out to be a gambler (the convolutions of the plot seem endless), Maggie establishes herself in business. She becomes an agent for a Madame Walker-like cosmetic entrepreneur. A second disappointment in love prompts a journey to a European battlefield as a war nurse. In this more conventionally feminine role, she is allowed a reconciliation with her first love.

The overall insistence on the primacy of romance in women's lives has another, unintended consequence. A minor character, Vera Manning, is "forced to devote her life" to civil rights work after her romance breaks up. She admits she is "almost glad" to travel through the South investigating lynchings and other racial crimes under the cover, as it were, of her very light skin. Yet, because Fauset subordinates everything in the novel to the marriage plot, this character's actions are devalued.

Writing an early notice for *The Crisis*, Locke called *There Is Confusion* "the novel that the Negro intelligentsia have been clamoring for . . . a cross section of the race life higher up the social pyramid." Locke's comment was double-edged, yet he was more generous than the *New York Post* reviewer who carped that "at times . . . it is a little overdone on the refined side." Montgomery Gregory caught the spirit of the novel exactly. Praising Fauset as "this modern Phillis Wheatley," he deemed the "great value" of her novel to lie "in interpreting the better elements of our life to those who know us only as domestic servants, 'uncles,' or criminals." Even more important, to blacks themselves who "have not dared so see ourselves as we really are," the novel represented "a sincere effort to view the life of the

race objectively."[55] Gregory, at least, was persuaded that Fauset had told "the truth about us." Many readers were not so sure, and few were ready to consider the actuality of multiple, contradictory, and competing truths about black people's lives.

No event better symbolizes the ambivalent response to *There Is Confusion* than the dinner at Manhattan's Civic Club, which was organized to mark its publication. What started out to be an informal gathering honoring Fauset turned into the well-orchestrated "debut of the younger school of Negro writers." The description is Charles S. Johnson's; the *Opportunity* editor was the event's guiding hand. If, as he wrote afterward, there had been "no formal, prearranged program," the evening's unwritten agenda was crystal clear. So was the fact that the proceedings had little to do with Jessie Fauset.

Almost all of the New Negro writers attended: Cullen, Hughes, Bennett, Locke, Eric Walrond, and Walter White. They were joined by their elders, Du Bois, James Weldon Johnson, and Georgia Douglas Johnson. Thus arrayed, they were presented to an audience including many of the most distinguished personages in the nation's literary life. From mainstream publishing houses came Frederick Allen of Harper Brothers, Horace Liveright of Boni, Liveright, and Walter Bartlett of Scribner's. The influential journal editors Carl Van Doren of the *Century*, Devere Allen of the *World Tomorrow*, Freda Kirchwey of the *Nation*, and Paul Kellogg of the *Survey Graphic* were on hand. Among the writers attending were Eugene O'Neill and Ridgely Torrence, playwrights whose representations of black life had won favor with blacks, and the novelist Zona Gale, who would write the foreword to Fauset's third book. Rounding out the hundred or so guests were sundry notables, including board members of the Urban League and the NAACP.

After making prefatory remarks, Charles Johnson presented Locke, the evening's master of ceremonies. Fauset's publisher, Horace Liveright, spoke next. Rather than the guest of honor's, he promoted another book on his list, Jean Toomer's *Cane*, and lamented its poor sales. Du Bois, introduced as a representative of the "older school," explained the shortcomings of earlier black writers who "were of necessity pioneers." Following his introduction as an anthologist and one

"who had given invaluable encouragement" to the younger group, James Weldon Johnson rose with salutations. In the main address, Columbia University professor Van Doren might have had Fauset in mind when he declared that "a Negro novelist who tells the simple story of any aspiring colored man or woman will call as with a bugle the minds of all just persons, white or black, to listen to him." He did not mention her name. Finally, after further remarks by Walter White, Montgomery Gregory, and art collector Albert Barnes, the evening's guest of honor was presented. One discerns a speck of irony in Charles Johnson's comment that "Miss Jessie Fauset was given a place of distinction on the program."[56]

Miss Fauset performed as her hosts expected. She thanked her friends for their assistance, and after singling out Dr. Du Bois as her "best friend and severest critic," she sat down. Years later, in a private letter to Locke, she vented the rage her good manners compelled her at the time to conceal. Accusing him of going out of his way to tell even her own brother that the dinner had not been for her, she fumed that she "still remember[ed] the consummate cleverness with which you that night as toastmaster strove to keep speech and comment away from the person for whom the occasion was meant."[57] Because she had by then several reasons to consider Locke an enemy, she found it easy to affix the blame.

More likely, Locke was adhering to the agenda set by Charles Johnson, one from which none of the speakers demurred. Its goal was to announce the existence of the black cultural awakening to the white men and women with the money and clout to sponsor its artists. They got the message. First to respond was Kellogg, the *Survey Graphic* editor, who offered to devote a special issue of his journal to the work of black writers; the issue was subsequently published in book form as *The New Negro*. Doubtless Fauset, a loyal race woman, welcomed this news. Still, she might have wondered whether procuring publishing contracts required slighting her achievement as a novelist or, for that matter, as an editor who, like James Weldon Johnson, had given "invaluable encouragement" to novice writers. Fauset was no prognosticator, but perhaps during the evening David Lewis calls "the dress rehearsal of what was soon to be known as the

'Harlem Renaissance,'" she divined: whatever she had done to produce it, Fauset would not have a starring role when the renaissance hit the big time.

The "Horizon" column in the November 1924 issue of *The Crisis* announced that "Miss Jessie Redmon Fauset had sailed for France" (29). She would be gone for six months but would continue to write for the journal while away. She was also hoping to complete her second novel. Fauset's first foreign dispatch, "Yarrow Revisited," was published in January 1925. Like Wordsworth in the poem to which her title alludes, Fauset found that reality did not accord with memory. In contrast to the Paris of her youth, the weather was gray, the pensions were cold and shabbily furnished, and the people were as courteous, but no more and no less courteous than anywhere else. Paris simply made Fauset feel more American, not African-American but American, than she ever did in America.

Two months later, her essay on the Sorbonne suggested that her affection for Paris had been rekindled. "The soul's deep valley was not slow / Its brightness to recover." Most of the piece gives a rather dry history of the greatest institution of learning in France. But the conclusion reveals Fauset's sensibility. It depicts two "absolutely black girls," moving across the university courtyard; their nationality is Haitian, their ancestry pure African. In an image that anticipates James Baldwin's "Stranger in the Village," Fauset evokes the figures of Pasteur and Hugo ruminating at the base of the Sorbonne church steps and regarding the black girls with "a benign indifference." But, unlike Baldwin's persona, the girls do not in this moment encounter the culture of the West as alien. Rather, in that culture they encounter themselves. Indeed, "so completely are they themselves that tolerance is a quality which they recognize only when they are exercising it toward others."[58]

In the interim, Fauset had told a reporter for the *Herald Tribune*: "I like Paris because I find something here, something of integrity, which I seem to have strangely lost in my own country." To put things simply, she went on: "I like to live among people and surroundings where I am not always conscious of 'thou shall not.'" Although, she asserted, "I am colored and wish to be known as

colored, . . . sometimes I have felt that my growth as a writer has been hampered in my own country. And so—but only temporarily—I have fled from it."[59] Fauset greatly appreciated the absence of the petty prejudice that shadowed her life at home. She usually took pains to avoid it abroad. When, on one occasion, she attempted to meet the proprietor of the famous bookstore Shakespeare & Company, she was rebuffed. Fauset confided to a friend, "Miss Beach has never acknowledged my note."[60] So although Fauset was well aware of the Anglo-American expatriate community, she had little contact with its members.

Her mood remained exultant. Writing from Venice, she told Arthur Spingarn that it was "the first time since I was seventeen that I have been—comparatively—free from fetters." She was particularly glad "to be for once outside the pull of routine duties." Moreover, Europe offered possibilities foreclosed to her at home: "I've had some taste of truly cosmopolitan life such as I should never have met with in America, not even in New York."[61] A rejuvenated Fauset returned to the United States.

She was, however, probably more eager to complete her novel than to resume her duties at *The Crisis*. Early in 1926, she wrote Spingarn confiding her plan to resign her post and requesting his assistance in her job search. But, as the letter made clear, she realized that no comparable career options existed. She was emphatic about her wish *not* to return to the classroom, but, to be on the safe side, she had taken the teachers examination anyway. Although she typed very well, she confessed she knew "nothing of shorthand." Her training was in French. She preferred a position as a publisher's reader, a social secretary, or a job in some capacity at a foundation. In the first instance, she was willing, "if the question of color should come up . . . to work at home." Fauset was surely aware that the question was inevitable; her willingness to compromise was no less agonizing for being deliberate. In closing, she admitted to Spingarn that "I am for various reasons very much at sea just now."[62]

Fauset's years of dedicated service, the high esteem in which she held Du Bois, and her decision not to specify her reasons for leaving the *Crisis* have prompted speculation about her motives. Sylvander reports Fauset's displeasure with Du Bois's slowness to repay a loan she and her sister advanced him. David Lewis insinuates the possibility that Fauset was in love with her distinguished boss. Certainly, she felt a deep emotional attachment to him; it was not necessarily romantic. In any case, it did not blind her to his flaws. Du Bois was not an easy man to work for.

In a biographical sketch, which she published anonymously in *The World Tomorrow*, Fauset was lavish with her praise ("an instinctive aristocrat," "a man born to lead," poet, *litterateur*, scholar). She took pains to defend him from the charge that he was embittered. As evidence, she offered snapshots of his life when he was not on the battlefield for the race and could be found dancing a Highland fling or eating hot dogs at Coney Island. Yet she acknowledged that Du Bois was arrogant, even haughty, and irascible. Moreover, in an essay replete with references to his personal accomplishments, she credited *The Crisis*, rather than its editor-in-chief, as having been "the greatest single contributing factor in the growth of significant Negro writers." In so doing, she retained some well-deserved credit for herself.[63]

Perhaps that provided consolation, for Fauset's hopes for a new position went nowhere. In 1927, she returned to the classroom at DeWitt Clinton High School, where she taught until 1944. She wrote her three remaining novels during school vacations.

Plum Bun (1928), Fauset's second novel, is generally considered her best. Although, like *There Is Confusion*, it relies on the marriage plot, to which it adds a complementary plot concerning "passing," the narrative is less digressive. Its arguments are more forceful. In its social critique, the novel represents the interlocking oppressions of race, gender, and class. Cautiously, but clearly, it anticipates what sociologist Deborah King calls "multiple jeopardy, multiple consciousness," her term for the forces that constrict black women's lives and that in their simultaneity multiply the negative effect each would exert alone.[64] It dramatizes issues of gender politics, including interracial romance and "free love," in ways that belie Fauset's reputation for propriety.

Through its shifting settings, the novel presents a broad view of the social hierarchies that constitute contemporary society. It high-

lights the contrasts between social reality and cultural myth. For example, when the protagonist Angela Murray reflects on the expression "free, white and twenty-one," she defines it as "this sense of owning the world, this realization that other things being equal, all things were possible" (88). Almost immediately comes the realization that other things are *not* equal: "'If I were a man,' she said, 'I could be president,' and laughed at herself for the 'if' itself proclaimed a limitation. . . ." She understands that freedom and opportunity are unequally distributed along racial and gender lines so that "men had a better time of it than women, colored men than colored women, white men than white women" (89). Within these categories, money or the lack of it brings a greater or lesser share of one's "inalienable" rights.

Light-skinned enough to pass for white, the protagonist is able to shift racial identities and gauge the gains and losses each shift makes. As a black woman, she lives constantly on edge, lest she be subjected to racial humiliation. In even the most trivial pursuits, going to a movie or to a restaurant for example, the possibility of public rejection looms. When the stakes are higher, as for a scholarship or a job, the cost is computed in material as well as psychic terms. By contrast, as a "white" woman, Angela has access to educational and employment opportunities, comfortable housing, and public accommodations. She moves freely through the world.

As a woman, she is nevertheless subject to sexual exploitation by men. A cynical white female acquaintance instructs Angela on the rules of courtship: "It is a game and the hardest game in the world for a woman, but the most fascinating. . . . [Y]ou have to be careful not to withhold too much and yet to give very little. If we don't give enough we lose them. If we give too much we lose ourselves" (145). Bold in her naivete, the protagonist looks forward to playing the game. It defeats her when, fearful of falling back into poverty, she submits to the wealthy white man who pursues her. Only when she denies her sister in order to safeguard her affair does she realize that she has lost herself.

Set mainly in New York during the 1920s, *Plum Bun* is in part a novel not only of, but about, the Harlem Renaissance. Like Fauset's essays, it explores issues of cultural politics, particularly the situation of the black artist, the vagaries of patronage, and the uneasy relationship between the uptown and downtown artistic and literary worlds.

Its protagonist is an aspiring artist; it fictionalizes historical figures, including Du Bois, as well as events from African-American cultural life. In *Plum Bun*, cultural politics are determined by the politics of race and class.

Several of the black characters are art students at New York's Cooper Union, and their narratives emphasize the obstacles black artists confront. When her race became known, Angela was forced to withdraw from art school in Philadelphia. In New York, she is passing, as is her fellow student Anthony Cross. Cross, whose name possibly alludes to the poem by Langston Hughes, carries the burdens of his mixed-race heritage furtively. Both he and Angela are aided in their subterfuge by the inability of whites even to imagine the existence of black artists. The one visibly black student, Rachel Powell, is gifted, hard working, yet isolated from her peers; the honorific "Miss" by which she is always addressed serves chiefly to mark her distance from the group. In a plot sequence derived from an actual incident involving sculptor Augusta Savage, the novel depicts Powell's winning a competition for a fellowship abroad; when the donors learn that she is black, they revoke the award and explain that they are interested "not in Ethnology but in Art" (359).[65]

As Deborah McDowell observes, the novel's epigraph introduces the tension between the fulfilled expectations promised by the rhyme and the cultural script for women it encodes and the thwarted expectations of the novel's black female characters (xvi): "To Market, to Market / To buy a Plum bun; / Home again, Home again, Market is done." A source of narrative cohesion, the rhyme reinforces the theme of sexual commodification. In addition, it anticipates the theme of departure and return, which is also explored in *Plum Bun*.

The protagonist travels from Philadelphia to New York to Paris. Along the way, she "passes" from the black world to the white and is thereby enabled to sojourn in Greenwich Village and to visit Harlem. In the novel's denouement, she is physically in Paris but spiritually at home. She has re-embraced her sister, her race, and the values of her childhood. As though disdaining its subtitle, "a novel without a moral," she has divined the moral of *Plum Bun*. Accordingly, she has learned to travel in place, to re-create the values of home wherever she goes. Hers is a view the novel endorses, for while it offers a keen-

eyed appraisal of cultural, racial, and sexual politics in its cosmopolitan settings, its representation of "home" is consistently nostalgic.

The novel's deployment of spatial metaphors reinforces this point. It opens with a description of Opal Street, home to the central characters and "as streets go, . . . no jewel of the first water." "Narrow, unsparkling, uninviting," without mystery or allure, it is "an unpretentious little street lined with unpretentious little houses, inhabited for the most part by unpretentious little people" (11).[66] The reader learns much more quickly than the protagonist that Opal is a semiprecious jewel nonetheless. As the narrator informs us, a little house on Opal Street represented to Angela's parents, who "had known poverty and homelessness, . . . the *ne plus ultra* of ambition." The stories of how they achieved it "would have made a latter-day Iliad." The unwritten epic in which the parents participate would relate the historical journey of African-Americans from slavery to freedom. But *Plum Bun* tells the less heroic tale of their daughter, who prizes the idea of freedom without having any sense of its meaning.

In contrast to the narrow, drab streets of her childhood, Angela determines to seek "paths which led to broad thoroughfares, large, bright houses, delicate niceties of existence" (12). Predictably, she is later awed by the grand streets of Manhattan: by the "canyon" of Fifth Avenue and "the broad-bosomed river" of Fourteenth Street. She feels "she was living on the crest of a wave of excitement and satisfaction, which would never wane, never break, never be spent" (87). Like a Christian pilgrim, however, Angela must learn that "broad is the way, that leadeth to destruction," while "narrow is the way which leadeth unto life" (Matthew 8:13, 14).

Although it draws heavily on Christian symbolism, the creed the novel advances is secular. Tellingly, the frequent allusion to Pope's "The Dying Christian" functions both as a reflection of the father's faith and as a comment on Angela's growing estrangement from both faith and family. The chief article of faith in *Plum Bun* is the primacy of the family, and the Murrays represent the ideal: "Father, mother and children, well-dressed, well-fed, united, going to church on a beautiful Sunday morning; there was an immense cosmic rightness about all this" (22). The novel proposes this ideal very seriously; one measure of how much so is the close resemblance between the descriptions of the Murrays' home life and Fauset's autobiographical essays, especially "Sunday Afternoon." But, while the narratives of the parents' lives in *Plum Bun* reflect the historical effects of segregation and racism, in their psychological configuration, the Murrays are a family drawn from the pages of nineteenth-century fiction.

The patriarch, Junius, is noble and industrious. By marrying Mattie, he "saved" her from the potential sexual exploitation to which her job as a domestic made her vulnerable. Proudly announcing his matrimonial intentions to her employer, he declines an offered gift and insists that the employer pay Mattie only what she has earned. A generous provider, he purchases a house and eventually earns enough so that Mattie can have household help herself. Unfailingly wise, he dismisses his wife's dream that their daughters be great artists. He maintains that they need "a good, plain education," and she recognizes that their "father's always right" (55). Unlike my account, the text notes without irony that to Mattie, Junius was "God." Upon his death, she wills her own.

To Junius, Mattie is "essentially feminine" and "perfectly harmless" (15). Pretty, charming, and frivolous, she loves clothes and relishes "being even on the fringe of a fashionable gathering." Light-skinned enough to pass racially and therefore to indulge the latter fancy, Mattie enjoys passing time in the foyers of grand hotels and other luxurious but forbidden public spaces. The novel draws no connection between Mattie's racial marginality and her vestibular relation to culture and society. Instead it treats her as a comic character, like Mrs. Bennett in *Pride and Prejudice*. Mattie does, however, convey one bit of putative wisdom. Despite the convenience her own color affords, she does not place a premium on it; instead she minimizes issues of race: ". . . you get so taken up with the problem of living, just life itself you know, that by and by being coloured or not is just one thing more or less that you have to contend with" (55). Having no cause to take her mother seriously, Angela ignores her counsel. Subsequent events in the novel seem to impugn it. Nevertheless, at its conclusion, the novel reiterates Mattie's conviction.

Toward the end of *Plum Bun*, Angela increasingly identifies with her mother. She has ended the affair and the episode has "left no trace of her moral nature" (245). Indeed, in the novel's moral scheme, Angela

can escape censure because even if she has tried to use her white lover, "he had been paid in full for any advantages she had meant to gain" (244). In the act necessary to reclaim her honor, she has reconciled with her sister. Beyond that, she has forged a wary sisterhood with Rachel Powell. To protest the retraction of Powell's scholarship, Angela renounces her own award and publicly claims her race. Having scaled down her ambition—she will be an illustrator rather than an artist—she considers marriage "the only, the most desirable and natural end" (274). What she perceives is not marriage as a divinely ordained union, but as a practical foundation on which a smart, ambitious woman might build a life. That life would be governed by conventions that constitute a "concentrated compendium of the art of living" and are as worthy of respect as "warm, vital impulses" (228). Hardly an artist's life, the life she envisions replicates her mother's.

That vision is delineated when Angela returns to Opal Street and visits a house identical to the one in which she was raised. "[I]t seemed a tiny island of protection reared out of and against an encroaching sea of troubles. In fancy she saw her father and mother almost a quarter of a century ago coming proudly to such a home, their little redoubt of refuge against the world" (366). At the close of the novel, Angela and Anthony reunite in Paris. But when and wherever they establish a home, the novel seems to assure, it will be one in which the social conventions are observed and in which societal conventions such as racism are not confronted but kept at bay.

Shortly after *Plum Bun* was published, on 10 April 1929, Jessie Fauset married Herbert E. Harris, an official of the Victory Insurance Company. According to an article in the *New York Amsterdam News*, the bride was given in marriage by her brother Arthur. Her attendants were women as socially prominent as she. The bride and groom had been feted at a string of prenuptial events—showers and luncheons, dinners and bridge parties. The article referred to the bride's academic and literary accomplishments, but it emphasized her social status; her novels and her membership in the Delta Sigma Theta sorority were given equal weight.

With due caution, one might connect the benign view of marriage in *Plum Bun* and Fauset's decision to marry for the first time at age forty-seven. After attaining a breadth of experience that her heroine craved and achieving a level of success far beyond that which she could realistically invent for any of her characters, Jessie Fauset might have sought for herself a little redoubt of refuge from the world.[67]

Admirably, she remained determined to write. But her next book, *The Chinaberry Tree* (1931), offers little worth admiring. As if to achieve the goal set forth in the foreword—to depict the "breathing-spells, in-between spaces where colored men and women work and love and go their ways with no thought of the 'problem'"—Fauset minimizes the most compelling narrative in the novel. Far more dramatic than the lifeless romance between protagonist Laurentine Strange and Dr. Denleigh or the courtship of the doomed young lovers, Melissa and Malory, is the love story involving the wealthy white Colonel Halloway and the black servant woman, Sal. Shadowed by the legacy of slavery, symbolized by the chinaberry tree, which has been transplanted from Aunt Sal's Alabama birthplace to the New Jersey home Halloway has purchased for her, the couple cannot legitimize their love. Yet love is what the novel insists they share. Furthermore, the novel argues that given the circumstances, Aunt Sal should not be judged according to the standards of conventional morality. However, her daughter, Laurentine, a post-slavery black woman, is free to be virtuous. Thus, after challenging the historical denigration of black women like Aunt Sal, the novel endorses the moral standards on which the denigration was based.

At no point does the novel adopt the perspective of Sal or her white lover. He dies before the story opens, and she is mainly silent. Given Fauset's tin ear for black vernacular, the few bits of dialogue Sal is given seem too many. By far the greater failure is Fauset's inability to imagine the character. Never an intrepid traveler, she does not even try to visit the inner life of an illiterate, southern black woman. She leaves it to Denleigh, who barely knows Sal, to sum up her character: "She wasn't a slave—she didn't have to yield to him. He loved her in spite of her being black and she loved him in spite of his being white. I don't advocate their line of action and yet there is something awe-inspiring" (160). That "something" remains unexpressed.[68]

What is reiterated, beyond many readers' capacity to endure, is the effect of Sal's actions on her daughter. Laurentine becomes a pariah whose constant plea is "Oh God, you know all I want is a chance to show them how decent I am" (36). For Laurentine, the breathing spells are few. Yet she never questions the right of "them" (the populace of the fictional New Jersey town of Red Brook) to judge her. The omniscient narrator is only slightly more willing to pass judgment on the blacks who shun the Stranges: "Gradually like the old definition of a simile, the case of Sal Strange and her daughter, Laurentine, became confused, the sign was accepted for the thing signified and a coldness and despite toward the unfortunate mother and child became a fetish without any real feeling or indignation on the part of the executioners for the offenses committed. Neglect of the two women became crystallized" (22). Their representation in the novel produces the same effect.

Fauset modifies the stock situation and stereotyped characters by creating a northern, post–Civil War setting. But the epithets, "Colonel" and "Aunt"; the descriptions of the house, which carry a vaguely antebellum odor; the stasis in which the protagonist remains, as if oblivious to twentieth-century notions of mobility, not to speak of modes of transportation; and the accursed mood that seems to envelop the entire family drain all feeling from the novel.

The Chinaberry Tree comes closest to expressing feeling in the admonition a rejected suitor offers Sal's niece, Melissa: "Be a good girl, a really good girl all the time." The warning baffles the immature teenage, who has never considered challenging the town's puritanical moral code. To the reader, the import is clearer. However much they might understand or at least condone Sal's actions, neither Laurentine nor Melissa could risk emulating them. On the contrary, propriety for the New Negro woman was virtually a racial obligation. Despite the novel's muted denials, in assuming the obligation, the New Negro woman censured her foremother and martyred herself. It was, indeed, a strange kind of freedom.

The elaborate structure of Fauset's final novel, *Comedy: American Style* (1933), announces its ambition. Reflecting Fauset's longstanding attraction to theatrical tropes, the novel is divided into six sections:

The Plot, the Characters, Teresa's Act, Oliver's Act, Phebe's Act, and Curtain. As is quickly evident, Fauset's reach exceeds her grasp; the scaffolding is more impressive than the narrative it supports. So uncertain is the author's control of the material that she saps the power of the novel's most dramatic incident by reporting it almost one hundred pages before staging it.

Despite its title, *Comedy: American Style* seems intent on representing the tragedy of race in America. But it achieves only melodrama.[69] Part of the problem is ideological. The view that racial prejudice is a burden that blacks simply overcome before they can attempt "the ordinary businesses of life" (124) does not lead to a tragic perspective. As she had throughout her career, Fauset continued to show how most blacks get on with the business of living. Also problematic is the relentless emphasis on the perils of courtship, which, while justifying the title, further undermines the novel's potentially tragic perspective. The novel's dramatic irony derives mainly from a series of misalliances that evoke the mood of "La Vie C'est La Vie." But Fauset cannot sustain such arch sophistication at book length. Nor should she have tried. To the extent that it recycles familiar themes and incidents, *Comedy: American Style* guarantees its own failure.

What is new and promising is the novel's antiheroine, Olivia Cary. A self-hating woman, a conniver, a shameless traitor to the race, and, most shockingly, an unloving mother, Olivia is a new character in African-American literature. Deliberately revising elements of the narratives of race men such as Du Bois (*The Souls of Black Folk*) and James Weldon Johnson (*The Autobiography of an Ex-Colored Man*), Fauset creates the narrative of an anti-race woman. Living in a small Massachusetts town, like the protagonists of Du Bois and Johnson, Olivia is called "nigger" by one of her playmates and is forced to recognize her difference from them. Soon after the family moves, and when a new teacher identifies her as Italian, Olivia sees a way to escape humiliation. The need to escape becomes an obsession.

When Olivia recognizes that she will be unable to escape completely herself—she decides that marriage to a light-skinned Negro physician is preferable to a union with a white man of lower status—she resolves that her children will be free of any racial stigma. Olivia's

hopes are thwarted when her third child, a son and namesake, betrays the mark of blackness. Her son represents "the totality of that black blood which she so despised. . . . To her Oliver meant shame. He meant more than that; he meant the expression of her failure to be truly white."[70] Unflinchingly, she acts out her hatred of her son; alternately banishing him from the family home or asking him to remain to impersonate a Filipino butler for her white friends, she ultimately drives him to suicide.

Through Olivia, the novel depicts racism's endless capacity to wound and to make victimizers of its victims. But it is a portrayal drawn very much from the outside; Fauset declines to develop the character from within. When Locke, among others, criticized the novel's characters for being one-dimensional types, Fauset defended herself by explaining that she had based them on a real family.[71] Her response indicates a naivete about the art of fiction and a refusal to consider that their real-life provenance might have deepened her aversion to speculating about her characters' innermost feelings. Such speculation might have been unseemly. So reluctant is Fauset to imagine an interior life for her protagonist that she does not even assign Olivia her own "act." Albeit for different reasons, Fauset is as loath to explore the psyche of a woman like Olivia as she is of a woman like Aunt Sal. To do so in this case would have meant confronting persistent contradictions in her ideology and art.

Several of these concern race. On the one hand, Fauset is ever conscious of the absurdity of classifying people according to a criterion as arbitrary as skin color. In fact, much of the comedy in her novel relies on the inability to determine, by looking, whether a character is black or white. In the case of the very light-skinned Phebe, for example, whites mistake her for a white woman when she is with a black suitor and attack him for transgressing racial boundaries; a prospective white suitor rejects her when she tells him she is black. While the novel treats these responses as absurd, it attempts to justify an equally arbitrary intraracial classification. For example, in the novel's moral calculus, the Cary in-laws lead altogether admirable lives. Most laudably, considering their own white-looking appearance, they are strong "race people." Yet, despite their devotion to racial uplift, "neither one of them would have married, nor would they have wanted their sons to marry with Negroes of unmixed blood" (190). As if to acknowledge the indefensibility of this view, the narrator quickly attributes it to "personal taste" and adds that the Carys chose their friends, if not each other, without regard to complexion. In other words, some of their best friends are black.

More than ever before, Fauset seems discomfited here by the resemblance between the racial views she endorses and those she censures. Both rely on discredited nineteenth-century notions of racial "blood"; both judge character on the basis of color; both assign greater value to light skin than to dark. Both have tragic consequences. In the only unhappy ending she wrote, Fauset acknowledges as much in *Comedy: American Style*. Olivia ends up living in Paris in a shabby pension, friendless and poor. In the final scene, she looks out of her window and fixes her gaze on a mother listening to her child read, "resting her dark head against his fair one" (327). In America, such contrasts are never simple, innocent, or happy. Yet, this novel seeks too often to deny the complexities.

Fauset's failure to write another novel suggests that she recognized the form she had chosen was inadequate for the story she wanted to tell. Couples marry at the end of *Comedy*, but their pallid passion is no match for Olivia's hatred. Even Marise, the show business character, said to outshine Josephine Baker, seems lifeless. At moments the novel seems ready to question assumptions regarding private and public life, family and work, as well as race, but it never quite does.

One brief scene intimates what might have been at stake. Olivia works outside the home; she is apparently a social worker, although the novel never depicts her on the job. She travels frequently, but she is not an adventurous traveler. The narrator mocks her "carefully planned tourist trip," on which "not a stop, not a sight varied from the usual." On one occasion she attends an International Women's Peace Conference, yet she was "unconscious of having assisted at a great feministic gesture" (103–104). What she remembered instead was sharing a cup of tea with a woman from Ohio. Despite the disparate genres and the obvious dissimilarities—Fauset was a woman who was always conscious of the historical significance of her endeavors

and a traveler who wandered off the beaten path—the scene recalls the conclusion of the essay "Dark Algiers the White." Although Olivia is not an autobiographical character, some of her attitudes were also Jessie Fauset's. In judging the character so harshly, Fauset might have been questioning the privileging of the private over the public, the retreat into domesticity, and the denial of difference, which ultimately cripple her fiction.

Three

Nella Larsen

Passing for What?

In January 1926, *Young's Magazine* published "The Wrong Man," a story about sexual transgression and its consequences. Fabricated, concealed, and mistaken identities are its theme. Against a glamorous backdrop in which the swirl of women's gorgeous dresses creates "a riotously hued scene," the scarlet-haired protagonist, dressed in smoke-colored chiffon, seems "even more flamingly clad than the rest." Images of fire and ice, suffocation and entrapment recur. Suddenly an orchestra, +clare which has been playing background music, "blare[s] into something wild and impressionistic, with a primitive staccato understrain of jazz." The action builds to the moment when the female protagonist, alternately paralyzed by fear of being unmasked and desperate to ward off discovery, commits an act that jeopardizes the life she has carefully constructed for herself. All of these elements make "The Wrong Man" of a piece with Nella Larsen's two novels, *Quicksand* (1928) and *Passing* (1929). But not until 1992 was the pseudonymous anagram "Allen Semi" transposed to reveal "Nella Imes," Larsen's married name.[1]

If the male pseudonym obscures the author's identity, so too does the absence of racial markers in the text. Although the story does not identify the race of its characters, plot details suggest they are not black. The setting is an exclusive Long Island estate that could have come right out of *The Great Gatsby*, which F. Scott Fitzgerald had published the year before. In dress and manner, the characters seem smugly upper class. The protagonist, Julia Romley, is an interior decorator who has "everything": love, wealth, and social position. Ralph Tyler, the man from her past, is a rich and famous adventurer. Julia's husband, Jim, Tyler's college classmate, fears that Tyler regards their social set as "a soft, lazy, self-pampering lot" (6). As if to confirm that judgment, he plans to host a "small, handpicked dinner party" in Tyler's honor.

Yet, despite the ambience, the relation of the main characters to the social elite is ambiguous. Implicitly, the story calls into question the definition of an elite. Looking over the crowd, the protagonist is reminded of the nursery rhyme "Rich man, poor man, / Beggar man, thief, / Doctor, lawyer, / Indian chief." No matter its source, anyone with money enough to pay the price of admission may join this club. But the protagonist does not question the legitimacy of the group; she just perceives her personal history to be dubious. Migrating eastward, Julia has left San Francisco and Chicago for New York and Boston. She does not speak of her past. Neither does Ralph Tyler, whom she knew in California. Tyler, too, has invented himself, though on a much grander scale. Not only his past, but his present is shrouded in mystery. Jim Romley knows only that Tyler is "an explorer, just back from some godforsaken place on the edge of nowhere. Been head of some expedition lost somewhere in Asia for years, given up for dead" (6).

The story invests Tyler with a mythic aura like Gatsby's, but it puts his history to a different use. Like the eruption of jazz, Tyler's history becomes a means by which the story inscribes issues of race. As is true in Larsen's mature fiction, the emphasis is on racial ambiguity. In this instance, Tyler's stint in the tropics has blurred his racial identity. Twice described as "a tall browned man," Tyler looks like the Indian chief of the rhyme. To Julia, his face has "yellowed." But, if Tyler has relinquished his white skin privilege, he has acquired an air of self-

sufficiency, superiority, and indifference that puts Jim Romley on edge. In his uneasiness, Romley makes an allusion to slavery in which he constructs whites as oppressed "others." To Jim, Tyler looks "as if he owned us all and despised the whole tribe of us" (6). In the same passage, Romley continues his fragmented narrative of Tyler's adventures: "Discovered a buried city or something; great contribution to civilization and all that, you know. They say he brought back some emeralds worth a king's ransom" (6). Here Tyler is both explorer and exploiter; the exploitation is duly rationalized as a boon to "civilization." Tellingly, while Jim can imagine the existence of jewels available for plunder, he cannot visualize an inhabited landscape. No Asians trouble his imagination; they are all dead and buried. By entering this world on the edge of nowhere, Ralph Tyler has risked the same fate.

His safe return threatens the far less adventurous Julia with a kind of death in life. Imagistically and thematically, Julia's narrative recalls Bonner's essay "On Being Young—A Woman—and Colored." Of course, Julia is not black. But the text associates her with the color gray, which in Larsen's novels becomes another sign of racial ambiguity. The controlling images of Julia's narrative are stasis and sterility. She shivers at the sight of Tyler and explains the shiver to a companion as "just someone walking over my grave." To find a place to think, she escapes to "a small deserted room." The final scene of the story begins with her sitting "motionless in the summerhouse in the rock garden" (7). Not surprisingly, she waits to be addressed. When she speaks, it is "in a low hesitating voice" (7).

The terrible secret that Julia fears will destroy her life is the story's most melodramatic aspect. She has been Tyler's mistress; his money has paid for her education, which is in turn the key to her comfortable life. Only after pleading with her companion to guard her secret does she realize she has confided in a stranger, the titular wrong man. More interesting than the turn of the plot is the explanation Julia offers for her transgression: "[W]hen a girl has been sick and starving on the streets, anything can happen to her; . . . she's grateful for food and shelter at any price" (8). She offers this unsentimental explanation without apology.[2] In order to survive in her present, less desperate

circumstances, Julia has concealed her history, recreated her self, and begun to pass.

Adopting a pseudonym, which Larsen did at least twice, constitutes a form of passing for a writer.[3] The motives may be various; in Larsen's case, they can only be conjectured. Perhaps she wanted to mask her insecurity as a novice or to explore forbidden issues or emotions; or, as scholar Charles Larson speculates, she wanted to send a coded and highly personal message to her philandering spouse. Whatever her reason was in this specific instance, Nella Larsen was, in general, pre-occupied with exploring strategies of concealment, self-invention, and passing in her fiction. In keeping with her reputation as "the mystery woman of the Harlem Renaissance," Nella Larsen's life has often been read as a text in which these same strategies recur.[4]

At the height of the Harlem Renaissance, Nella Larsen published two novels, *Quicksand* and *Passing.* They were widely and favorably reviewed. Applauded by the critics, Larsen was heralded as a rising star in the black artistic firmament. She was treated accordingly: invitations to speaking engagements and social affairs came her way, as did significant honors. In 1930, she became the first African-American woman to receive a Guggenheim Fellowship for Creative Writing. Her star then faded as quickly as it had risen; by 1934, Nella Larsen had disappeared from Harlem and from literature. This chapter will examine some of the factors that led to her disappearance and the thirty-year silence that followed. It will also sketch some elements of the cultural zeitgeist that shaped and was reflected in Larsen's writing. But it will concentrate on the novels that she left behind, for these novels prove that at least some of her promise was realized.

Among the best written of the Harlem Renaissance, her books comment incisively on issues of marginality and cultural dualism that engaged Larsen's more famous contemporaries, including Jean Toomer and Claude McKay. However, Larsen's most striking insights are into psychic dilemmas confronting certain black women. These women, like those drawn by Jessie Fauset, are by virtue of their appearance, education, and social class atypical in the extreme. Unlike Fauset, however, Larsen makes no claim for them as representative or worthy of emulation. Swiftly viewed, they resemble the tragic mulat-

toes of literary convention. On closer examination, they become the means through which the author demonstrates the psychological costs of racism and sexism.

For Larsen, the tragic mulatto was the most accessible convention for the portrayal of middle-class black women in fiction.[5] But her protagonists subvert the convention consistently. They are neither noble nor long-suffering; their plights are not used to symbolize the oppression of blacks, the irrationality of prejudice, or the absurdity of concepts of race generally. Larsen's deviations from these conventional representations signal that her concerns lie elsewhere, but only recently have critics begun to decode her major themes. Perhaps Larsen's most effective act of passing was masking the subversive themes that frequently shimmered beneath the surface of her fiction. Both *Quicksand* and *Passing* contemplate the inextricability of the racism and sexism that confront the black woman in her quest for self-hood. As they navigate between racial and cultural polarities, Larsen's protagonists attempt to fashion a sense of self—free both of suffocating restrictions of ladyhood and fantasies of the exotic female Other. They fail. The tragedy for these mulattoes is the impossibility of self-definition. Larsen's protagonists assume false identities that ensure social survival but result in psychological suicide. In one way or another, they all "pass." Passing for white, Larsen's novels remind us, is only one way this game is played.

Nella Larsen was herself an enigmatic figure to those who came in contact with her during the Harlem Renaissance years. The public faces she wore were inconsistent, the flippant and frivolous socialite alternating with the serious novelist. Her professional commitments were similarly diverse: nurse, librarian, and, most briefly, writer. Larsen's racial identity was ambiguous as well. She claimed to be a child of that most-detested union in American society, a white mother and a black father. She had the option to pass in and out of the white and black worlds, but she seems rarely to have exercised it, and then, much like Fauset's Mattie Murray, only for temporary social convenience. Alluding to the possibility of passing offered one way to intensify the mystery she cultivated about her past. The shadowy portrait she drew suggested many parallels between Larsen's fictional

Nella Larsen Imes, ca. 1930.
Photograph by Pinchot Studio.
Courtesy Yale Collection of American
Literature, Beinecke Rare Book and
Manuscript Library, Yale University.

characters and their creator. But like all self-portraits, it should be approached warily, particularly since even her contemporaries knew nothing of her pre-Harlem past except what she told them.

Larsen was born Nellie Walker on 13 April 1891 in Chicago.[6] As Larsen told it, her mother had immigrated to the United States from Denmark, and her father was from the Virgin Islands, formerly the Danish West Indies. Her mother's family bitterly resented the marriage. Their reprieve came when the marriage ended abruptly. Nellie was two years old. Shortly afterward, her mother remarried a man of her own race and nationality. One may infer from the novels that Larsen's stepfather found her presence in the home vexing. Years later, she told an interviewer, "I don't see my family much now. It might make it awkward for them, particularly my half-sister."[7]

Cross-checking old city directories, census data, records of vital statistics, and school registers, Thadious Davis has unearthed a history more incredible than any of Larsen's biomythographies. According to Davis's biography, Larsen's mother, Mary Hanson, was Danish; her father, Peter Walker, was "colored" and probably an immigrant from the Danish West Indies. Although they applied for a marriage license in 1890, no record of their marriage is extant. The father of Hanson's second child, Anna, born in 1893, was Peter Larson. Mother, father, and daughter were all "white." Peter Larson (later Larsen) and Mary (now Marie) Hanson (or Hansen) married on February 7, 1894. Davis speculates that Peter Walker and Peter Larsen might well have been the same person. If so, Peter Larsen became, like the protagonist of James Weldon Johnson's novel, an ex–colored man. The subsequent dislocations his child Nellie (later Nellye and finally Nella) experienced, possibly including a stint in the Erring Woman's Refuge for Reform, stemmed from the inconvenient fact that she remained "colored" in a family that was passing for "white."[8]

Along with the alienation she experienced at home, she was ostracized at school and in the neighborhood. Her elementary school classmates were mostly the children of German and Scandinavian immigrants. Like their elders, these children had quickly assimilated American racial attitudes. Larsen later attended Wendell Phillips High School, which did have a substantial number of African-American students, but her status as outsider remained unchanged.

Estranged from her family, Larsen enrolled in the high school department of Fisk University in Nashville, Tennessee, in 1907. Fisk was among the most prestigious institutions for Negroes in the country. Many, though far from all, of its students were children of the nascent Negro middle class. Evidently Larsen felt no more at home in the black bourgeois environment of Fisk than she had in the white working-class neighborhoods of Chicago. She left after one year.[9] Evidently, she was no more at home in an all-black community than she had been in a white one. In an autobiographical note she wrote as a preface to an article on Scandinavian games, published in *The Brownies' Book*, Larsen referred to a sojourn in Denmark, where she claimed to have attended the University of Copenhagen. Eight years later, the section of her novel *Quicksand* set in Denmark seemed to corroborate the autobiographical sketch. But both stories were fictions. In fact, Larsen did not leave the United States.[10]

What she did instead remains a mystery, a part of her past that she went to great lengths to conceal. Records verify that from 1912 to 1915 Larsen was enrolled at New York's Lincoln Hospital Training School for Nurses, and upon her graduation in 1915, she accepted a position as an assistant superintendent of nurses at Tuskegee Institute in Alabama.[11] Whatever idealistic hopes she had harbored were quickly dashed; Larsen found conditions at Tuskegee appalling. Along with their academic and vocational training, students were schooled in subservience and docility. A stringent behavior code was applied to students, faculty, and staff alike. The now urbane, outspoken Larsen quickly ran afoul of the conservative administration, and after a year she and the school authorities "parted with mutual disgust and relief."[12]

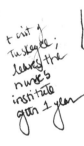

Larsen quit Tuskegee, but she retained her identity as a black American woman. She came back to New York and found work as a nurse, first at Lincoln Hospital and later with the Department of Health. Now, however, she was dissatisfied with her profession. Characteristically, she resolved to pursue a new one. This career brought her to Harlem and an association with the New Negro intelligentsia. In 1922, Larsen took a job as an assistant with the New York Public Library, earned a certificate from its training school in 1923, and soon after became children's librarian at the 135th Street branch. The

Harlem library was an extraordinarily vibrant center during the 1920s, a public forum for readings and debates and an informal meeting place for the community's literati. When Nella Larsen was ready to play a part in the Negro Renaissance, she would find herself center stage.

Young, intelligent, and strikingly cosmopolitan, Larsen's New Negro credentials were almost impeccable. Her marriage to Elmer Imes in 1919 had provided the only missing element, a proper social pedigree. Handsome and debonair, Imes was a research physicist with a Ph.D. from the University of Michigan; at the time of their wedding at New York's Union Theological Seminary, he was employed by a Manhattan engineering development firm. Within the next decade, he would become chair of the physics department at Fisk. In 1931, Boston journalist Eugene Gordon named Imes one of the thirteen most gifted blacks in the United States. In 1925, Imes's brother, William, assumed the pastorate of St. James Presbyterian Church, among the wealthiest and most elite congregations in Harlem. Though Larsen described herself as a "modern" woman who did not believe in religion or churches, the family connection had a definite cachet.

Even before they moved from Jersey City to an apartment on 135th Street in April 1927, Elmer and Nella Larsen Imes were active participants on the Harlem social scene. Walter White, (newly appointed assistant secretary of the NAACP) became a close friend, as did Carl Van Vechten, doyen of Harlem night visitors. James Weldon and Grace Johnson extended invitations. The writer/physician Rudolph Fisher and his wife, Jane, and Dorothy Peterson, a schoolteacher and devotee of the arts, were less well known members of the couple's social group.[13]

In an admiring letter to Van Vechten, her mentor and confidant, Larsen observed: "It *is* nice to find some one writing as if he didnt [*sic*] absolutely despise the age in which he lives. And surely it is more interesting to belong to one's own time, to share its peculiar vision, catch that flying glimpse of the panorama which no subsequent generation can ever recover."[14] It was by becoming a writer that Larsen became truly a woman of her time. For a few brief years—no more than ten in all—Larsen was caught up in the Harlem panorama, but her vision was distinctively her own.

Larsen's earliest publications, descriptions of children's games in Scandinavia, had appeared in *The Brownies' Book* under the byline Nella Larsen Imes. According to Jessie Fauset, who solicited those pieces, it was Stribling's 1922 novel *Birthright* that inspired Larsen, along with Walter White and Fauset herself, to attempt their own novels. Their work, written from inside the black community, was intended, in Fauset's phrase, to "tell the truth about us." No such statement of purpose from Larsen seems extant.[15]

Privately reflecting on "what things there are to write, if one can only write them," Larsen catalogued "society ladies, children, acrobats, governesses, businessmen, countesses, flappers, Nile green bath rooms, beautifully tiled, gay moods and shivering hesitations, all presented in an intensely restrained and civilized manner, and underneath the ironic survival of a much more primitive mood. Delicious."[16] The randomness of the list stands in vivid contrast to the political obligation implied in Fauset's credo. Larsen's sensuous phrases find no counterpart in Fauset's utilitarian fiction. Yet Fauset would have been loath to use a word like "primitive" because she understood her time well enough to know that the word could not be shorn of its racial connotations. In the mid-twenties, when Larsen turned her hand to fiction, expectations of what she as a black woman would write were rigidly defined. They suggest another reason she might have chosen to publish her first short stories under a pseudonym.[17] By 1926, when those stories were published, Larsen had completed the first draft of *Quicksand*; its byline would read Nella Larsen.

Chances are, a decade earlier or later, Larsen would not have attempted a novel. Her decision to do so was doubtless in large part a response to the zeitgeist. As Thadious Davis maintains, "The writer during the Renaissance was just as often *made* as born." Davis asserts that *Quicksand* represented Larsen's attempt to "cash in" on the fad for black literature.[18] In an unpublished interview with Harlem journalist Marion Starkey, Larsen had presented herself in a nobler light. If what was going on was a fad, she reasoned, "it's an awfully good fad." Editors, she averred, "seem to be eager to give us an opportunity to show ourselves to the world as we appear to each other, and not as we formerly appeared in magazine literature, as a strange race of black-

face comedians engaged in putting on a perpetual minstrel show."
Citing the range of writers whose work had come into print and calling
McKay, Du Bois, Toomer, Cullen, Fauset, and Walter White by name,
Larsen concluded that "even if the fad for our writing passes pres-
ently, as it is bound to do I suppose, we will in the meantime have laid
the foundation for our permanent contributions to American culture."[19]

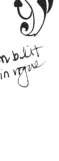

my b lit
in vogue

However noble her intentions were, or how mixed her motives,
Larsen was alert to some of the pitfalls of being a writer in vogue.
When, for example, she considered entering her manuscript in a contest for black writers sponsored by the publishers A. & C. Boni, she
confided to Van Vechten: "I understand, though, that they are a bit
disgusted with what is being submitted. It is being whispered about
that anything literate is sure to be awarded the honor. That's discou-
raging. Of course, it would be nice to get a thousand dollars, just so,
and—the publicity. Not so nice, however, to be merely the best of a
bad lot."[20] She did not enter the competition. Yet she was capable of
advising a friend: "Dorothy, you'd better write some poetry, or something. I've met a man from Macmillans who asked me to look out for
any Negro stuff and send them to him. (Rather mixed grammar but
you get the implication.)"[21] Privately, Larsen was frequently cynical
and, all too often, downright disparaging in her references to the race.
She recognized, though, that the best defense against the exploitation of the marketplace, as against self-abasement, was hard work.

Larsen strove to write a book that met her own standard. She revised extensively, telling Van Vechten on one occasion that she had
resumed work and "celebrated the return by destroying a good half
of what was completed. It *was* awful." Perhaps the changes improved
the manuscript, but the revisions were inadequate. She solicited Van
Vechten's advice—as well as Walter White's—then added her own
critique. "I do think the thing is perhaps not so much *too short*, as *too
thin*. . . . I should hate to have to write even one more word for the
damned thing, but I suppose I could if I absolutely had to."[22] More
than once she wondered if she could see the work through. An illness
in 1926 and a temporary move to Jersey City had caused her to resign
her position at the library. The saving grace of the forced sabbatical

negms
library job
'26 bad
illness +
writes
Quicksand

was the time it had given her to write. Periodically, she berated herself for what she termed her "lack of self driving power." But she stayed the course. In March 1928, *Quicksand* was published by Knopf, a firm whose integrity Larsen respected and one that, she believed, was "very hard to please."[23]

Quicksand explores the choices open to educated and middle-class black women in western society. Superficially broad, they are profoundly restrictive. Intelligent, idealistic, and attractive, Helga Crane, Larsen's memorable protagonist, embarks on a journey toward self-discovery that seems destined to succeed. When it ends with Helga mired in poverty and hopelessness, the victim seems willing to accept the blame. Throughout the novel, Helga has pondered her "difference," which she perceives as a personal flaw that makes her unable to take advantage of the opportunities she is offered. In truth, the flaw is Helga's accurate perception that to succeed on the terms she is given, she must play herself false. While Helga, alone among Larsen's major characters, never considers passing for white, she is keenly aware that the image she projects is fraudulent.

As the novel opens, Helga is teaching at Naxos, a southern black college where she is doomed to be an outsider, unable to conform or to be happy in her nonconformity. Initially, the self-righteous, stultifying atmosphere of the school seems to be at fault. Clearly modeled on Tuskegee, Naxos tolerates neither innovation nor individualism. Moreover, the institution, for all the lip service it pays to race consciousness and race pride, seems intent on stamping out those qualities in its students, which Helga characterizes as racial. Naxos is more true to its name, which, as Deborah McDowell points out, is an anagram of "Saxon," than to its rhetoric. On reflection, Helga realizes that her problems go even deeper than conditions at Naxos. She understands that her battles with school authorities and snobbish co-workers are symptomatic of her personal struggle to define herself.

Helga recognizes that, superficially, her more sophisticated taste in clothing and furnishings sets her apart at Naxos and conditions the way in which others respond to her. For example, when she mentions resigning, a colleague urges her to stay because "we need a few decorations to brighten our sad lives."[24] The dark-skinned young

woman making this statement reveals not only a negative self-image, but the expectation that light-skinned, "pretty" women like Helga should assume an ornamental role. Helga's interracial parentage—her father is black and her mother is white—troubles her, too, but it is not the primary cause of her uneasiness. Her real struggle is against imposed definitions of blackness and womanhood. Her "difference" is ultimately her refusal to accept these definitions even in the face of her inability to define alternatives.[25]

In the class-conscious community of Naxos, however, her heritage is a practical liability, and Helga is concerned lest it jeopardize her engagement to James Vayle, the son of prominent black Atlantans. Vayle, whose name evokes the "veil" of Du Bois's famous metaphor, lives shrouded by the narrow, petty ideas of the college; his only ambition is to rise within its ranks. He is as impatient with Helga's inability to win the acceptance of their peers as she is contemptuous of his self-satisfaction. She analyzes their relationship thus:

> She was, she knew, in a queer indefinite way, a disturbing factor. She knew too that something held him, something against which he was powerless. The idea that she was in but one nameless way necessary to him filled her with a sensation amounting almost to shame. And yet his mute helplessness against that ancient appeal by which she held him pleased her and fed her vanity—gave her a feeling of power." (7–8)

Here is an incipient realization that sexuality is political; it is "power." But Helga mistakenly assumes it is hers to wield. Actually, she is trapped by the need to repress her sexuality, to assume the ornamental, acquiescent role of "lady," which not only Vayle but the entire Naxos community expects. Her reflection that "to relinquish James Vayle would most certainly be social suicide" (8) is followed by a scene in Helga's ornately furnished room in which "faintness closed about her like a vise." Revealingly, the words that prompt Helga's actual departure are not spoken by Vayle, but by the "apparently humane and understanding" administrator, Robert Anderson, who argues that she is needed there because she is a "lady."[26]

Taking flight, Helga travels first to Chicago, the city of her birth but a place where she has "no home" (27). When the opportunity

arises, she takes off for Harlem, where, in happy contrast, she has that "strange transforming experience . . . that magic sense of having come home" (43). Here Helga meets people who share her tastes and ideas. "Their sophisticated cynical talk, their elaborate parties, the unobtrusive correctness of their clothes and homes, all appealed to her craving for smartness, for enjoyment" (43). Better yet, they are extremely scornful of institutions like Naxos, and Helga feels her own actions have been vindicated. Even Robert Anderson has traded Naxos for New York. Then there is the "continuously gorgeous panorama of Harlem" that, to Helga, is so fascinating that she rarely finds occasion to venture to other areas of the city. In short, she feels a sense of freedom in Harlem; she is accepted there, and she chooses not to risk the rejection of the white world. Besides, she is convinced that Harlem offers a complete, self-contained life. "And she was satisfied, unenvious. For her this Harlem was enough" (45).

Of course, Larsen's point is that Harlem is *not* enough. Life there is "too cramped, too uncertain, too cruel" (96). Shallow and provincial, Helga's Harlemites are possessed of a race consciousness at once consuming and superficial, proud and ineffectual. They immerse themselves in the race problem, scanning newspapers to tabulate every injustice against the race. But, of course, they keep their distance from the suffering masses. Indeed, though they proclaim their love of blackness, they imitate the values and ways of white folk down to the smallest detail. They dislike Afro-American songs and dances, the inflections of black southerners' speech, and "like the despised people of the white race, . . . preferred Pavlova to Florence Mills, John McCormack to Taylor Gordon, Walter Hampden to Paul Robeson" (49). Floundering in this maze of contradictions, these New Negroes are unable to confront themselves and their situation honestly.

The peculiar demands of the Jazz Age further complicated matters for the Harlem bourgeoisie. As more and more white New Yorkers, like Americans generally, were drawn to black culture—or at least what they believed to be black culture—the New Negroes felt compelled to increase their own identification with their traditions. Often as ignorant of these traditions as anyone else, however, many embraced the popular imitations instead. Larsen uses a nightclub scene,

an almost obligatory feature in Harlem novels, to examine the packaging of manufactured blackness:

> For the while, Helga was oblivious of the reek of flesh, smoke, and alcohol, oblivious of the oblivion of other gyrating pairs, oblivious of the color, the noise, and the grand distorted childishness of it all. She was drugged, lifted, sustained by the extraordinary music, blown out, ripped out, beaten out, by the joyous murky orchestra. The essence of life seemed bodily motion. And when suddenly the music died, she dragged herself back to the present with a conscious effort; and a shameful certainty that not only had she been in the jungle, but that she had enjoyed it, began to taunt her. She wasn't, she told herself, a jungle creature. (59)

Helga is correct about not being a jungle creature, but then neither were any of the club's other patrons. This image was nonetheless foisted on blacks as Harlem barrooms were refurbished to resemble African jungles; as bands, even the best ones, like that of Duke Ellington, advertised the latest in "jungle music." It all made Harlem a more exotic tourist attraction while it increased the confusion of some local residents. In Larsen's interpretation, the ersatz culture marketed to blacks as their own was clearly insufficient. It borrowed enough of the authentic traditions to retain some power, but it existed dysfunctionally in a vacuum. The reference to the "grand distorted childishness of it all" applies to the spectacle of these urbane, middle-class New Yorkers attempting to find their cultural roots in the basement of a Harlem speakeasy. For Helga, the artifice was repelling.[27]

Both Vayle and Anderson reappear in the Harlem sequences of the novel, thereby demonstrating that the expectations for women remain the same. Helga's meeting with Vayle confirms the wisdom of her decision to reject him, social suicide being preferable to spiritual death. For his part, he wants to resume the engagement and tries to impress upon Helga her obligation as a member of the Talented Tenth to marry and have children. "Don't you see that if we—I mean people like us—don't have children, the others will still have. That's one of the things that's the matter with us. The race is sterile at the top" (103). This is a responsibility Helga neither recognizes nor accepts, and she is happy to leave Vayle to Naxos. Robert Anderson is

another matter, however. On seeing him again, she becomes aware of a strong and mutual sexual attraction. Taught too well to repress any sexual feelings, she denies them. Anderson's behavior is equally circumspect. Larsen introduces a minor character named Audrey Denny to highlight the psychic cost of Helga's self-denial. Audrey is glamorous and bold, ignoring the outraged reactions her appearance and behavior elicit from respectable Harlemites like Anne Grey, the wealthy young widow with whom Helga lives. Most objectionable is her refusal to limit her socializing to Harlem; Audrey has white friends and possibly white lovers. However disreputable her character, she is the object of eager attention from black men as well. In the nightclub scene, Robert Anderson joins her circle of admirers. When he does, Helga's envious approbation gives way to jealousy. Larsen concludes the scene with well-placed references to asphyxiation, as her heroine escapes the smoke-filled cabaret for the brisk night air.

Helga is emerging too from the restricting definitions of ladyhood so accepted in the middle-class black world. She does not consider chastity the supreme virtue the women at Naxos insist it is; though she notes that as "sophisticated" as Anne Grey is, she has preferred a passionless marriage. Helga is also aware of the energy black women waste trying to conform to a white standard of beauty. Straightened hair, she reflects, does not beautify, though as her own is naturally straight, she cannot voice this opinion. Ever conscious of clothes, she resents the prohibition of bright colors by those who want it understood that black women do *not* love red. She does. She further seeks the adventure that color usually symbolizes. That is what makes Audrey Denny so appealing to her. Audrey is unencumbered by the norms that define Negro ladies. Having white friends is the least of her daring. More to the point, Audrey has declined to play the husband-hunting game. She need not marry to find someone to pay for all those tasteful, elegant things with which real ladies surround themselves.

Eventually, Harlem becomes as oppressive an environment as Naxos. The constant superficial race consciousness seems to demand that Helga deny a part of herself, and when a white uncle gives her five thousand dollars, she uses his conscience money to escape to Copenhagen. As soon as the ship sets sail, Helga feels free. Denmark

promises "no Negroes, no problems, no prejudice," though Helga is slightly wary of the reception she will receive from relatives there. Her fears prove unfounded, the Dahls, her well-to-do aunt and uncle, welcome her warmly, but the kind reception is proffered with an eye to the role the young woman can play in advancing the couple's social fortunes. Immediately, they inform Helga that she should capitalize on her "difference." She should wear "striking things, exotic things" so she will make an impression. They are more than happy to supply the necessary wardrobe. Though she comprehends their motives and resents being a decoration, a curio with which her relatives hope to capture the notice of influential people, Helga enjoys, as always, the expensive clothes, the physical freedom, and the fact that her dark skin so despised in America makes her the source of endless fascination to the Danes. Forced to discover and parade her own beauty, she feels new confidence and self-acceptance.

Her satisfaction does not last. Like Edith Wharton's Lily Bart, Helga finds that the admiration she elicits for making herself into a beautiful object and the material comforts her pleasing appearance bring carry too high a price. Helga's blackness, of course, complicates the issue. To the Danes, Helga's beauty is "exotic, almost savage." In Copenhagen, no one requires that Helga be a lady. Instead she is made into an exotic female Other—symbol of the unconscious, the unknowable, the erotic, and the passive.[28] Her aunt and uncle conspire to this end, by dressing her in batik dresses, leopard-skin coats, turban-like hats made out of metallic silks, feathers, furs, and glittering jewelry.

It is Axel Olsen, a fashionable portrait painter, who most fervently wants to re-create Helga. Olsen is an odd man, given to overwrought, theatrical gestures. It is he who demonstrates most sharply the confluence of racism and sexism, in both the way he paints Helga and the way he courts her. In their first meeting, he examines the specimen before him and pronounces her amazing and marvelous; her smile becomes a "mask" as he announces his findings to his audience. Larsen borrows vocabulary from anthropology throughout the Copenhagen section, but never to greater effect than when Olsen is on view. Helga's role, as she realizes, is to be exhibited, to "incite" a

voluptuous impression in sedate Danish drawing rooms. Soon she finds herself enjoying "the fascinating business of being seen, gaped at, desired" (74). When she sees the resulting impression reproduced on Olsen's canvas, she disowns the image. "It wasn't, she contended, herself at all, but some disgusting sensual creature with her features" (89). Olsen is, of course, sure he has captured the essential Helga; but, although he has discerned the sensuality she had concealed in America, his portrait is not the mirror of Helga's soul he believes it to be. As Anne Hostetler observes, the sensuality Helga confronts "staring out at her from Olsen's portrait . . . disgusts her, for in the painting, it is abstracted as a commodity, a stereotype, the focus of the portrait, rather than one of its multicolored strands."[29] After Helga ignores his insinuations that they have an affair, he proposes marriage. He is mystified by her refusal.

Critic Hortense Thornton has suggested that because Helga stresses their racial differences in her rejection of Olsen, perhaps "her acknowledgment of race is used as a mask for her sexual repression."[30] In my view, this scene more than any other shows how inextricably bound sexual and racial identity are. Olsen follows his marriage proposal with a frank admission that he would have preferred that she be his mistress. At that point she protests, "In my country the men, of my race at least, don't make suggestions to decent girls" (86). Olsen cannot hear her objection. He rants instead about her "deliberate lure" and declares that, for him, marrying her will be "an experience." And finally he sums up her character:

> You know, Helga, you are a contradiction. You have been, I suspect, corrupted by the good Fru Dahl, which is perhaps as well. Who knows? You have the warm impulsive nature of the women of Africa, but, my lovely, you have, I fear, the soul of a prostitute. You sell yourself to the highest buyer. I should of course be happy that it is I. And I am. (87)

Only the spell of racial mythology could lead a man to mistake such insults for gallantry. Olsen knows nothing of African women, but that does not shake his belief in their exotic primitivism. Black women were completely sentient, sexual beings. Helga Crane should confirm that belief. When she does not, it proves that she has been contaminated by the West and has suffered the primordial female corruption. Even so damaged, she is the closest approximation of the exotic female Other that he is likely to find. He is willing to settle.

Olsen makes explicit the connection between prostitution and marriage Larsen had earlier implied in the scene with Audrey Denny and in Helga's musings about marriage as a means to acquire things. His words evoke from Helga a declaration of independence: "But you see, Herr Olsen, I'm not for sale. Not to you. Not to any white man. I don't care at all to be owned" (87). Shortly after this confrontation, Helga leaves Denmark.

Contrary to the impression Nella Larsen created, the Copenhagen plot sequences are not autobiographical. She never went to Denmark.[31] But the narrative she invented echoed the experiences of an African-American woman who spent the 1920s in Europe and whose public feats and private affairs were chronicled in the American press. Dancing the Charleston on the stage of the Paris music hall, Josephine Baker brought the vogue for Harlem to Europe, where it was transformed into "*Le Tumulte Noir*." She became its emblem. On both sides of the Atlantic, Baker was a vivid figure in the panorama of Larsen's time.

In the mid-twenties, Josephine Baker's image was as commodified as Michael Jackson's or Madonna's in the nineties. There were Josephine Baker dolls, costumes, perfumes, and pomades. Parisian women wore their hair slicked down, à la Baker's; to affect the look, some purchased a product called Bakerfix. In 1926, according to *Vanity Fair*, the magazine that served as a major arbiter of contemporary culture, the cabaret star and Woodrow Wilson were the two best-known Americans in post-war Europe. Even if Larsen was correct when she avowed that no later generation could ever "catch that flying glimpse of the panorama" of an earlier time, Josephine Baker's fabulous career offers a cynosure. Moreover, Baker's experiences—the freedom she won and the constrictions she could not overcome—suggest an analogue to those of Larsen's protagonist.

To Europeans, Baker embodied the exotic primitive. One commonplace held that "Baker dancing looked like an African sculpture come to life."[32] Finding her dance "a wild splendor and magnificent

Josephine Baker. Yale Collection of
American Literature, Beinecke Rare Book
and Manuscript Library, Yale University.

animality," an eminent critic concluded that the effect of her performance ("the frenzy of African Eros swept over the audience") was
akin to that of the black Venus that haunted Baudelaire.[33] Baker herself adopted "Black Venus" as a favorite epithet. Onstage she usually
appeared bare-breasted, either with feathers around her neck, waist,
and ankles or girdled with her infamous bananas. Offstage she turned
heads as she walked her pet leopard down the Champs Élysées. She
traveled with a veritable menagerie. Wherever she went, Baker was
always costumed to intensify the effect.

The iconographic use of clothing in *Quicksand* produces a similar
dynamic. In Copenhagen, Helga becomes "a striking exotic thing"
(68). The public discourse by and about Josephine Baker reverber-
ates in the descriptions of Helga's clothes and her emotional response
to wearing them. Dressed in "a shining black taffeta with . . . bizarre
trimmings of purple and cerise," Helga feels "like a veritable savage"
(69). In another dress, cut down until it is practically "nothing but a
skirt," Helga feels so naked that she is "thankful for the barbaric
bracelets, for the dangling earrings, for the beads about her neck. . . .
No other woman in the stately, pale-blue room was so greatly exposed" (70). Her managers, the Dahls, arrange that everywhere
Helga goes she is "incited to inflame attention and admiration. She
was dressed for it, subtly schooled for it" (74). This incitement cap-
tures the attention of Olsen, under whose gaze Helga, though fully
clothed, once again feels naked.

The sensation Josephine Baker created likewise attracted the notice
of leading artists. Picasso (who called her the "Nefertiti of now"),
graphic artist Paul Colin, cubist Henri Laurens (who depicted her
doing the Charleston), Domergue (whose nude portrait of Baker hung
in the Grand Palais) and sculptor Alexander Calder (whose caricature
of Baker became the prototype of the mobile, the form for which he is
famous) captured "Le Baker" in media as varied as the art they created. Yet the woman must rarely have recognized herself in the images
they created. Unlike Helga, however, Josephine Baker was able to
mock the role of exotic primitive even as she played it to the hilt.

Born in Saint Louis, Baker first achieved success as a chorus girl in
the road company of the legendary Broadway show *Shuffle Along*;

eventually she joined the New York cast. In recognition of her appeal, lyricist Noble Sissle and composer Eubie Blake composed special material for Baker in their next show, *Chocolate Dandies*; Baker was billed as "That Comedy Chorus Girl." But the role called for a persona more pickaninny than chanteuse. A photograph from the play shows Baker in blackface, wearing a schoolgirl dress with floppy bows, black stockings, and oversized shoes, sitting with her legs wide open and her eyes crossed. The brown-skinned Baker could not hope to become a star on the American stage.

Fortune intervened when producer Caroline Dudley hired Baker for *La Revue Nègre*, a musical show that she planned to take to Europe; it became one of the great stage sensations of the early twentieth century. Its cast was "unmistakably black" because, according to Baker, the producer "did not share New York's infatuation with 'white,' blond-haired Negro girls."[34] The troupe of twenty-five black Americans, including blues singer Maud de Forest and the pianist Claude Hopkins, who organized a band featuring clarinetist Sidney Bechet, sailed for Paris aboard the SS *Berengaria* on the evening of 15 September 1925. In a statement reminiscent of a scene in *Quicksand*, Josephine Baker recalled standing on deck: "'My life passed in review before me. I saw Bernard Street and my raggedy playmates. . . . When the Statue of Liberty disappeared over the horizon, I knew I was free.'"[35]

To generate publicity for the show, its producers hired Paul Colin, an unknown young artist, to design a poster. Since he thought that the leading lady, de Forest, looked "like a washerwoman," he decided to feature the chorus girl instead. He asked her to pose nude and years afterward recalled that "in spite of her magnificent body, she was extremely modest." Baker was only nineteen, already twice married. Whether or not the modesty was an affectation, she soon shed it—along with her clothes. Later she expressed gratitude to the artist: "Paul gave me self-confidence. For the first time in my life, I felt beautiful."[36]

Her autobiographies do not record her response to the finished product. In the poster, which helped make both Baker and Colin famous, a caricature of Baker stands with arms akimbo and hips in

motion. The figure is not nude but is clothed in a form-fitting white dress with a fringed hem that stops well above midthigh. Its large eyes look out in opposite directions and its full red lips border a mouthful of bright white teeth. "REVUE NÈGRE" is drawn in red boldface at the top of the poster, so that the top of the figure's head touches the base of the V. Along the bottom border, the poster announces the Paris venue of the show. Flanking the female figure and foregrounded are two larger male figures, one of which wears a white bowler hat large enough to balance the white of the dress. The size and shape of the eyes, lips, and teeth disclose the minstrel origins of all three figures. While the figure of Baker is far more sexualized than in the photograph from *Chocolate Dandies*, the image is at best comic, at worst crude. It is in no way beautiful.[37]

As it turned out, beauty was hardly the point. Colin's work succeeded beyond anyone's expectations. Not only did it sell tickets in Paris, "copies of the poster sold as far away as New York, fetching handsome prices in Harlem."[38] Conceivably, Nella Larsen might have seen it and responded to the contrast between the sensual stereotype it depicted and the lithe, sinewy, sensuous woman who had danced across the Broadway stage.[39]

If she did, she was hardly alone. Baker's European stardom was soon the talk of black America. In an unsigned column in the February 1927 issue of *Opportunity*, the writer, probably Countee Cullen, wrote that "all that remains now is for her to try on the glass slipper and marry the Prince."[40] The public's curiosity about her was insatiable. If the press reported her public triumphs, the press and the grapevine chronicled her private exploits.

For example, after the premiere of *La Revue Nègre*, Baker attended a reception at the theater. She was escorted by Paul Colin, already rumored to be her lover and soon to be her guide into the world of painters, artists, and writers which would open its doors to her. Her dress was designed by Paul Poiret, a leading couturier. In his studio, Baker had also felt reborn, this time when Poiret draped her body "in the most beautiful silvery material I had ever seen. It looked like a flowing river. . . . I felt like a sea goddess emerging from the foam." In Baker biographer Phyllis Rose's account, "the contrast was lost on

Paul Colin's poster for *La Revue Nègre*.

no one and underlined a message Parisians were ready to hear: put a pretty savage in a Paul Poiret dress and she could be a princess."[41] A torrent of invitations followed; Baker's presence gave any party cachet.

Larsen's protagonist enjoys a more local celebrity. At one point, Helga revels in "that sensation of lavish contentment and well-being enjoyed only by impecunious sybarites waking in the houses of the rich" (67). However much she relished its perquisites, Josephine Baker understood that "to be a curiosity is a painful profession."[42] Even as she sought the glare of publicity, Baker tried to maintain control of the image she projected. In interviews and memoirs, she referred proudly to private situations that she had negotiated with skill. For example, she explained that when she was "summoned to a social function to be shown off like a circus animal in fancy dress, I would glue myself to the buffet table instead of joining the expectant guests on the lawn, then quietly slip away." In Berlin, where *La Revue Nègre* enjoyed a popular run after leaving Paris, Baker was told that she symbolized primitivism. She retorted, "What are you trying to say? I was born in 1906 in the twentieth century."[43]

However ably she parried insults in private, Baker's personal life became a succession of scandals and personal calamities. Public moments presented greater opportunities. In contrast to Helga, who (like Toni Morrison's protagonist Sula) is an artist without an art form, Baker was accomplished in several metiers. Through dance, mime, and song, she could wage resistance to the images that confined and demeaned her. In her performances, she created a persona that both played to racist and sexist fantasies and allowed her to retain a modicum of control and even achieve a measure of freedom.

The odds were formidable. Like the Plantation Club in New York, where Baker was performing when Caroline Dudley hired her, *La Revue Nègre* was designed to evoke and conflate the images of plantation and jungle. Against a backdrop of a Mississippi levee, complete with riverboats, trees dripping Spanish moss, and ubiquitous bales of cotton, stood black women in headrags, bandannas, and aprons. Suddenly Baker entered the scene clowning. The audience had never seen a figure like hers.[44] Dressed in tatters, wearing her short black

hair slicked down, her face made up with the exaggerated lips characteristic of minstrels—minus the blackface paint—Baker darted across
the stage, walking on all fours. No one could be sure whether the
figure was female or male. To one reporter, more insightful than most,
it seemed to be "something as exotic and elusive as music."[45] Then,
as the orchestra played "Yes, Sir, That's My Baby!" Baker stood and
started to Charleston. The crowd went wild. When she finished, she
exited as she entered, on all fours with her head down and her der-
riere in the air.

In one description, Baker looked like "a weird cross between a
kangaroo, a bicyclist, and a machine gun."[46] What she did *not* resemble was the stereotyped black woman the setting prepared the
audience to expect. The Tin Pan Alley tune and the latest U.S. dance
craze multiplied the anomalies and permitted Baker to create a context for her performance that partook of century-old fantasies of Africa
and the American South but was clearly a new and imaginary site.

The dances were another matter. Baker, who began her career
with the Dixie Steppers, a vaudeville troupe headlined by blues
queen Clara Smith, was schooled in the traditions of black American
vaudeville.[47] She had been an accomplished dancer since childhood.
What she was amazed to learn in Europe was the sensation she could
create by doing her old dances in new dress, or undress, as it were.
She read "with astonishment" descriptions of how she "personified
the savage on the stage," though she was eager to exploit the celebrity the personification brought her. At the same time, she seemed
aware of its absurd and comic aspect. Her talent as a comedienne
gave her the means to express the absurdity.[48]

A film clip of Baker's famous banana dance, which she introduced
in 1926 at the Folies-Bergère, provides an illustration. The setting is
the "jungle," and the extras are "natives" who either beat their drums
or serve a "white hunter" on one corner of the stage. Baker enters
from above, pausing warily to survey the territory, then climbs down
the tree that is the scene's largest prop. Although the setting might
lead one to presume she would dance for the white hunter, she does
not glance in his direction. Instead, center stage, she faces the audience and begins a dance that features continuous pelvic rolls and

thrusts. Her skirt of bananas accentuates the movements. The bananas may signify Baker's status as denizen of the jungle (some commentators thought she climbed down the tree like a monkey) or the symbolic phalluses of the male onlookers, but Baker, jangling her oversized earrings and waving her manicured hands, begins to dance for the audience and ends up seeming to dance for herself alone.

Several of Helga's epiphanies in *Quicksand* occur in the theater. Rather than an onstage performer, however, Helga is "an ironical and silently speculative spectator" (183). As Helga sits with a group of Danish acquaintances that includes Axel Olsen, two black men dance across the stage of the Circus, a vaudeville house in Copenhagen. Helga is shocked by their presence and stunned by the avid delight that her companions take in the way the dancers "cavort." During the loud applause that follows, Helga sits "silent, motionless" (82). A spectator is by definition an onlooker at a spectacle. Helga's response to the spectacle at the Circus is to grow reflective. In one of the ironies she begins to decipher, Helga recognizes the degree to which she has herself become a spectacle for the Europeans she has met. Speculative in another sense as well, she begins to understand that she has been engaged in a business transaction that requires considerable risk for the chance of larger gains.

Unlike Josephine Baker, who was similarly speculative but savvy enough to understand the business she was in, Helga speculates and loses. Significantly, the scene in the theater and a performance of Antonín Dvořák's "New World Symphony" frame the scenes with Olsen. In both cases, Helga has no agency, no way of acting on or acting out the deepening awareness she achieves. Her only option is flight. The awareness Helga develops in the vaudeville house, to which she returns again and again, governs her actions with Olsen. After observing his response to "stage Negroes," she declines to become one for his private audience. In effect, the song the black entertainers perform, "Everybody Gives Me Good Advice," which Helga recognizes as an old ragtime number, defines aptly the role they play in the text. Similarly, the "New World Symphony" inspires Helga's decision to leave Copenhagen. According to the text, "those wailing undertones of 'Swing Low, Sweet Chariot' were too poignantly familiar" (92). She flees.

Another of the symphony's themes, the neo-spiritual "Going Home," might serve as a more apt, if equally ironic, leitmotif for the Copenhagen section of *Quicksand*. If Helga has traveled to Europe in quest of a spiritual home, the performances she observed abroad compel her return to the United States, the land to which by birth and culture she "belongs." *Quicksand* highlights the complexities of cultural "belonging" through the highly mediated versions of African-American culture it represents. The black vaudevillians are twentieth-century minstrels, whose performance is packaged for European consumption. Its impact on Helga suggests that the performance, like Josephine Baker's dancing, retains a semblance of the authority of its vernacular roots. Yet, given Helga's distant relation to those roots, her response is an unreliable barometer. The reference to Dvořák is even more ambiguous and is central to the novel's cultural critique. A Czech, Dvořák appropriated Negro spirituals for use in the European genre of symphonic composition. On one level, "New World Symphony" paid tribute to the intrinsic beauty of African-American folk music. On another, as European art music, it existed in hierarchical relation to its source. By having Helga respond to the spiritual on which a section of the symphony is based, *Quicksand* honors the source. But it respects as well the integrity of Dvořák's orchestration. "Wonderfully rendered," Dvořák's variation on the spiritual has the power to "move" Helga. Analogously, in their own act of reappropriation, black college and church choirs soon made "Going Home" a staple in their repertoire. Absent the hierarchies that govern relations between white/black and Old World/New World, the products of cultural exchange would enrich the lives of all. The hierarchies persist, of course, and for Helga Crane the ambiguities of cultural belonging prove destructive.

Returning to Harlem, Helga is haunted by the images of herself refracted in the European cultural mirror. In particular, Axel Olsen's constructions of her influence her actions. Determined not to sell herself, she gives herself away. Even this proves more difficult than Helga imagines. Unwilling to repress her sexuality any longer, she misconstrues Robert Anderson's intentions when he drunkenly kisses her. She is ready to have an affair, but Anderson, now married to Anne Grey, declines. Helga's subsequent turmoil is marked by an increasing number of asphyxiation metaphors. As several critics have noted, "quicksand" is not merely a title, but a unifying metaphor supported throughout by concrete images of suffocation, asphyxiation, and claustrophobia. Moreover, Larsen, like many nineteenth- and twentieth-century women writers, used rooms as metaphors of female confinement and frustration.[49] She had used Helga's room at Naxos, the Jim Crow car on which she journeyed North, a car on the Chicago "El," and a Harlem cabaret among other examples. With the narrowing of choices available to Helga, such references redouble and intensify. In a tiny Harlem storefront church, Helga loses her soul.

In the mission's heightened emotional atmosphere, a predominantly female congregation purges itself of discontent and despair. The church sisters attend Helga until she, too, achieves a temporary catharsis. They crowd around the drunk and desperate Helga, who, dressed in red, appears to them the very reincarnation of Jezebel. They pray for her soul. As Hostetler asserts, "In her shattered state Helga gives in, not to passion, but finally to this construction of herself as a scarlet woman, in order to be at 'home,' immersed in a sense of belonging that is an utter betrayal of her personality" (43–44). The musical allusions—the refrain of one hymn is "less of self and more of thee"—and the overheated prose describing the scene underscore Helga's loss. At one point, "the women dragged themselves upon their knees and crawled over the floor like reptiles, sobbing and pulling their hair and tearing off their clothing" (114). Little wonder that in the instant before Helga is "saved," or rather, lost, she thinks, "This is terrible. I must get out of here." But she cannot escape.

In large measure, Helga is trapped by her stereotyped view of what "true" black culture is. Perhaps by representing such a caricature of the religious aspect of the culture, the novel demonstrates the futility of pursuing such purity. Only in her mental and emotional exhaustion would it occur to Helga Crane to seek a church home. Earlier in the novel, when she arrives in Chicago, Helga feels momentarily the sensation of homecoming. Food is a familiar signifier of home, but the "agreeable, exotic food" Helga savors at this moment exemplifies the conflict between her personality and the cultural stereotypes that would define who she is. Helga relishes "sweet-

breads, smothered with truffles and mushrooms" (30). The chapter ends with a fittingly discordant antiphony: "[S]he felt, too, that she had come home. She, Helga Crane, who had no home" (30).

The calm that descends upon the restless Helga is only a chimera; it only seems to offer a resolution. More accurately, it represents a retreat, which is personified by the aptly named Reverend Pleasant Green, whom Helga hurriedly marries. In rural Alabama, where she moves with her new husband, Rev. Green's female parishioners assume the role played by the women in the Harlem mission. But their ministrations cannot sustain her. Neither can the sexual release she finds in marriage. Reality is too harsh and the confinement of the birthing room is inescapable. Her five children tie her permanently to a life she loathes.[50]

Helga Crane's tragedy is reminiscent of Edna Pontellier's, Kate Chopin's heroine in *The Awakening*. Edna is also a sensitive, idealistic woman who seeks spiritual fulfillment and sexual freedom, the mere desire for which puts her in conflict with society. Chopin even introduces a minor theme involving cultural dualism; she juxtaposes the rigid, puritanical manner of Edna's Kentucky forebears with the relaxed, fluid mores of Louisiana Creoles. But the more important polarities in the novel are represented by Mademoiselle Reisz and Adele Ratignolle, who symbolize the two roles available to Edna. Lacking the dedication and discipline to pursue the solitary life of the artist and recoiling from the compulsive intimacy of domestic life, Edna is unable to navigate a middle course. She does not struggle vainly, however, because in the process she is awakened to beauty, to passion, and to self-knowledge. Reflecting a basic impulse in American literary tradition, Edna chooses experience over innocence and pays a high penalty for doing so. In the end, unable to live life on her own terms, she chooses to die. Her suicide is a painstakingly deliberate act. By contrast, Helga's actions are rarely deliberate. At the end of *Quicksand*, she muses that she has years of living and perhaps even of happiness ahead of her. The crucial difference between Chopin's vision and Larsen's is expressed best in the central metaphors they chose for their novels.

Nella Larsen may or may not have been familiar with Chopin's novel, but one can reasonably assume she knew the work of Jean

Toomer. Five years before *Quicksand*, the publication of *Cane* had sent tremors through the African-American literary community; it represented a new plateau of achievement, a new yardstick by which black writers were to measure their work. Toomer's book also set forth many of the major themes that were to preoccupy black artists for the remainder of the decade and beyond. In a sense, Toomer strove to create a usable past, to assert the regenerative power of the African-American folk tradition—a tradition dying in the onslaught of "civilization." For him, western civilization was indeed the moral and spiritual "wasteland" Eliot had proclaimed it. The folk culture offered a necessary alternative. Yet *Cane* does not evoke the folk tradition uncritically; neither does it suggest that reclaiming it will be easy. Female characters like Karintha and Fern, for whom Toomer fashions exquisite prose poems praising their physical and spiritual beauty, are permeated by the folk ethos, but it has not prevented the tragic waste of their lives. The figure most a part of this tradition, the old former slave Father John, has been rendered mute, blind, and motionless. The folk tradition has not enabled him to transcend his oppression, though in the most elemental sense, it has enabled him to survive. "Survival" is a key word; the book implies that for blacks to survive they must embrace the past that is alive in the tragic pain and triumphant beauty of the rural black experience. Doing this can be difficult, however, especially for those impeded by middle-class and intellectual inhibitions as most of the males in *Cane* are.

Nella Larsen viewed the folk experience far more ambivalently. Although she had not immersed herself in it as Toomer had (albeit briefly), she was aware of its strength and beauty. She had written of "the dark undecorated women unceasingly concerned with the actual business of life, its rounds of births and christenings, of loves and marriages, of deaths and funerals, [who] were to Helga miraculously beautiful" (201). Still the folk experience did not engage her imagination the way it did Toomer's. Perhaps Toomer, the idealist and mystic, was able to ferret out beauty invisible to the eye of a writer whose romanticism was strongly tempered by realism. The gender difference was surely significant. As a woman, Larsen was unable to romanticize the unceasing toil and continuous childbearing that was the particular oppression of rural women. Their unyielding religious faith is, in her portrayal, at once inspiring and pathetic. Helga tries for a time to emulate it, but only when "the curtain of religion [is] rent" can she see her situation clearly. The Alabama women never do. Transcending one's training and class status was also problematic for Larsen; it meant denying who one was. Although Helga Crane in her alienation and lack of direction is very much a soulmate of Toomer's Kabnis, it is inconceivable that Larsen would describe her in these terms: "a promise of soil-soaked beauty, uprooted, thinning out. Suspended a few feet above the soil whose touch would resurrect him. Arm's length removed from those whose will to help . . ."[51]

For Larsen it is enough that Helga has fought against the white world's definition of a Negro; Helga knows she is neither exotic nor primitive, "savage" nor sharecropper. At the same time, she has resisted male definitions of her womanhood. Having no foundation on which to base one, Helga never achieves true self-definition. Her quest ends in defeat, yet her struggle is admirable. Inevitably, her courage avails little when it is pitted against the quicksand of racism and sexism. Larsen's depiction of a memorable protagonist, her adept narration, and her skillful development of the novel's central metaphor have all won praise. Most critics agree that *Quicksand* is one of the best novels of the Harlem Renaissance.

Contemporary reviewers found much for which to commend it. The writer for the *New York Times* deemed it "an articulate and sympathetic first novel," while the reviewer for the *World Telegram* exulted, "The book makes you want to read everything that Nella Larsen will ever write." Headlines like "A Mulatto Girl" and "Mixed Blood" accurately reflected the aspect of the novel white reviewers found most interesting. Black critics noted Helga's mulatto identity but were not persuaded that it was the subject of the novel. Indeed, an unsigned review in the *New York Amsterdam News* entitled "Miscegenation? Bah!" began by assuring readers that, contrary to rumor, miscegenation was not what Larsen's novel was about. Neither "a plea" nor a "long scream of hate," *Quicksand* was "a story, and mostly a well-told one."[52] The writer expressed the common judgment that the ending of the novel was flawed.

Perhaps the most influential contemporary criticism of Larsen's novel came from W. E. B. Du Bois in a joint review of *Quicksand* and Claude McKay's *Home to Harlem*. Praising Larsen at McKay's expense, Du Bois concluded that Larsen "has done a fine, thoughtful and courageous piece of work in her novel. It is, on the whole, the best piece of fiction that Negro America has produced since the heyday of Chesnutt and stands easily with Jessie Fauset's *There Is Confusion*, in its subtle comprehension of the curious cross currents that swirl about the black American."[53] Du Bois's choice of adjectives is apt enough, but the comparison to Fauset, a lead which too many other critics have followed, does Larsen a disservice.

Larsen is a far better writer, an author capable of the subtlety Du Bois wrongly ascribed to Fauset. The quality of her prose as of her perception distinguishes Larsen from her predecessor. Although they both wrote about middle-class black life, Larsen did so keenly aware of its limitations, of the hypocrisy and materialism that too often masked insecurity and self-hatred. She was not a propagandist for the Negro bourgeoisie. Indeed, Larsen's novel is not a polemic for any cause. She scorned purpose novels and mocked the sometimes sententious rhetoric of racial uplift. A minor character in *Quicksand*, Mrs. Hayes-Rore is a professional "race" woman. To Fauset, such a woman would be heroic; to Larsen she is the object of caricature. (Suffice it to say that Larsen's lively cynicism can make one hanker for Fauset's duller high-mindedness.) More significantly, Larsen did not agree with Fauset that the New Negro woman's freedom to be virtuous was worth celebrating. She recognized, as Zora Hurston would later, that too much respectability was deadening.

Du Bois was on firmer ground when he cited Larsen's comprehension of "the curious cross currents that swirl about the black American." As the formulator of the double-consciousness concept, Du Bois was attuned to Larsen's explorations of the possibilities and restrictions in both the black and white worlds. As had Du Bois, she stressed the duality of the Afro-American experience, the psychic pull between the African (the supposedly primitive and spiritually liberating folk experience) and the American (the apparently refined and intellectually liberating urban experience). Unable to mediate

between these two inadequate constructs, Helga becomes a psychological exile. Thus the philosophical content of Larsen's work resembles that of Jean Toomer's and Claude McKay's more than that of Jessie Fauset's. But the bourgeois ethos of her novels has obscured the similarities.

In his joint review, Du Bois wrote of *Home to Harlem*, "[It] for the most part nauseates me, and after the dirtier parts of its filth I feel distinctly like taking a bath." To Du Bois, McKay was guilty of catering to white readers' "prurient demands."[54] What McKay had done, in fact, was to re-create the underside of Harlem life, the cabarets and buffet flats, giving some attention to the working class but ignoring the New Negro elite altogether. The protagonist, Jake, is a "natural man," who lives by his wits and answers only to his instincts. He is beyond any solemn appeal to race pride, let alone race responsibility. His search is not for self, but for a beautiful prostitute, Felice, whose name is appropriate for the male fantasy she represents. As a character, Jake could have "something appealing," as Du Bois conceded, but he could do little to advance any political cause. Of course, Helga Crane was an equally undependable ally, but she did struggle in her way, and she conformed to at least some of Du Bois's notions of gentility and refinement. Moreover, she was the victim of the "cross currents" Du Bois believed were inherent in a racist society, "cross currents" from which Jake was completely insulated. Although McKay had introduced the character Ray, a young Haitian intellectual, to articulate concerns similar to Du Bois's and Larsen's, the scenes of Harlem after dark had overshadowed his presence in the novel. These scenes seemed also to reinforce racial stereotypes, not to mention gender stereotypes, and, in Du Bois's view, could only harm the cause of African-American advancement. Claude McKay had defaulted on his obligations to the race.

In his review, Du Bois rightly emphasized the importance of racial identity as a theme in *Quicksand*. He was less discerning about Larsen's exploration of gender issues. Before the publication of revisionist criticism in the 1970s and 1980s, few of the novel's commentators paid any regard to this aspect. Gwendolyn Bennett came closest when she described it as "the story of the struggle of an interesting cultured Negro

woman against her environment" and identified "the psychological struggle of the heroine" as the central subject of the novel.[55]

However flawed the commentary, Larsen's novel did garner notice. It was widely and favorably reviewed. Larsen was feted by community groups including the women's auxiliary of the NAACP. She received recognition from outside the community as well. From 1926 to 1930, the William E. Harmon Foundation sponsored an annual competition designed to acknowledge and foster black achievement in the arts. Countee Cullen, James Weldon Johnson, Eric Waldrond, Walter White, and Langston Hughes were recipients of literary honors. In 1928, Larsen won the foundation's Bronze Medal for literature; the Gold Medal went to McKay.[56] As Larsen's public profile rose, she began to receive attention from the press. The coverage is significant because it was representative of the treatment accorded black women writers. Its emphasis was on Larsen's appearance, her possessions, her background, her personal life in general—on everything except her work.

Larsen was the subject of a feature story in the *Amsterdam News*, Harlem's most influential newspaper, soon after the publication of *Quicksand*. Although the headline reads "New Author Unearthed Right Here in Harlem," nowhere in the article is the novel discussed. Instead, the reader is treated to a detailed description of Larsen's apartment, which the reporter thought possessed "the air of a Greenwich Village studio," presumably because it contained "vari-colored pillows," flowers, paintings, and books. Larsen herself was presented as "a modern woman" who smoked, wore short dresses, did not believe in religion and churches, and felt that "people of the artistic type can definitely help with the race problem." Of course, she played bridge, apparently a social necessity judging from the prominence it is given in interviews with both Fauset and Larsen. As if to account for Larsen's unconventional and, by implication, improper lifestyle, the article ends with a reference to her mixed parentage.[57]

A major point of contrast between this article and those that appeared in the white press was that white reporters made certain Larsen's background was mentioned *first*. They also seemed more preoccupied with her appearance. One interviewer introduced her subject thus: "Nella Larsen . . . has skin the color of maple syrup. The costume of shading grays makes it seem lighter than it really is." With this statement, the reporter both differentiated Larsen from "ordinary Negroes" and conveyed to the paper's readers that necessary distinctions could still be drawn. Larsen, perhaps assuming she would not be taken seriously or understanding that to take herself seriously would make her vulnerable, offered flippant responses to her questioner. Political issues were disposed of quickly, with Larsen contending that "recognition and liberation will come to the Negro only through individual effort." The interview concentrated on more personal concerns. The "unforgivable sin" was being bored, so she selected only amusing and natural people, not too intellectual. She would never "pass," because "with my economic status it's better to be a Negro. So many things are excused them. The chained and downtrodden Negro is a picture that came out of the Civil War." And while she claimed to be "not quite sure what she wanted to be spiritually," she knew she "want[ed] things—beautiful and rich things."[58]

In *Quicksand*, Larsen had definitely been more dubious about the value of materialism and more aware of the psychological costs of racial passing. Perhaps the tongue-in-cheek stance she adopted in her interviews constituted another form of passing. By declining to take herself seriously, she anticipated the inability of the press and the public to respond to her as a serious writer. She went to considerable lengths to project a frivolous image. For instance, in an application submitted to the Harmon Foundation, she, or someone acting on her behalf and presumably with her approval, noted that "Mrs. Imes loves bridge and feels particularly moved by the color green."[59] This could merely have been an attempt to mock the pretense and hypocrisy Larsen believed characterized organizations devoted to social causes. But everything about Larsen's public demeanor seemed designed to assure that she posed no threat to anyone; she was pretty, perhaps a little foolish, and clever enough to choose in literature a diversion slightly more demanding than bridge. In clinging to this image, she was certainly adopting a pose long common among women authors. Behind its mask, one supposes, she felt safe. To be sure, concealed, fabricated, and mistaken identities are at the heart of Nella Larsen's second novel, *Passing*, which was published in 1929.

Two characters, Irene Redfield and Clare Kendry, dominate the novel; both are attractive, affluent, and able to pass for white. Irene identifies with blacks, choosing to pass only for occasional convenience, while Clare has moved completely into the white world. Each assumes a role Helga Crane rejects; Irene is the perfect lady and Clare, the exotic Other. A chance meeting in the tea room of an exclusive Chicago hotel, on an occasion when both women are "passing," introduces the action of the novel. Clare recognizes the childhood friend she has not seen in twelve years, and she is anxious to renew the acquaintance. Irene, assured and complacent in her life as the wife of a Harlem physician, is more cautious. Reluctantly, she accepts Clare's invitation to tea, where they are joined by another school friend, Gertrude, who is married to a white man, and by Clare's husband, Jack Bellew. Bellew proves to be a rabid racist, and Irene vows never to see Clare again. Two years later, her resolve is shaken. Now visiting New York, Clare longs for the company of blacks; the longing is in part a response to her husband's bigotry. Clare presents herself at Irene's house uninvited and, over Irene's objections, makes increasingly frequent jaunts to Harlem. Distressed by the unsettling effect produced by Clare's presence, Irene begins to suspect that Clare is having an affair with Dr. Redfield. But before Irene can act on her suspicions, Bellew follows Clare to Harlem and confirms his. Clare Kendry falls through a sixth-story window to her death.

Unlike Helga Crane, who is both spectator and performer, the two characters in *Passing* seem at first to divide the roles of the black female performer and the black female spectator.[60] The performer, Clare, is introduced metonymically. In the opening paragraph of the novel, a letter is described in terms that anticipate the description of the novel's antagonist: out of place, alien, mysterious, furtive, sly, and flaunting. The handwriting on the envelope is an "almost illegible scrawl," and it bears no return address "to betray the sender." Without reading the letter, Irene, the addressee, presumes to know not only who it is from, but what it says. She is certain that its contents will be consistent with all she knows of Clare, "stepping always on the edge of danger." In a flashback, Irene remembers Clare as a young child nimbly evading the blows of a drunken father and seeming all the

while unperturbed. Whatever her flaws—and Irene thought Clare to be selfish, cold, and hard—Irene considers her capable of almost *"theatrical* heroics."[61]

In ironic contrast to her name, Clare is an opaque character, impossible to "read," but one who is read for us by Irene, the character from whose point of view the narrative is told. As she peruses the letter, for example, "puzzling out, as best she could, the carelessly formed words or making instinctive guesses at them," Irene gives us her sense of Clare, as a dangerous woman who is always onstage. When the two meet for the first time in the text, Irene recognizes Clare by her laugh, which is described variously as "a small sequence of notes that was like a trill," "like the ringing of a delicate bell" (151), and "the very essence of mockery" (154). If Clare's laugh connotes beauty and aesthetic pleasure, it also conveys ridicule and derision. But who and what is the object of her mockery? Irene recognizes that if it is she, she is somehow performing for Clare.

Irene prefers to keep Clare onstage. In Irene's eyes, racial passing is the latest in the series of performances that constitute Clare's life. Among the earliest is Clare's melodramatic grieving over her father's death. After her father was murdered in a barroom fight, Clare unleashed a torrent of tears that, in Irene's interpretation, expressed mourning less than fury at the tawdry circumstances of his death and at the abuse he had meted out to her in life. Similarly, Irene remembers the rumors of the glamorous life Clare was said to live after passing out of the black world. The rumors were based in part on Clare's having been glimpsed at a fashionable hotel with one "white" woman and two "white" men. Irene never questions the ability of black people to discern race, although the reader notes that in their first meeting, Irene mistakes Clare for a "white" woman. According to yet another rumor, Clare was seen riding in a chauffeured limousine with a man, "unmistakably white and evidently rich" (153). Later in the novel, Irene refers to "that old suspicion that Clare was acting, not consciously, perhaps—that is, not too consciously—but, none the less acting" (182). Against backdrops that convey glamour and danger in equal measure, Clare acts out her life's dramas.

The setting for the characters' reunion is such a backdrop. But the scene that unfolds confirms that Irene, no less than Clare, participates in a masquerade. When she first arrives, Irene thinks the rooftop cafe at an expensive Chicago hotel is like "another world." To enter it, she is required to pass, which she does without reflection or regret. She admires another apparently white woman, whose spring-like appearance seems, like the cafe itself, an antidote to a sweltering summer day. The "sweetly scented woman in a fluttering dress of green chiffon whose mingled pattern of narcissuses, jonquils, and hyacinths was a reminder of pleasantly chill spring days" turns out to be Clare (148).

Struck by Clare's peculiar, odd, caressing, and inappropriate smile—"just a shade too provocative for a waiter" (149)—Irene is intrigued and fascinated, until Clare begins to fix Irene in her gaze. Clare stares boldly at Irene and refuses to be embarrassed about it. Irene, by contrast, chafes at the scrutiny and quickly averts her eyes. Although she is confident of her ability to pass for an Italian, a Spaniard, a Mexican, a gypsy, anything but what she is, Irene begins to fear being unmasked as a Negro. When Clare rises to approach Irene, Irene is frightened that she will be turned out of the restaurant and thus made into the kind of spectacle she associates previously with Clare.

Having failed to recognize Clare, Irene is at a practical disadvantage; she has lost the moral edge she covets as well, for each character knows the other is passing. Subsequently, Irene tries to regain the upper hand by declining to answer Clare's questions about the rumors surrounding her disappearance from the black community. Clare finds Irene's convenient memory lapse amusing. Later, Irene purposely forgets to ask Clare about her current life, which she assumes is an immoral one. In every case, Clare intuits the reason behind Irene's dissembling. Moreover, the reader is privy, as Clare is not, to a preceding scene in which Irene ignored a stricken pedestrian whom she passed on the street. Hardly a Good Samaritan, Irene has no grounds for the moral superiority she claims. Little wonder Irene finds Clare's mocking laughter unsettling; she assumes her old friend is laughing at her.

The mocking laughter betokens the ways in which the novel breaks with literary conventions of passing and the tragic mulatto. Although her death is typical of the tragic mulatto fate, the Clare Kendry character breaks the mold in every other respect.[62] Her

motives for passing are ambiguous. Though she seeks the freedom to define herself, she also wants the material comforts the white world offers. As she explains, "I was determined to get away, to be a person and not a charity or a problem, or even a daughter of the indiscreet Ham. Then, too, I wanted things. I knew I wasn't bad-looking and that I could 'pass'" (159). The psychic rewards are few, but at first Clare is sure the money is worth its price. Bellew is an international banking agent, apparently as rich as Croesus, who indulges his wife's love of luxury. Clare can chat glibly of travels to pre-war Paris and post-war Budapest.[63]

Despite the ease with which Clare crosses racial and cultural borders, she refers to herself as a "deserter." Yet Irene looks in vain for traces of pain, fear, or grief on her countenance. Even when Clare begins to doubt the wisdom of her choice, she claims no noble purpose, merely loneliness and a vague yearning for "my own people." In fact, her trips to Harlem involve more pleasure-seeking than homecoming. Like Helga Crane, Clare is profoundly homeless; unlike Helga, she is never in despair over it. She remains instead cool and calculating. At one point, she confesses to Irene: "Why, to get the things I want badly enough, I'd do anything, hurt anybody, throw anything away. Really, 'Rene, I'm not safe" (210). In drawing such an unsympathetic character, Larsen seems initially merely to flout the tragic mulatto convention.

Rather than emphasize the pathos of the "passing" situation, Larsen stresses its attractive veneer. Clare Kendry always looks exquisite, whether wearing a "superlatively simple cinnamon-brown frock" with a "little golden bowl of a hat" or a "shining red gown." Clothes, furnishings, notepaper—all the accoutrements of Clare's life are painstakingly described. At times Larsen's intentions seem definitely satirical, as when on one occasion Clare chooses a dress whose shade not only suits her but sets off her hotel room's decor. But at other points, Larsen seems to solicit the reader's admiration for the graceful, elegant Clare.

Clare's survival depends literally on her ability to keep up appearances. She must look like the white society matron she pretends to be. But her looks, clothes, and facile conversation are the envy of the other female characters. They, too, spend an inordinate amount of time shopping and preening. The narrative pauses frequently to offer detailed descriptions of clothes and home furnishings. But what seems at first an annoying preoccupation with "minutiae" (to borrow Hoyt Fuller's apt term) becomes instead a statement on the condition of women in the book.[64] In their lives, maintaining the social niceties is an obligation, and pouring tea is, in the words of one, "an occupation." Each of these characters, like Clare, relies on a husband for material possessions, security, and identity. Each reflects and is a reflection of her husband's class status. Clare's is merely an extreme version of a situation they all share.

These characters join in the masquerade described by feminist theorist Luce Irigaray as "what women do . . . in order to participate in man's desire, but at the cost of giving up their own."[65] Some characters perform the masquerade with great flair, while for others, their lack of finesse becomes a marker of integrity. Irene is one of the former. Her husband, Brian, is a physician, whose professional success provides for her materially—a Harlem town house and household staff—and psychologically—she takes comfort in the security and status attendant to his position. To an extent, the Redfields' life is one Irene has "arranged." She has dissuaded Brian from pursuing his dream of a new life in Brazil. She has spun a cocoon around her sons, forbidding discussion of racism as too disagreeable, and she plans someday to send the boys to European boarding schools (like the one Clare's daughter attends in Switzerland). But the price she pays is a marriage devoid of passion. The couple sleep in separate bedrooms, and Brian argues that the sooner their children learn that sex is "a grand joke," the better off they will be.

If Irene plays the role of bourgeois wife with style, Gertrude Martin looks "as if her husband might be a butcher" (167). Her dress is too frilly and too short; her stockings are cheap and badly dyed. But if style is the basis of Irene's judgment, as of the society's, it is not the standard the novel ultimately endorses. During the conversation with Bellew, three women (Clare, Irene, and Gertrude) are passing for white; none steps out of her role. Irene is certain that she alone takes offense at Bellew's racist vitriol, but when they leave, it is Gertrude

who expresses outrage. Irene imagines, by contrast, that "under other conditions," she could like Jack Bellew. Gertrude is hardly heroic. Not only has she also kept silent during Bellew's insults, she shares Clare's relief that her children are not dark. Nevertheless, she does not conceal her racial identity. Her husband is white, but he, his family, and his friends know that Gertrude is not. In this small measure, she displays a greater sense of integrity than her glamorous peers.

Irene's response to Bellew's racism is laughter, which in this case proves an ineffective tool of resistance. Bellew jokes that Clare is getting darker by the day and, if she does not look out, "she'll wake up one of these days and find she's turned into a nigger" (171). Irene laughs hysterically. Bellew laughs, too, although he is not joking when he declares that there are "no niggers in my family." In response, Irene laughs again, too loud and too long. Eventually, she catches herself but not before realizing that she has risked unmasking Clare and making a spectacle of herself.

The injection of racial difference into the masquerade of femininity, even when performed in well-appointed hotel suites or tastefully elegant town houses, threatens to produce a public spectacle. White feminist critic Mary Russo, recalling admonitions she heard in childhood, observes that "making a spectacle out of oneself seemed a specifically feminine danger." The danger of exposure could present itself at any time, for rather than requiring a deliberate act, it had "more to do with a kind of inadvertency and loss of boundaries."[66] Such danger imperilled the personal reputation of white women. Revealingly, as long as the characters in *Passing* play the role of white lady, that is the danger they run. Gertrude's slovenliness and Irene's unseemly laughter jeopardize their individual reputations. But the black woman who makes a spectacle of herself may not only embarrass herself; she may disgrace the race. Consequently, the admonitions (as the numerous examples in Fauset's fiction confirm) as well as the risks are intensified. Transgressing racial boundaries means running the risk of being turned out of public places and being put out of house and home.

Racial boundaries in most of America during the 1920s were rigidly policed, but less so in Harlem, which attracted a stream of white

intellectuals, celebrities, and other tourists. Not only is *Passing* set in Harlem at the height of its vogue, it is itself a product of the vogue. Aptly then, it acknowledges the opportunities as well as the risks that the more fluid racial and cultural boundaries of the period created. The National Welfare League dance is the scene that best depicts the possibilities and the limits.

The National Welfare League (N.W.L.) is Larsen's fictionalized amalgam of the NAACP and the Urban League, and the scene is doubtlessly inspired by the NAACP Ball, an annual Harlem social event. On occasion, the Imeses attended the ball with Carl Van Vechten and his wife, Fania Marinoff, to whom *Passing* is dedicated. The Van Vechtens appear in the novel as well, thinly disguised as the novelist Hugh Wentworth and his wife, Bianca. Appropriately, Wentworth is the bellwether of the white elite who flock to Harlem. Clare is surprised that a famous white man would attend a black social event. Smugly, Irene informs her that it "was the year 1927 in the city of New York, and hundreds of white people of Hugh Wentworth's type came to affairs in Harlem, more all the time" (198). According to Irene, the reason was simple: they wanted "to see Negroes." In an irony that is lost on neither Irene nor the reader, Clare quickly decides she wants to do the same. Of course, as Clare's ambiguous situation illustrates, the issue of who is seeing and who is being seen is far from simple.

The Negro Welfare League dance is "a public thing," a spectacle where a few whites come merely to enjoy themselves; more come to collect material with which they hope to capitalize on the Negro vogue; and most come "to gaze on these great and near great while they gaze on the Negroes" (198). Even as they are onstage, blacks can turn the tables and watch the white folks watching them. If places can be so easily traded, however, one is at risk of losing his or hers. Larsen seems aware both of how acutely blacks want to break free of the place that society assigns them and of how profoundly they fear being displaced. On one level, the former constituted the political agenda of civil rights organizations like the N.W.L., while the latter constituted the social service agenda. But the novel is concerned as well with the psychological displacement experienced by middle-class black women. It was on no one's agenda.

Irene's fear of displacement complicates her response to Clare's request. Declining to invite her, Irene casts about for a reason. She fears Clare will be recognized by acquaintances of John Bellew or mistaken for a prostitute. After all, she points out, "all sorts of people go, anybody who can pay a dollar, even ladies of easy virtue looking for trade" (199). Clare laughs at the absurdity of the first possibility and is amused by the second. Passing allows her to evade the obsession with propriety described by Marita Bonner and experienced by many New Negro women, an obsession fueled by the fear that racist and sexist stereotypes would render their individual selves invisible. Although Irene relents and promises to include Clare in her party, she fears the consequences. Having slipped the bonds of propriety, Clare might provoke a scene, some "unpleasantness" or "danger" that could implicate Irene.

No scene erupts at the dance, but the event itself is a spectacle. The dance attracts people from all over, a point that Larsen underscores by quoting the nursery rhyme "Rich man, poor man, / Beggar man, thief," as she had done in "The Wrong Man." On the dance floor, blacks and white cross lines that are impassable elsewhere. Interracial couples only seem to flirt with the possibility of the illicit; the boundaries are carefully preserved. After the ball, blacks and whites will return to their segregated lives.

Even in the public moment, blacks and whites occupy unequal positions. Nathan Huggins's comment on Van Vechten's *Nigger Heaven* is pertinent. Noting that the title was derived from the Jim Crow practice that required black theatergoers to be seated in the balcony, Huggins argues that "Harlem was no segregated balcony to Manhattan's 'theater,' where black people sat up high to watch the show of life go on. Rather, it was a stage; the performers played for all they were worth to a white world" (245). Allegedly in the interest of "Negro welfare," so do the dancers in *Passing*.

As if she were a stand-in for the Negro in vogue, Clare dresses to steal the spotlight: "Clare, exquisite, golden, fragrant, flaunting, in a stately gown of shining black taffeta" (203). To Hugh Wentworth, she looks like "the blonde beauty out of the fairy tale" (204). But the information he seeks—name, status, and race—is more the stuff of crime fiction than fairy tales.

At the least, Wentworth's questions suggest an impulse to put Clare in her place. Giving these words to a character so obviously based on Van Vechten is an intriguing choice on Larsen's part. While Hugh Wentworth is generally depicted as an admirable character, the portrayal is tinged with irony. For example, although the reference to whites who came to Harlem to "get material to turn into shekels" does not name Wentworth, knowledgeable readers might recall that *Nigger Heaven* outsold every book produced by the Negro vogue. Moreover, in *Passing*, Irene tutors the Wentworth character continually; he becomes the device through which historical and sociological data are conveyed. In the novel, Irene assures Hugh Wentworth that she is not "slipping" or mocking him; she would not do that to one so "sincere." As author, Nella Larsen responded differently to the character's real-life counterpart.[67]

Most telling is the revision *Passing* makes of a key element in *Nigger Heaven*. Structurally, Van Vechten's novel consists of dual plots. One chronicles the dull and proper courtship of two New Negroes, librarian Mary Love and aspiring writer Byron Kasson. The second depicts a scandalous affair between Byron and Lasca Sartoris, a sybaritic sex goddess who is fond of cocaine and devil worship. Lasca fits to a tee the black female stereotype that repelled Marita Bonner: "only a gross collection of desires, all uncontrolled."[68] In the sensational climax, the jilted Byron goes to a Harlem speakeasy to exact revenge by murdering the man who has replaced him in Lasca's bed. But a notorious pimp—with the unlikely name of Anatole Longfellow, alias the Scarlet Creeper, and a score of his own to settle—beats Byron to the draw. Not surprisingly, the second plot eclipses the first; the netherworld of lust, drugs, and violence is so much more vivid than the wholly separate world of the respectable bourgeoisie that the novel reinforces the racist stereotypes it purports to demolish.

Far less sensational, *Passing* uses doubled characters rather than a dual plot to represent a more complex world than either of those portrayed in *Nigger Heaven*. Its most sensational event does not take place in a nightclub, but in the home of respectable Harlemites. Its most profound insights concern the psychological damage done when black women internalize the racist and sexist stereotypes omnipres-

*[handwritten margin notes: "examine
example
to draw II's
from the
2 gen?
antagonist
Irene's
objections —"
"is
she?"]*

ent in the society. What happens when one performs neither for the public nor for one's own pleasure, as a singer or dancer might? What happens when one performs a masquerade for oneself?

Throughout the narrative, while Irene continues to call attention to the differences between herself and Clare, Nella Larsen, more often than not, minimizes those differences to great effect. For example, Irene craves stability and abhors the risks Clare thrives on; she is a devoted mother, whereas Clare professes little interest in the welfare of her daughter, and Irene prides herself on her loyalty to the race. However, Irene's world is barely more secure than that of her friend, and when it is threatened, she is every bit as dangerous. In effect, Irene becomes Clare's double. As an educated, middle-class black woman, Irene is in as much danger of being made into a spectacle as the daring, passing-for-white Clare.

Partly in self-defense and partly because Clare invites the role, Irene has begun to view her friend as an exotic Other. Watching her, she has the sensation of "gazing into the eyes of some creature utterly strange and apart" (172).[69] Her face is "an ivory mask" (157). Then again, Clare's look is "unfathomable, utterly beyond any comprehension of Irene's" (176). Irene invents for Clare a complex inner life. But she is not responding to the person before her as much as to her own notions of Otherness. Clare's "Negro eyes" symbolize the unconscious, the unknowable, the erotic, and the passive. In other words, they symbolize those aspects of the psyche Irene denies within herself. Her confused sense of race becomes at last an evasion by which she avoids confronting her deepest feelings.

*[handwritten margin notes: "✓"
"?"
"But
one's
are
passive in
many ways,
than
Clare"]*

Clare's repeated assertions of her own dangerousness reinforce Irene's fears and allow Irene to objectify Clare completely. At the same time, they allow Irene to emulate Clare. After her suspicions grow that Clare is interested in Brian and Clare becomes a menace she must eliminate, Irene begins to act with the same deviousness she attributes to Clare. For example, she conceals her encounter with Bellew in which she was in fact unmasked and begins to contrive plots that would unmask Clare. Irene's language becomes increasingly arch and her gestures increasingly theatrical. At the climactic moment, Irene becomes the performer, enacting the clichéd role of the female Exotic. Although the evidence is all circumstantial, Larsen strongly

implies that Irene pushes Clare through the window.[70] Irene is certainly capable of it, for by the end of the novel, she is indeed Clare's double, willing to "do anything, hurt anybody, throw anything away" to get what she wants. A psychological suicide, if not a murderer, Irene too has played the game of passing and lost.

Clare's death is at the center of a spectacle that commences when Jack Bellew knocks on the door of the Freeland home in Harlem. His entry signals the imposition of the rigidly prescribed boundaries of race, gender, and class. The private (free?) space becomes the site of "a public thing," which ends with "a frenzied rush of feet," "the slamming of distant doors," and the clamor of voices including that of "a strange man, official and authoritative," who arrives to conduct an investigation. In the official inquiry, individual motives and culpability will not be at issue. Bellew is the only individual suspected of foul play, and Irene absolves him. That the suspicion falls on him at all suggests that the drama will be played out according to a preordained script in the press and the courts. The element of race ensures that private affairs become public spectacle.[71]

In both its imagery and its themes, *Passing* revisits the territory Larsen explored in *Quicksand*. Like "quicksand," "passing" is a metaphor of death and desperation, and it is similarly supported by images of asphyxiation, suffocation, and claustrophobia. Unlike "quicksand," "passing" provokes definite associations and expectations that Larsen is finally unable to transcend. In Larsen's novel, "passing" does not refer only to the sociological phenomenon of blacks crossing the color line. It represents additionally both the loss of racial identity and the denial of self required of women who conform to restrictive gender roles. Though less fully developed than Helga Crane, Irene and Clare likewise demonstrate the price black women pay for their acquiescence and, ultimately, the high cost of rebellion. As these characters deviate from the norm, they are defined—indeed too often define themselves—as Other. They thereby cede control of their lives. But, in truth, the worlds these characters inhabit offer them no possibility of autonomy or fulfillment.

Nathan Huggins has observed that of the Harlem Renaissance writers, "Nella Larsen came as close as any to treating human motivation with complexity and sophistication. But she could not wrestle

free of the mulatto condition that her main characters had been given."[72] I would argue that Larsen achieves a good measure of complexity and sophistication, yet Huggins's point has merit, especially in regard to *Passing*. Much more than *Quicksand*, this novel adheres to the pattern—the victim caught forever betwixt and between until she finds in death the only freedom she can know. The inevitable melodrama weakens the credibility of the narrative and diverts attention from the author's more compelling concerns. Its plot still reveals something of the predicament of the middle-class black woman, and the book itself illuminates problems facing the black woman novelist.

Among the images of black women presented in fiction before the Harlem Renaissance, the tragic mulatto was the least degrading and the most attractive, which partly explains its prominence in Jessie Fauset's novels and in those of her predecessors dating back to Harriet Wilson and Frances Watkins Harper. In light of this literary history, depicting the tragic mulatto was probably the surest way for a black woman fiction writer to gain a hearing. Nella Larsen's personal history doubtless increased the appeal for her, as the reality behind the image was in part her own story. Nevertheless, working with an image long stereotyped in the literary and popular imaginations proved difficult. No matter how much she tried to vary it, deepen it, and make it live, she was hindered by the expectations it engendered.

In what became her final publication, Larsen experimented with a totally different kind of character. Such an experiment might have freed her from the limitations of worn formulas. Instead, the furor that developed soon after the short story appeared helped to ensure her silence. "Sanctuary" was published in the January 1930 issue of *Forum* magazine. Set in the rural South, the story revolves around Annie Poole, an old black woman who possesses "some quality of hardness that belied her appearance of frailty" (15). Out of a sense of race loyalty, she hides a young fugitive who believes he has murdered a white man. With the arrival of the sheriff, both the woman and the man she is protecting learn that it is Annie Poole's son who has been murdered. Though the sheriff and his men are anxious to capture her son's killer, Annie Poole refuses to yield to her own desire for re-

venge. Race loyalty has a stronger claim on her emotions, and she allows the grief-stricken young man to go free. Larsen handles the story's narration with detachment, as usual offering no judgment on the actions of any of the characters; she allows the ironies to speak for themselves. In this instance, however, the ironies are so heavy that they almost sink the story. Mrs. Poole's son, Obadiah, is as upright as his name; he has goodheartedly befriended the ne'er-do-well Jim Hammer. The mother is a keener judge of character, yet she offers Jim, with his "soiled body and grimy garments," sanctuary in her immaculate home because she believes he cannot expect justice from the law. Everything in her life has confirmed her conviction that "white folks is white folks" (15). With an irony that badly strains the reader's credulity, Larsen portrays the sheriff as a man in sympathy with the Pooles, as a man who does in fact seek justice. Such just and humane southern lawmen were surely as rare in life as they are in fiction. Larsen's portrayal of Jim is more convincing. Shocked and remorseful, he reveals some of the qualities that might have won him Obadiah's friendship initially. Of course, nothing he can do now can assuage Mrs. Poole's grief. She keeps her word nevertheless and bids him safe passage by telling him to be thankful for his black face.

In a sense, "Sanctuary" explores the impulse toward race solidarity that had been a concern in Larsen's earlier work. Her conclusions had been similarly ambiguous in *Quicksand* and *Passing*, but the situations had been more believable. Clearly, Larsen understood too little about the realities and psychology of southern blacks to render them credibly. The best that can be said of "Sanctuary" is that it is a failed experiment. Some *Forum* readers said far worse.

In a letter to the editor, one of several submitted, a reader noted a "striking resemblance" between Larsen's story and one by Sheila Kaye-Smith, "Mrs. Adis," published eight years before in *Century*. The charges were specific and devastating: "Aside from dialect and setting, the stories are almost identical. The structure, situation, character, and plot are the same. One finds in Miss Larsen's story the same words and expressions used by Sheila Kaye-Smith . . ."[73] The similarities *are* unmistakable. The action of each commences at nightfall as the protagonist prepares the evening meal. Each woman

sees the lawmen pass in the distance and warns the fugitive of their approach. The lawmen arrive bearing the body of the son. However, no final confrontation between mother and murderer occurs in "Mrs. Adis." Moreover, race solidarity supplies a far stronger motivation for the characters in Larsen's story than the hints of class conflict in Kaye-Smith's. Flawed as it is, "Sanctuary" is a much better story than "Mrs. Adis."

Needless to say, the issue in 1930 was not literary merit; it was theft. Nella Larsen had to prove, publicly, that she was not a plagiarist. To demonstrate her innocence, she submitted four preliminary drafts of the story to the magazine's editors. Then, in a long letter printed alongside that of her accuser, she recounted the circumstances that she claimed inspired her work. An elderly woman who had been her patient at Lincoln Hospital had often expressed dismay at the racial politics in an institution staffed completely by black nurses and white doctors and administrators. The woman, a highly vocal proponent of race unity, according to Larsen, told how she had shielded her husband's murderer because she intended to deal with him herself "without any interference from 'white folks.'" Only with the advent of the controversy generated by "Sanctuary" had Larsen discovered that the woman's story was "so old and so well known that it is almost folklore."[74]

Larsen's account may not be a total fabrication, but it contains a signal flaw. No source for the story in the "folk" tradition has ever been identified. "Almost" folklore is what scholar Richard Dorson calls "fakelore." What seems a more likely scenario for the genesis of "Sanctuary" is that Larsen had read Kaye-Smith's story and recognized the affinity of its theme to African-American life. Then, perhaps unconsciously, when she began to write "Sanctuary," Larsen adapted key elements of "Mrs. Adis," much as was done in the theater where "black" versions of classic and contemporary plays were common. But she failed to acknowledge her debt.[75]

Larsen's explanation and the four drafts convinced the editors of *Forum* that she was blameless. But the accusations remained lodged securely in the minds of many. Those Harlemites who disliked Larsen took more than a little pleasure in her pain. Harold Jackman,

a familiar figure in Harlem salons, kept his good friend Countee Cullen, then living in Paris, abreast of the controversy. Never doubting the truth of the charge, he judged, "But isn't it a terrible thing." When he saw Larsen at a party, he could hardly contain his outrage. As he vented it to Cullen, "She thinks she is so much hell—I could have strangled her that night. . . ." Part of the venom is explained by Jackman's succeeding lament: "I have been so broke I haven't been going anywhere."[76] The rest is more difficult to explicate. Whatever its cause—and misogyny seems the most obvious possibility—Alice Walker had good reason to think of Nella Larsen fifty years later when she reflected: "[O]ur oral tradition, which works as well as ever, kills successful black women off at house parties."[77]

These attacks on her professional integrity could not have come at a worse time, for they coincided with a personal crisis that would also become a public scandal before it was done. Sometime early in 1930, Nella Larsen discovered that Elmer Imes was having an affair. Imes had accepted a professorship at Fisk and moved to Nashville, while Larsen remained in New York. He had become involved with a Fisk staffer. To complicate matters for all concerned, the woman was white. An interracial affair represented a potential scandal no southern black school could afford. When the Fisk administration learned of the affair, they insisted that Larsen come to Nashville. She arrived in May. As she described the trip to Van Vechten, she was "a dutiful wife going down to visit her husband."[78] She could have hardly missed the final irony: in this instance, the race, as much as her philandering husband, required her loyalty. Her presence did not save the marriage, but it did quiet the gossip, as it was intended to do.

No scandal could completely overshadow Larsen's success in 1930. In March, she became the first African-American woman to receive a Guggenheim Fellowship for Creative Writing. The achievement compelled recognition. Only two other black writers, Cullen and Walter White, had been awarded this fellowship. The terms of the grant were propitious. Larsen was awarded two thousand dollars to support her travel abroad, especially in Spain and France, where she was to write a novel on "the different effects of Europe and the United States on the intellectual and physical freedom of the Negro."[79] This was an oppor-

tunity to explore anew themes that had resonated in Larsen's best work, and she welcomed it. But although Nella Larsen sailed for Europe that fall and remained abroad until the spring of 1932, she was never to publish another novel.

That she tried to satisfy the conditions of the award is evident from her correspondence. Very soon after her arrival in Europe, she wrote Van Vechten expressing her grim determination "to work like a nigger." The letter continued: "Thinking it over, I've come to the conclusion that I've never expended any real honest-to-God-labour on anything in my life (except floors and woodwork) and perhaps that's not being quite fair either to myself or the very few people who—."[80] Clearly, the year's events had taken their toll. Nevertheless, Larsen continued working, in Majorca, where she lived for a time with Dorothy Peterson, and even in Nashville, to which she returned in April 1932. Eventually, she completed the novel begun in Europe and entitled *Fall Fever*. By the summer of 1933, she was at work on a second book, to be called *The Wingless Hour*, and was co-authoring a third, *Adrian and Evodne*.[81] None of this work reached publication, and none of the manuscripts is extant.

Larsen's last public notice was a scurrilous article in the *Baltimore Afro-American*; its headline read "Fisk Professor Is Divorced by N.Y. Novelist: Friends Think Love Cooled While Wife Wintered in Europe." The scandal had surfaced with a vengeance, with Nella Larsen cast as its prime villain. The article had a few of its facts straight. Larsen had divorced Elmer Imes in Nashville in September 1933. She had tried, unsuccessfully, as the article evidences, to do so discreetly. Imes's lover, Ethel Gilbert, had resigned her position; he remained on the faculty.[82]

Her personal life shattered, Nella Larsen began her withdrawal from both the black community and the world of letters. In 1932, she had shared a Harlem podium with Rudolph Fisher discussing the role of the Arts, and, in 1933, she had been elected assistant secretary of the Writers' League Against Lynching, an organization founded by Walter White, among others. But after her divorce, she ceased to be involved in such activities.[83] She moved from Harlem to Greenwich Village, where for a time her social circle included writers and artists

who knew her as a novelist. Gradually, she broke off her few remaining friendships, including those with James Weldon Johnson and Carl Van Vechten. In 1937, she tried to disappear completely by pretending to sail for South America.[84]

Having been unable to find acceptance in either the white world of her youth or the black world of her young adulthood, Larsen subsequently declined to identify with either. But she did not pass. When the alimony with which she supported herself ended upon her husband's death in 1941, Larsen returned to nursing. For seventeen years, Nella Imes, as she was known, worked the night shift at Gouverneur Hospital on the Lower East Side. She lived in a one-room apartment, also in lower Manhattan. The hospital and her book-lined studio marked the perimeters of her life. She read extensively, but if she wrote, she did not publish. Her friends were few and drawn almost exclusively from her hospital coworkers, first at Gouverneur, then at Metropolitan Hospital, to which she transferred in 1961. Outside this circle, Nella Larsen succeeded in achieving the anonymity that by that time she preferred.

The facts about Nella Larsen's later life are important because they suggest the reasons for her long silence. Certainly, the crises of the early thirties propelled her flight into obscurity. On the one hand, the "Sanctuary" controversy raised doubts among Larsen's readers and perhaps within Larsen herself about her talent and integrity as a writer. The marital crisis was even more wounding. If Larsen's domestic troubles were "personal," they illustrate, again, the impossibility of drawing neat categories labelled "personal" and "professional" or "public" and "private" in an examination of a writer's work. Surely, Larsen's marital woes proved so overwhelming in part because the private became public. Surely, too, her career made her a target for the scandalmongers in the press. Larsen the writer was excoriated for the alleged shortcomings of Larsen the woman.[85] Larsen's work made her vulnerable on more profound levels as well. Her novels had explored the ambiguous meanings of race and the false allure, grounded in racial mythology, that could catalyze interracial liaisons. Her husband's affair with a white lover raised these issues in the most intimate way. As we have seen, the situation also called into question the issue of

race loyalty. In her correspondence, Larsen never mentions these issues. But it seems reasonable to conclude that the pain and confusion attending them, along with a desire not to sort them out publicly, sped her flight.

To some degree, Nella Larsen must have been aware all along that the work she did was dangerous. Examining the intersection of race, class, and gender was a perilous business. She could derive no safe or simple truths. Ambiguity may be a mark of complexity and sophistication in modern literature, but a black writer whose political commitment is not patently clear is suspected of ideological confusion at best, evasion and cowardice at worst. Nella Larsen has been charged with all of these. In fact, her novels often raise questions, forthright, difficult questions, about the significance of race and racial difference that Larsen does not always presume to answer—an act of honesty and courage, not cowardice. At other times, her conclusions are limited by a class bias she discerns more clearly in her characters than in herself.

Perhaps to fend off the inevitable criticism, Larsen masked her most subversive concerns, speaking so subtly about gender questions in particular that only after half a century are readers beginning to explore the tentative answers her novels insinuate. Part of the mask was the dialogue she fashioned for her characters. This stylized speech enervates her prose; but because it calls attention to itself rather than to the ideas it conveys, it also deflects the criticism those ideas would otherwise have evoked. Without question, the mask's most deceptive aspect was the convention of the tragic mulatto. Readers were so sure they knew the story Larsen was telling they misread the story she actually told. In this sense, one might say Larsen tried to "pass" as a novelist and to an extent succeeded. Using the tragic mulatto as a cover, she set forth a vision far more complex and daring than even her most enthusiastic critics imagined. She paid a price. Her success was measured by those who *knew* what they were seeing and thereby missed the point. Passing is and ever was a losing game.

Four

Zora Neale Hurston's Traveling Blues

When Nella Larsen's *Quicksand* was published in March 1928, Zora Neale Hurston was in the field, living at the Everglades Cypress Lumber Company in Loughman, Florida. Situated in Polk County, "where the water tastes lak cherry wine," the sawmill camp drew workers from across the South. Hurston recognized immediately that she had struck a mother lode of material: folktales, work songs, proverbs and sermons, children's rhymes, and blues. In *Dust Tracks on a Road*, she gives a compressed, poetic account of her Polk County expedition. The blues ethos is unmistakable. "Polk County . . . Singing, laughing, cursing, boasting of last night's love, and looking forward to the darkness again. They do not say embrace when they mean slept with a woman." Everlasting love is a lie. Love is made and "unmade"; one welcomes it when and wherever it is found. Hurston quotes a blues that expresses a philosophy not only of love, but of life:

Got on de train didn't have no fare
But I rode some

Yes I rode some.
Got on de train didn't have no fare
Conductor ask me what I'm doing there
But I rode some
Yes I rode some.
Well, he grabbed me by de collar and he led me to de door
But I rode some
Yes I rode some.
Well, he grabbed me by de collar and he led me to de door
He rapped me over de head with a forty-four
But I rode some
Yes I rode some.[1]

Even on the printed page the insistent refrain of this song resonates with what critic Stephen Henderson calls the "survival motion" inherent in the blues.[2] The folk singer insists on the value and breadth of his life, realizing that the powerful had neither granted him permission to live it nor understood that he had. The song duly records the oppressive circumstances of the singer's life, but more important, it proclaims his triumph over them. In doing so, it expresses a central premise of Hurston's work: material poverty is not tantamount to spiritual poverty or experiential deprivation. Life in the Polk counties of the nation was rich and complex, as the blues and other vernacular forms confirmed. "It would be a tremendous loss to the Negro race and to America," Hurston once told a reporter, "if we should lose the folklore and folk music, for the unlettered Negro has given the Negro's best contribution to America's culture."[3]

In keeping with this belief, the sources of Hurston's imagination and the texture of her prose are radically different from those of her female contemporaries. No tragic mulattoes people her fiction. Characters do not ponder emotional dilemmas while pouring tea. Plots do not resolve themselves in sentimental clichés. The reasons for these differences are several, but one of the most important is suggested by the affinity between Hurston's aesthetic and that of the blues singer. Zora Neale Hurston was the one literary woman who was free to embrace Bessie Smith's art, who was also heir to the legacy evoked in the blues.[4]

As a daughter of the rural South, Hurston claimed this legacy by birthright. As an anthropologist, she reclaimed it through years of in-

tense, often perilous research. As a writer, she summoned this legacy in her choice of setting, her delineation of character, and, most devotedly, in her distillation of language. All these elements provided sharp contrasts to the formal poetry and fiction discussed earlier in this book, but the discursive differences are crucial. Jessie Fauset's characters shifted between a pseudo-literary language that no one spoke and a mundanely popular one that everyone did. Despite the complex metaphorical patterns of her novels, Nella Larsen wrote only serviceable prose. Zora Neale Hurston's writing is, by contrast, what her biographer terms a series of "linguistic moments."[5] With a keen sensitivity to the rhythms of southern black speech, Hurston had recorded the language of informants in the field, she understood the priority placed on verbal agility in black expressive culture. As the blueswoman fashioned her lyrics from the storehouse of rural blues, Hurston drew from the repository of African-American oral tradition to construct a literary language that is distinctly her own.

Hurston's respect for the cultural traditions of black people is one of the most important constants in her career. This respect threads through the short fiction of her youth; her ethnographic research in the rural South and the Caribbean (reported in *Mules and Men* and *Tell My Horse*); her novels, plays, and autobiography; and the journalistic essays she authored in later years. In all, she published more than fifty short stories and articles in addition to her seven books. Because her focus was on black cultural traditions, she rarely explored interracial themes.[6] Hurston appreciated and approved the reluctance of blacks to reveal "that which the soul lives by" to the hostile and uncomprehending gaze of outsiders. But the interior reality was what she wished to probe. In that reality, blacks ceased to be "tongueless, earless, eyeless conveniences" whose labor whites exploited; they ceased to be mules and were men and women.

For Hurston, the measure of a people's self-respect was the love they had for "their own things": "their songs, their [stories], and proverbs and dances."[7] The documentation of these expressions was crucial. So Zora Hurston traveled the South collecting folktales; recording sermons, spirituals, and blues; and apprenticing herself to hoodoo doctors to learn their curses and cures. The years she spent in the field not only yielded *Mules and Men* but shaped Hurston's entire

oeuvre. As she put it, "I picked up glints and gleams out of what I had and stored it away to turn to my own use" (*Dust Tracks*, 51). Hurston's writing is suffused with the similes, the metaphors, and the rhythms that are the poetry of black vernacular expression. Her desire, in Karla Holloway's phrase, "to render the oral culture literate" led to the technical innovations of her prose.[8] Her effort was not merely to interpolate folk sayings in her fiction; it was to create a literary language informed by the poetry as well as the perspective of the "folk."

The first stop on Hurston's journey back was her hometown, Eatonville, Florida, the "first Negro community in America to be incorporated." It was not, she emphasized in *Dust Tracks*, "the black back-side of an average town," but "a pure Negro town—charter, mayor, council, town marshal and all" (1). Her parents, John and Lucy (Potts) Hurston, had been tenant farmers in their native Alabama, but in Eatonville John Hurston was thrice elected mayor and wrote the village laws. His experience exemplifies the political and psychological significance of Eatonville; it allowed black people to assume roles in keeping with their image of themselves rather than internalizing the subservient images the dominant society prescribed. Finally, Eatonville's significance was cultural. Joe Clarke's store was "the heart and spring of the town," the site of the "lying sessions" that defined the town's cultural identity (45). In these folktales or "lies," "God, Devil, Brer Rabbit, Brer Fox, Sis Cat, Brer Lion, Tiger, Buzzard, and all the wood folk walked and talked like natural men" (47). For the child Zora, the store porch was the most interesting place in town. Hurston the writer retained the fascination, even as she remarked on the exclusion of women from the store-porch ritual.

John Hurston was a carpenter by trade but a minister by calling; as a preacher/poet, he played a major role in Eatonville's cultural life. From her father's example, Zora Hurston perceived how verbal agility conferred status within the community. His sermons demonstrated as well the power of his language to convey the complexity of the lives of his parishioners. In her fiction, she honed in on the connection between voice and selfhood, between the power of speech and personal status. Revelatory moments in her novels occur when a character claims his or her own voice.

Lucy Hurston was a smart, feisty woman who was strong willed enough at fourteen to marry a man of whom her parents disapproved. The marriage endured, but the bonds of union were often strained. In their daughter's view, John Hurston, with less education than his wife and less money than her father, was never fully convinced that his later success matched his wife's ambitions. Unlike her husband, Lucy had no public forum from which to speak, but she knew how to turn a phrase. Zora recalled that Lucy "exhorted her children at every opportunity to 'jump at de sun.' We might not land on the sun, but at least we would get off the ground" (*Dust Tracks*, 13). Lucy refused to circumscribe her children's dreams. Perhaps, too, she saw in her most rebellious child Zora's spunk a reflection of her own.

Only in the third chapter of her autobiography, *Dust Tracks*, does Hurston begin the story of her own life, and its presentation is highly evasive. She begins with a warning: "This is all hear-say. Maybe some of the details of my birth as told me might be a little inaccurate, but it is pretty well established that I really did get born" (19). Although Hurston had identified the precise date on which Eatonville was incorporated, the closest she comes here to dating her birth is January, during "hog-killing time." In practice, Hurston celebrated her birthday on January 7 and most frequently gave 1901 or 1903 as the year of her birth. She lied. According to the 1900 census, Zora L. Hurston was born in January 1891. She was her parents' fifth child and their second daughter. Her birthplace is listed as Alabama.[9]

Hurston's birthplace was Notasulga, Alabama, a rural hamlet a few miles from Tuskegee and home to at least two generations of Hurston's family. One of her grandfathers, Alf Hurston, founded three Baptist churches in the town. Her older siblings, Hezekiah Robert (Bob), John Cornelius, Richard William, and Sarah Emmeline, were also born in Notasulga, as was Clifford Joel. Sometime between Clifford's birth in 1893 and Benjamin's birth in 1895, the family moved to Eatonville. Everette (b. 1898), who visited his big sister in New York, must have been amused when he read that Zora had been born five years after he. He might have found some humor in it, too, since, in *Dust Tracks* at least, she made the claim with the verbal equivalent of a wink.[10]

When and why Hurston invented the deception is not clear. Certainly, by the time she became a public figure, it was to her advantage to project a youthful, up-and-coming image. Scholarship donors were more likely to support a twenty-four-year-old, the age Hurston was thought to be when she entered Barnard in 1925, than one thirty-four. Achieving publication by the earlier age was likewise more impressive. As one who never admitted embarrassment on any score, Hurston may have found it difficult to own up to her educational deficiencies. Then, too, coming from a background alien to the experience of her classmates in every discernible way, she may have decided simply to let well enough alone. Of course, Hurston may have intentionally suppressed information about her past that could have discredited her. Acknowledging an early marriage, for example, would have been problematic. At Morgan or Howard, the two black universities she attended, as at Barnard, married women did not become "coeds." Whatever her reasons, Hurston persuaded all she met that she was at least ten years younger than she in fact was—no mean accomplishment. The discrepancy concerning her birthplace is altogether less important. Whether she was born there or not, Eatonville was assuredly Zora Hurston's home.

Her recollections of life in Eatonville are vivid and detailed. The beauty of central Florida, with its sumptuous blossoms and pristine lakes, was etched sharply in the memory. At home, as a counterweight to her mother's urging her to "jump at de sun," her father had warned that "it did not do for Negroes to have too much spirit" (13). At Hungerford School, disciples of Booker T. Washington had taught basic academic skills and self-reliance. But the child's elaborate fantasies had been more satisfying than school. In *Dust Tracks*, Hurston recalled at length imaginary playmates, her intense conversations with trees and lakes, and the man who turned into an alligator for her benefit. Recounting her fantasies, Hurston realized they had been inspired by the tales she had overheard on the porch of Joe Clarke's store.

Lucy Potts Hurston's death in 1904 was the pivotal event of Zora's childhood. Her mother, having instructed her daughter to protest the ceremonial acts the village performed for the dying, lay silent upon her bed: "But she looked at me, or so I felt, to speak for her. She depended

on me for a voice" (63). The passage might be accorded wider significance.[11] Although one could argue that Zora Hurston set out to honor
her father's art and that of the Eatonville storytellers, the history of
her career is, to a considerable degree, the history of her efforts to recover her mother's voice. Reflecting these dual motives, her evocation
of African-American vernacular culture is always part celebration and
part critique.

With her mother's death, Hurston's idyllic childhood came to an
abrupt, traumatic end.[12] "That hour began my wanderings. Not so
much in geography, but in time. Then not so much in time as in
spirit" (*Dust Tracks*, 65). A reader might take this as another elliptical
warning, for Hurston leaves many of her wanderings unmapped.
Among those she marks are a year of school in Jacksonville, unhappy
sojourns with relatives, a long series of domestic jobs in unspecified
locations, and an eighteen-month stint as an actress's maid. Poverty
was her constant companion, but like the blues singer, Hurston
seems pleased to say she rode the train anyhow.

Two of her most important destinations were Baltimore, where she
enrolled in night school at Morgan, and Washington, where she
became a student at Howard in 1918. In terms of both geography and
spirit, she was less a solitary traveler than her autobiography depicts.
The protagonist of *Dust Tracks* describes herself as falling ill and being
stranded in Baltimore after the theatrical troupe with which she was
traveling disbands, causing her to lose her job as a maid. In fact,
Hurston's sister, Sarah Hurston Mack, lived in Baltimore: if Zora fell
ill there, it was providential.[13] Zora lived with Sarah's family while she
attended Morgan. While Sarah's schooling had ended with an early
marriage, Hurston's brothers had outstripped the forces of segregation
and poverty to pursue an education. Eldest brother Bob was already a
physician in Memphis; Benjamin would eventually open a pharmacy
in the building that housed Bob's medical practice. Joel was the principal of a high school in Decatur, Alabama. Zora's thirst for education
equalled theirs.[14]

In all likelihood, her brothers offered inspiration and challenge,
but they did not provide financial support. During her years in Baltimore and Washington, she was usually a part-time student and a

full-time worker. Among other jobs, she worked as a waitress at the Cosmos Club and a manicurist in George Robinson's barbershop on Washington's G Street, a black-owned business that served whites only. Whatever the task, she kept her eye on the prize.

Literature was her subject. At Howard, Hurston joined the Stylus, the campus literary club sponsored by Alain Locke and Montgomery Gregory, who quickly recognized her talent. The second issue of the club magazine featured two of her pieces, a short story, "John Redding Goes to Sea," and a poem entitled "O Night." Likely it was Locke who introduced her to Georgia Douglas Johnson; Hurston became a frequent participant in the Saturday Nighters' discussions.[15] "O Night" and several other poems that betray Johnson's probable influence were later published in, of all places, *Negro World*, the official journal of Marcus Garvey's U.N.I.A. With titles like "Passion" and "Journey's End," the poems are wholly apolitical. They are also derivative and inept. Wisely, Hurston soon abandoned poetry and Johnson's model, though not her friendship, in favor of fiction and a sustained effort to make the Eatonville experience accessible to literature. Doubtless, her resolve was strengthened by the response of one influential reader of the *Stylus*. From New York, Charles S. Johnson, editor of *Opportunity*, wrote to congratulate the author of "John Redding Goes to Sea" and to request more material. Locke had alerted him to Hurston's potential, and when her second story, "Drenched in Light," arrived, Johnson agreed to publish it. Zora Neale Hurston's literary career was launched.[16]

In *Dust Tracks*, Zora Neale Hurston remembers that, "feeling the urge to write," she moved to New York City in January 1925, with "$1.50, no job, no friends, and a lot of hope" (122). She had arrived in Baltimore and Washington in roughly the same situation, yet she had achieved academic success. Literary success in New York seemed within her grasp.

Good notices came quickly. In May 1925, her short story "Spunk" took second prize at the Opportunity Awards; a dinner marking the first annual competition sponsored by the magazine *Opportunity* was attended by an array of well-known literary figures, both black and white. "Spunk" was subsequently published in *The New Negro*. The

following year, Hurston was one of several associate editors of *Fire!!*, an avant-garde journal whose single issue won it a place in African-American literary history. The young artists who produced *Fire!!* included Gwendolyn Bennett, who lived in the same house as Hurston on West 66th Street; painter Aaron Douglas; Langston Hughes; bohemian writer and artist Bruce Nugent; and the venture's guiding spirit, novelist Wallace Thurman. Hurston's contributions to the journal were the play *Color Struck* and the remarkable short story "Sweat." Not only was Hurston's work being published and garnering modest attention, she seemed to have found an artistic community whose members shared similar goals and sensibilities. Neither the incipient fame nor the sense of community would endure.

Years later, Langston Hughes referred to the Harlem Renaissance mordantly as the period when the Negro was in vogue. Alain Locke and other intellectual leaders of the New Negro movement, including Jessie Fauset, Charles S. Johnson, and James Weldon Johnson, hoped, vainly as it turned out, that cultural recognition the artists achieved would be translated into social and political progress for the race. As Hurston made clear in "How It Feels to Be Colored Me," she was not sympathetic to the political project. As she put it, she refused to "belong to the sobbing school of Negrohood who hold that nature somehow gave them a lowdown dirty deal and whose feelings are all hurt about it" (153). Recognizing that this definition renders her a victim and nothing more, she rejects it. But she finds it difficult to express her identification with the race as an adult in positive terms. Moreover, when she claims that discrimination "astonishes" rather than angers her, she seems hopelessly naive.

"Sweat" was by far the best of Hurston's apprentice efforts. Unlike "Drenched in Light" and "Spunk," she concentrated here less on presenting a novel situation and more on developing fully drawn characters. Hurston had joined her friends Langston Hughes, Gwendolyn Bennett, and Wallace Thurman as an associate editor of *Fire!!* because she believed black Americans needed "a purely literary magazine," not one "in literature on the side," as were *Crisis* and *Opportunity*.[17] In "Sweat," Hurston claimed the voice that animates her mature fiction; the themes of marital conflict and female exploitation

Jessie Fauset, Langston Hughes, and
Zora Neale Hurston at the statue of
Booker T. Washington, Tuskegee,
1927. Langston Hughes Papers,
Beinecke Rare Book and Manuscript
Library, Yale University.

were introduced as well. Black women like Delia Jones, Hurston's protagonist, "sweat" for everybody, their employers and families alike, but the conflict that propels the narrative occurs between husband and wife. No simplistic encounters between blacks and whites mar the credibility of this story. Folklore is used sparingly and only to illuminate character. "Sweat" transcends the category of local color fiction, and in so doing, evokes a reality that Bessie Smith's admirers could verify.

Delia Jones is a washerwoman, the family breadwinner, and an abused wife. These roles exist in a causal relation, for Delia's work is both an economic necessity and a psychological threat to her husband, Sykes. In the story, Sykes seems never to work at all, and he asserts his manhood mainly by intimidating and betraying his wife. Although Hurston does not explore the economic motives fully, they are clearly important. No matter how onerous the labor, Delia, as a woman, can always find work; a black man, her husband has more difficulty. Typically, Hurston is more interested in the psychology of her characters than in their material existence. Delia is a devoutly religious woman whose faith helps her weather the storms of her marriage, while at the same time, it imbues her with a meekness that makes her more vulnerable to her husband's cruelty. Conversely, when Delia gains the strength to stand up to Sykes, she jeopardizes her spiritual peace.

In the manner of Hurston's later protagonists, Delia Jones claims a self by claiming her voice, but the result is more ambiguous for her than for her successors. As the story opens, Sykes has returned home on a Sunday evening, a time he knows Delia will be sorting the week's laundry. Initially, he frightens her by playing on her fear of snakes. Then, he accuses her of religious hypocrisy because she is working on the Sabbath. Finally, he threatens to force her to give up her work completely. With this, "Delia's habitual meekness seemed to slip from her shoulders" and she begins to "change some words" of her own. So cowed by her verbal defiance, Sykes does not hit her as he usually does. Delia takes no joy in her victory, however; instead she seeks refuge in her faith. After much reflection, she is able to build a "spiritual earthworks" against Sykes. She takes comfort in the

belief that "whatever goes over the Devil's back, is got to come under his belly. Sometime or ruther, Sykes, like everybody else, is gointer reap his sowing." Thereafter, she endures his cruelty in silence.[18]

Delia's complacency does not defuse Sykes's anger. It may in fact intensify it, for Delia's anger, like all her other passion, is subsumed by her faith. Even if she has turned to religion after Sykes's sexual interest in her waned, her reliance on it obviates any emotional need she has for him. Sykes's next actions test Delia's resolve. He begins to flaunt his girlfriend before the townsfolk and determines to remove Delia from the house Delia's labor has paid for. A self-proclaimed "snake charmer," Sykes brings a rattler home in the hope that Delia will be terrified into leaving. The snake becomes Sykes's symbol, imaging his sexuality and his evil. Through her deft manipulation of this symbol, Hurston transforms "Sweat" from a story of marital conflict to a spiritual allegory. Ultimately, Sykes becomes a threat not so much to Delia's person as to her soul.

In a bitter final argument, Delia acknowledges Sykes's victory, or more correctly her defeat. Unable to sustain her stoic indifference, Delia confesses that she now hates Sykes as much as she once loved him. The calm with which she pronounces her hatred is even more sinister than the invective itself ("Ah hates yuh lak uh suck-egg dog"). Sykes is understandably stunned, but he does not perceive the grave danger in which Delia's "fall" places him. The problem is partly Hurston's. Here as elsewhere, she is unable to resist a vivid linguistic turn even when it deflects attention from the central meaning of a passage. Delia struggles to hold on to her faith by attending a church service, a "love feast," that brings her temporary solace. As she returns home, she sings the spiritual that will echo throughout the rest of the story:

> Jurden water, black an' col'
> Chills de body, not de soul
> An' Ah wantah cross Jurden in uh calm time. (205)

The story moves to a beautifully controlled, if predictable climax. Sykes uses the snake to set a trap for Delia, but he is the one ensnared. Delia makes no effort to warn, rescue, or even comfort him. Instead, she "waited in the growing heat while inside she knew the cold river

was creeping up and up to extinguish that eye which must know by now that she knew." She exacts her revenge, but at a terrible spiritual cost. This good Christian will never cross Jordan in a calm time.

The culmination of a five-year apprenticeship, "Sweat" might have signaled the beginning of the mature phase of Hurston's career. It did not. Hurston had come to New York in 1925 because she felt "the urge to write." By day she worked as a domestic for the novelist Fannie Hurst and the philanthropist Annie Nathan Meyer; by night she thrashed out plans for a new literature with the Young Turks of the Renaissance.[19] That fall, with Meyer's assistance, she entered Barnard College to complete the literary studies commenced at Howard. Then her plans abruptly changed. A paper she wrote for an elective course in anthropology so impressed the professor, Gladys Reichard, that she brought it to the attention of Franz Boas. Preeminent in his field and to Hurston, "the greatest anthropologist alive," Boas inspired her to rechannel her ambitions; she abandoned literature for social science.

Anthropology exerted a powerful appeal, because it gave her a profoundly altered view of her past. The Barnard training ultimately allowed Hurston to appreciate the Eatonville experience intellectually as well as intuitively. No longer were her homefolk simply good storytellers whose values were commendable, superstitions remarkable, and humor penetrating. As such, they had been well suited for local color fiction. Now, however, "they became a part of cultural anthropology; scientific objects who could and should be studied for their academic value."[20] The cultural relativity of anthropology freed Hurston from the need to defend her subjects' alleged inferiority. She could discard behavioral explanations drawn from racial mythology. Eatonville blacks were neither exotic nor primitive; they had simply selected different characteristics from what Ruth Benedict, another pioneering anthropologist trained by Boas, called the "great arc of human potentialities." Such truths could pay literary dividends, but by the time she graduated from Barnard in 1927, Zora Hurston was convinced her future lay elsewhere.

Even before graduation, she had set forth on the first of a series of field expeditions. Not surprisingly, her initial stop was Eatonville,

where she was confident a storehouse of material awaited her. Cha-
grined that she could not unlock it on the first try, she returned to
prove her confidence had not been misplaced. As she crisscrossed
Florida, braved Louisiana bayous, and ventured onto Bahamian plan-
tations, Hurston immersed herself in the cultures she studied.
Whether sitting on the porch of Joe Clarke's store or signing on at saw-
mill camps or apprenticing herself to hoodoo doctors, she became a
member of each community she entered. Clearly her race and
personal heritage gave her an entree previous researchers lacked.
Beyond that, Hurston felt herself part and parcel of the cultures she
investigated. The diligence and skill with which she pursued her research enabled her to capitalize on these advantages.

Fieldwork was arduous business nonetheless. However exciting
and glamorous it may have appeared from the distance of Morning-
side Heights, up close it was physically grueling and psychologically
demanding. After a month in Florida, Hurston had written a New
York friend: "Flowers are gorgeous now, crackers not troubling me at
all—hope they don't begin as I go further down state. I'll be very
glad to be back in N.Y.C., however."[21]

She soon made her peace with the South, but her professional
commitment had numerous personal consequences. A marriage was
an early casualty. In the midst of a collecting trip, she had wed Herbert Sheen on 19 May 1927. The couple had met while both were
students at Howard, and their romance had outlasted Hurston's New
York move. Within four months, however, the marriage was broken.
Unable to reconcile the competing demands of marriage and career,
Hurston resumed her collecting while Sheen returned to medical
school.[22] Her work strained other relationships as well. It was extremely unusual, after all, for an educated young woman to travel
alone to desolate shanty towns and turpentine camps. Even the subjects of her research viewed her with suspicion. In one town, she
recalled, "they all thought I must be a revenue officer or a detective
of some kind" (*Dust Tracks*, 60). Her explanation that she was a boot-
legger's girlfriend on the lam put these suspicions to rest. The doubts
of her college classmates, many of whom did not share her conviction
that African-American folklore was worth preserving, were harder to

allay. One woman opined that after years in the field, "Zora seemed to go backward. It was a complete change from the Zora I had known at Howard, where she wrote poems 'in very good English.'"[23]

With her deep belief in the value of her work, Hurston could disregard the judgments of her friends; but conviction alone could not supply the wherewithal to proceed. She needed money. To obtain it, she secured a patron, Charlotte (Mrs. Rufus Osgood) Mason, who underwrote her expenses from December 1927 to September 1932. Theirs was an intense, problematic, and highly controversial relationship. Locke had introduced them in the fall of 1927, Hurston being one of the first of numerous young artists he shepherded to the dowager's Park Avenue apartment. Locke succeeded in exploiting Mason's longstanding interest in "primitives," diverting some of her attention from the Indians of the Southwest to the black artists of Harlem. Over the years, the recipients of her largesse included Langston Hughes, Claude McKay, sculptor Richmond Barthé, painter Aaron Douglas, and choirmaster Hall Johnson. Only Hurston broke the vows of silence Mason imposed, never to reveal her name publicly as a patron. In committing some details of their relationship to print, Hurston exposed herself to contemptuous criticism.

She wrote in *Dust Tracks* of the "psychic bond" between her and the beloved Godmother who "was just as pagan as I." Mason could read her mind, Hurston averred, even when she was thousands of miles away. Letters would find Hurston in Alabama or Florida, which accused: "You have broken the law. You are dissipating your powers in things that have no real meaning . . . Keep silent. Does a child in the womb speak?" Hurston claimed such admonitions always arrived when she was in fact misusing her time, but they strike most readers as demeaning. Talk of pagan godmothers and psychic bonds seemed spurious to many of her peers, who assumed she was "puttin' on ole massa." Yet Hurston described the following scene in Mason's drawing room quite artlessly:[24]

> There she was sitting up there at the table over capon, caviar and gleaming silver, eager to hear every word on every phase of life on a saw-mill "job." I must tell the tales, sing the songs, do the dances, and repeat the raucous sayings and doings of the Negro farthest

down. She is altogether in sympathy with them, because she says truthfully they are utterly sincere in living. (*Dust Tracks*, 129)

Recently, more private correspondence of Renaissance figures has been made available to scholars; it confirms that Hurston's response to Mason was not unique. Locke and Hall Johnson testified to psychic experiences with their benefactor, and in an incredible correspondence stretching from 1927 to 1943, Locke adopted a most ingratiating tone to the woman he regarded as a surrogate mother. For her part, Mason referred to Locke, who was forty years old when they met, as her "precious brown boy." Nothing that is known about this woman accounts for the galvanizing effect of her personality. Born Charlotte van der Veer Quick in Princeton, New Jersey, in 1854, she boasted a rich and powerful lineage; the misses Chapin and Biddle were her handmaidens. Her husband had been a physician, but she owed neither her wealth nor her social eminence solely to him. Arthritic and frail in the late twenties, she had to dictate the letters that told Hurston, "That is nothing! It had no soul in it."[25] Whatever other powers she possessed, and Charlotte Mason believed devoutly they were telepathic, the power to write checks was paramount.

The terms of her agreement with Hurston were anything but ethereal. In a contract—signed, witnessed, and notarized—Mason spelled out exactly what she was offering and what she expected to receive. She employed Hurston, "but as an independent agent, forthwith diligently to seek out, compile and collect all information possible, both written and oral, concerning the music, poetry, folk-lore, literature, hoodoo, conjure, manifestations of art and kindred subjects relating to and existing among the North American negroes . . ." But it was Charlotte Mason who was "desirous of obtaining and compiling" said data. Only "because of the pressure of other matters" was she unable "to undertake the collecting of this information in person." The material collected would *belong* to Mason; Hurston was forbidden to "make known to any other person, except one designated in writing by said first party, any of said data or information." For services rendered, Hurston was to receive a stipend of $200 per month. She had to account for each nickel spent. Her ledgers list expenditures for everything from dues to professional organizations to Kotex.[26] The period of

the original contract was one year, but its terms were subsequently extended. To all intents and purposes, Hurston's independence was limited to independent liability for any damage resulting from the use of the automobile Mason agreed to provide.[27]

Given the terms of this Faustian compact, it is remarkable that Hurston ever found any voice of her own to claim. She devised what loopholes she could. She corresponded with Boas, seeking his counsel about her work, and later aided, clandestinely, one of his protégés investigating music in New Orleans. Early on she apprised Boas of her situation, without, however, revealing Mason's name; he urged that she persuade her "angel" to sponsor graduate work for Hurston, but Hurston could not convince her to do so.[28]

She could secretly share her findings with Langston Hughes, who realized as well as she that a people's folklore could not be owned. At the end of her sojourn in New Orleans in 1927, Hughes met up with her and, in the car she nicknamed "Sassy Susie," they drove back to New York together, stopping along the way in Tuskegee, where they joined Jessie Fauset in paying tribute to the gravesite of Booker T. Washington, and in Macon, Georgia, where they watched Bessie Smith perform and afterward enjoyed a private audience with the Empress of the Blues. They also traveled southern back roads, and Hughes, who had never been South before, understood more fully the lives of black folk.[29]

Several years later, Hurston and Hughes collaborated on the ill-fated comedy *Mule Bone*; its characters, situations, and dialogue sprang from Hurston's memories of Eatonville. But she hoped to deploy these memories onstage to fulfill a new concept of drama, which she and Hughes were developing in tandem. The concept, which Hurston alone would formulate in the essay "Characteristics of Negro Expression," derived from an understanding of the drama that pervaded the daily rituals of life in African-American communities. Produced in a context of music and dance, as they were enacted traditionally, such rituals might form the foundation of "the *real* Negro theatre" Hurston wanted to establish.[30] She wrote Hughes and invited him to share in the project; deferring to his greater practical sense, she thought he might be the senior partner.

Mrs. Mason had other ideas. Theatrical ventures were not on the definite agendas she had set for her protégées. To evade her detection, Hurston and Hughes collaborated on *Mule Bone* in secret. Based on a folktale, "The Bone of Contention," which Hurston had collected and set in Eatonville, *Mule Bone* was a series of oral and musical performances connected by a whisper of a plot. When word of the project got out, the consequences were even worse than its authors feared. The collaboration produced a bitter rivalry and abundant recriminations, but no play. Its greatest casualty was the friendship between Hurston and Hughes.[31] Hurston's interest in the theater did not die. She continued to believe that it was the ideal medium for presenting her research to the public.

Although she had completed the bulk of her research by 1932, Hurston found it exceedingly difficult to organize the voluminous material she had collected into a book. Knopf editor Harry Block reviewed the manuscript and deemed the material "glorious," but advised that the conjure material in particular had to be rewritten "into a geographical and chronological narrative." Professing not to be "cast down" by Block's implication that she "had no book, but *notes* for a book," she continued to make scant progress toward its completion.[32] The pressure of her arrangement with Mason was assuredly a factor. Not only did she have to write to suit her patron's requirements, she would not "own" the finished product.

An added pressure was Hurston's secret knowledge of an earlier failed attempt at scholarly writing. An article published in the October 1927 issue of the *Journal of Negro History* had been heavily plagiarized. "Cudjo's Own Story of the Last African Slaver" was based on interviews Hurston had with Cudjo Lewis, reputed to be the sole survivor of the last-known slave ship to dock on United States shores. Hurston had fleshed out the essay by copying, almost verbatim, passages from *Historic Sketches of the Old South*, by Emma Langdon Roche. The fraud went undetected for nearly fifty years. After the article was published, Hurston returned to interview Lewis several times and completed a book-length manuscript inspired by his life. Interestingly, Lewis knew enough about Charlotte Mason to write her and inquire about her "goddaughter."[33] Hurston's problems with the Lewis piece began when her initial investigations yielded too little material for an article. With the folklore manuscript, the problem was that Hurston had more material than she knew how to use. A substantial portion of it would first take written form in her novel *Jonah's Gourd Vine*, published in 1934.

Before it was done, *Mules and Men* went through several drafts, and with each unsuccessful one its author's hopes for the future dimmed. In her letters, praise for Mason grew more fulsome, perhaps out of the knowledge that the depression was forcing her patron to shed unprofitable investments and the fear she would soon be dropped from the payroll. Any such fears were well founded, as by June 1931, Alain Locke was advising Godmother that Hurston had become too much of a burden for her to carry. His solution was a job, for "if Z. [Zora] isn't doing creative work, she should for the time being do some bread and butter work."[34] As Hurston maneuvered to hold on to her economic lifeline, she expressed to Mason both deep-seated doubt and residual determination.

"You see," she explained, "I am trying to get some bone in my legs so that you can see me standing so I shall cease to worry you . . . Thus I feel that I must let no grass grow under my feet . . . So I shall wrassle me up a future or die trying." In another letter, she rued her lack of productivity: "When I look back on the three and a half years that I have known you, Godmother, I am amazed. I see all my terrible weaknesses and failures, my stark stupidity and lack of vision and I am amazed that your love and confidence has carried over." Yet a few weeks later, resigning herself to accepting whatever financial decision Mason would make, she maintained: "Personally I feel that it has all been to good purpose and that I shall succeed."[35]

Mason's money had been a boon as well as a bane, insofar as it allowed Hurston to conduct research she otherwise would have had to forego. Still, being forced off the payroll was a blessing; it freed Hurston to declare her artistic independence. Significantly, the platform she chose was the theater. In a series of concerts variously entitled *The Great Day* (1932), *From Sun to Sun* (1933), and *Singing Steel* (1934), she presented her material to audiences in New York, Chicago, and Florida. Of course, she had to proceed cautiously, ever mindful that

her notes were locked in her patron's vault. And Mason granted access sparingly, warning Hurston that "it is vital to your people that you should not rob your books, which must stand as a lasting monument, in order to further a commercial venture."[36] But, attractive as financial independence must have been under the circumstances, Hurston's goal in these productions was not simply to turn a profit, which, in any case, she failed to do. It was rather to offer her version of "the real voice" of her people.

To do so, she had literally to raise her own. Although she acknowledged that she was neither a singer, a dancer, nor even a musician and professed no ambition to make a reputation in any of these fields, Hurston not only conceived these concerts, she performed in them. If Mason controlled what material she could adapt for her concerts, much as recording executives controlled what Bessie Smith could sing, onstage Hurston could do with it what she chose. Through her performances, singing "East Coast Blues" or "Evalina," she was able to lay claim to her material in a far more intimate way than academic publication allowed. In the process, she settled on the format for her book.[37]

Although not her primary mission, Hurston had collected African-American folksongs of every description in the field. She found them superior to the "ersatz Negro music" now frequently performed on the concert stage. Her reference was to the "arranged" spirituals that had become staples in the repertoire of classically trained singers like Marian Anderson and Roland Hayes and of the Negro college choirs, which, following in the tradition of the Fisk Jubilee Singers, balanced the budgets of their schools through their music. "Highly flavored with Bach and Brahms, and Gregorian Chants," Hurston not only judged these "neo-spirituals," as she later dubbed them, inferior to the originals, she impugned the motives of their composers. Calling Hall Johnson (with whom she was feuding) by name, she suggested that his arrangements, like those of Harry Burleigh, Nathaniel Dett, J. Rosamond Johnson, and John Work, constituted "a determined effort to squeeze all of the rich black juice out of the songs and present a sort of musical octoroon to the public. Like some more 'passing for white.'"[38]

The effort to identify the "authentic," the "real," or the "original" impresses late-twentieth-century thinkers as misguided and futile.[39] Moreover, the value of "arranged" spirituals now seems unarguable. Not only did they preserve the legacy of the slave's song, but they have their own intrinsic beauty. Hurston's rejection of them and her quest for the authentic served an important purpose nonetheless: in her concerts she grew determined to reproduce not merely the songs themselves but the context in which they were created. Although they went through several versions, the spine of her productions was always the dramatization of a working day on a Florida railroad camp. Scenes included "In the Quarters—Waking the Camp," "Working on the Railroad" (which featured the lining and spiking songs she would publish in *Mules and Men*), "Dusk Dark" (game songs), "Itinerant Preacher at the Quarters," "In the Jook," and "The Fiery Chariot" (based on Hurston's story written in the folk tradition). In part because Charlotte Mason had forbade the use of any conjure material, and in part because Hurston thought "that we had nothing in America to equal it," the climax of the concerts was the Bahamian Fire Dance.[40] Of the many lessons she learned in what she called the concert field, this one was especially apt: to re-create what she considered "Negro singing in a natural way," she had to re-create the action that accompanied or occasioned it. In *Mules and Men*, she would not only present folktales, she would recreate the context in which they were told.

Mules and Men, the first book of folklore by a black American, is a widely recognized if underdiscussed classic in African-American literature and American anthropology. It records seventy folktales, including the well-known Brer Rabbit tales and the less familiar stories of the heroic slave John. It is, however, more than a compilation of tales. Hurston devises a unifying narrative that provides a context for the tales and allows her to present a range of Southern verbal art. Hurston uses it as well to interrogate the process of narration. Not only is the narrative concerned with showing by whom, to whom, and to what purpose the tales she collected are told, the text repeatedly raises these same questions about the narrative Hurston constructs. Moreover, this narrative offers a subtle revelation of the ways in which women are relegated to subordinate roles in the culture Hurston

otherwise celebrates and the means by which these women gain access to creative expression and power.

In effect, the subtext of *Mules and Men* is the narrative of a successful quest for female empowerment. In the opening scenes, the narrator "Zora" introduces both herself, diffident and naive, and her hometown, where despite its unusual customs and memorable patterns of language, all too familiar gender roles are strictly imposed. On the journey South, the narrator is changed by her encounter with Big Sweet, the powerful figure who becomes Zora's guardian and guide. Finally, under the providential guidance of the spirit of Marie Leveau, the great New Orleans hoodoo priestess, Zora is completely transformed. In this outline, *Mules and Men* is a paradigmatic immersion narrative that prefigures the movement of Hurston's classic novel *Their Eyes Were Watching God*.[41] As much as that novel, *Mules and Men* deserves to be considered an "Ur-text" in the tradition of black women's writing.

The first line of *Mules and Men* reads "I was glad when somebody told me, 'You may go and collect Negro folk-lore.'"[42] The biblical allusion establishes both Hurston's sense of mission and the high value she places on the material she is out to preserve. Divided into two parts, headed "Folk Tales" and "Hoodoo," *Mules and Men* is a compendium of expressive forms featuring tales and aphorisms, prayers and sermons, children's rhymes and games, blues and work songs, curses and cures. One might define the text in a phrase from Houston Baker's richly nuanced reading of it: "a condensed, poetic distillate that constitutes earned, improvisational cultural wisdom."[43] *Mules and Men* is, in sum, the brief Hurston offers the world in support of her contention that the "unlettered Negro has given the Negro's best contribution to America's culture."[44]

After its initial joyous proclamation, however, the introduction is ambivalent at every turn. First, the narrator declares collecting would not be a new experience for her since she had known the lore "from the earliest rocking of my cradle." On the other hand, she had not been able to appreciate this old experience until college had given her the "spy-glass of Anthropology" through which to view it. "New" to the field, she is relieved and happy to make the familiar ground of

Eatonville her first stop. Seasoned in their ways, she knows how jealously black folk guard "that which the soul lives by." Even "Lucy Hurston's daughter Zora" might have problems probing the minds of strangers, but her Eatonville homefolk would be eager in every way to help. She would, it seems, need all the help she could get.[45]

At its close, then, the introduction leaves us with a persona who is idealistic but timid, inspired but insecure, and one who is far more sure of her mission than of herself. The shy self-consciousness is at odds with everything we know about the real-life Hurston in the late 1920s—a woman for whom the adjective "bodacious" could have been coined—but it is totally consistent with what the book's Eatonville expects of Lucy Hurston's daughter.

Driving across the Maitland-Eatonville township line, a line that separates the white world from the black, the narrator is delighted that her first sight is the store porch. The sight confirms her expectation expressed in the introduction that Eatonville's cultural riches have been preserved during her absence. "The same love of talk and song" animates the store porch. But Hurston's relation to the scene has changed. She must now convey the scene's significance to outsiders. An exchange between Zora and one of the porch sitters dramatizes the importance of the lore.

When B. Moseley wonders who would be interested in "them big old lies we tell when we're jus' sittin' around here on the store porch doin' nothin," Zora responds, "They are a lot more valuable than you might think. We want to set them down before it's too late" (8). How much more than nothing goes on on the store porch is evidenced by a narrative that seems often filled to overflowing with wordplay and incident (an effect Hurston reinforces by representing informants interrupting each other in their eagerness to share the lore). At bottom, of course, the opposing views of folklore as "valuable" and "nothing" represent a conflict less between Zora and her informant than between Hurston and the audience for her book. Ultimately, leaving the "we" unspecified invites the reader to identify with Hurston's project.

On the store porch, a card game is in progress, and, significantly, all of the participants and onlookers are male. The narrator's comment is

typically slant: "'Hello, boys,' I hailed them as I went into neutral." Read figuratively, this comment connotes Zora's desire to praise her homeboys as well as her need to assume the objectivity fieldwork required. Neutrality is also the mask the narrator dons when confronted by the issues of sexual politics that soon prove to be the subject of the first section of *Mules and Men*.

Throughout the early scenes of the text, Hurston represents the ways in which gender roles are imposed, resisted, and, more often than not, accepted. The scenes range from the overtly benign to the protoviolent. An example of the former is the first event Zora attends, a toe-party, at which women stand behind a curtain, revealing only their feet, as men bid for their company. Not surprisingly, the totally passive Zora, who defers to someone else for every decision made in the first chapter, is selected five times. After the toe-party, this Zora recedes from the narrative, and a presumably more assertive figure begins to choreograph the action. The group that gathers on the store porch at Zora's invitation the following morning is made up of women and men. Interspersed among the tales are highly charged exchanges between couples; these constitute another narrative, the subject of which is male-female relationships.

This narrative is constructed of what Hurston once referred to apologetically as the "between-story conversation and business" she inserted "because when I offered [the manuscript] without it, every publisher said it was too monotonous."[46] She feared, rightly, that this concession to commercial pressure would damage the reputation of the book among professional folklorists. For a long time it did. More recent commentary from folklorists emphasizes the value of the context Hurston provides because of what it conveys about folklore process.[47] Literary critics are apt to praise it for the narrative skill it demonstrates. One aspect of that narrative skill, the manipulation of the "between-story conversation and business," is the means through which Hurston is able to give voice to women in her text.

Drawing on the same field notes from which she produced *Mules and Men*, Hurston penned a groundbreaking essay on African-American aesthetics, "Characteristics of Negro Expression," in which she argued:

> Every phase of Negro life is highly dramatized. No matter how
> joyful or how sad the case there is sufficient poise for drama. Every-
> thing is acted out. Unconsciously for the most part of course. There
> is an impromptu ceremony always ready for every hour of life.
> No little moment passes unadorned.[48]

Here Hurston states one of the principles that informs the structure
of *Mules and Men*. In accord with this principle, the text presents a
series of brilliant performances that reflect what Hurston termed the
African-American's "will to adorn."[49]

Anticipating the work of current-day anthropologists by several
decades, Hurston in the 1930s both theorized about and put into
practice the concept of performance. For Hurston, performance is, as
Richard Bauman defines it, "the enactment of the poetic function,
the essence of spoken artistry."[50] What becomes clear in *Mules and
Men* is the extent to which the most highly regarded types of performance in African-American culture, storytelling and sermonizing,
for example, are in the main the province of men.

Only three of the tales told in the Eatonville section and cited in the
table of contents are told by women; only one is about women. The
relative scarcity of woman-centered tales in the oral tradition must
have been one of the revelations of Hurston's fieldwork. Although tales
about women created by men, many of them virulently misogynistic,
exist in some quantity, tales about women told from a female point of
view are rare. In "Characteristics," Hurston had noted the "scornful at-
titude towards black women" expressed in African-American folksongs and tales.[51] Yet she noted they were respected in "real life."

How women "assert their image and values as women" is not
found in the folklore literature because, according to Roger Abrahams, women negotiate for respect in the "apparently spontaneous
interpersonal exchanges of everyday interactions." Only apparently
spontaneous, black women's presentations in these exchanges are in
fact often as formulaic as the more formal performances in which
men engage. "Ideally a woman has the ability to *talk sweet* with her
infants and peers but *talk smart* or *cold* with anyone who might
threaten her self-image."[52] Respect is never a permanent given, as
the "between-story conversations" in *Mules* amply demonstrate.

Some of the fiercest exchanges on the store porch take place between a man and woman named Gene and Gold. After one tale, which uses "rounders and brick-bats" as terms of address for women, Gold negotiates for respect by commenting that the teller knows he has told a "lie." He laughingly denies it and thus confirms her charge, which encourages Gold to continue: "Dat's all you men is good for—settin' 'round and lyin'. Some of you done quit lyin' and gone to flyin'." Though he is not the storyteller, Gene responds and his retort shifts the focus from the tale to the tensions between men and women. Initially, the tensions stem from economics; Gene allows that "you women ain't good for nothin' exceptin' readin' Sears and Roebuck's bible and hollerin' 'bout, 'gimme dis and gimme dat' as soon as we draw our pay."

Continuing the formulaic exchange, a woman named Shug interjects that the only way women get anything is by working for it: "You mens don't draw no pay. You don't do nothin' but stand around and draw lightnin'." The tension escalates when Gold moves from the general to the specific and addresses Gene directly: "Aw, shut up, Gene . . . You tryin' to talk like big wood when you ain't nothin' but brush" (24). At this point another woman, Armetta, sensing "a hard anger creepin' into the teasing," defuses it with a joke. With a similarly humorous gesture, Hurston defuses the anger with a prayer that the group conveniently overhears in the pause it takes to restore good humor to the porch. In this instance, Hurston is, to borrow Barbara Johnson's formulation, both describing and employing a strategy.[53]

Among the other formal devices Hurston employs to link text and context is the incorporation of the structural patterns of the folktales into the unifying narrative. As the scene continues to unfold and the porch sitters break down into two camps, both the folk stories and the between-story conversation follow the thematic parallel of people asking God for the wrong thing. The comments of the men grow more crudely sexist; George Thomas proposes, for example, that a woman "could have had mo' sense, but she told God no, she'd ruther take it out in hips . . . [so] she got plenty hips, plenty mouf and no brains." Thomas's remark anticipates the structure of the tale Mathilda Moseley jumps in to tell in women's defense. While Moseley's ability to respond to Thomas's challenge proves she can *talk smart*, "Why Women Always Take Advantage of Men" finally reinscribes the inferior position of women.

The story begins with an invocation of a faraway past in which "de woman was just as strong as de man and both of 'em did de same things" (31). This, to summarize briefly, is more than the man can stand, and he entreats God to give him more strength than woman. God grants his request. When the woman finds out what has happened, she angrily asks God to restore the balance. He refuses to comply. Turning then to the Devil, she gains the keys to the kitchen, the bedroom, and the cradle; with these she can counter man's greater power.

As is true of most of the women on the porch, Mathilda Moseley's smart-talking, or "sass," is ultimately resistance of a passive kind. It produces important transformations: women become subjects in their own discourse rather than the objects they generally are in the discourse of black men and white men and women. But the discursive transformations do not make them the subjects of their own lives. Before the scene is concluded, more stories are told, but between men and women, nothing is changed.

When Zora explains that her townspeople have lied "good but not enough," one of them suggests that she go down to Polk County, "where they really lies up a mess" and "where dey makes up all de songs and things lak dat" (55). On this journey, Zora crosses a boundary as significant as that which divides white Maitland from black Eatonville: "twelve miles below Kissimmee I passed under an arch that marked the Polk County line." She has reached Polk County, where, according to the blues, the "water tastes lak cherry wine." Following the directional markers the narrative provides, she has traveled South, *down* to an almost mythic space that represents the matrix of African-American expressive culture.

In Polk County, both the narrator and the women of the book grow more assertive. When Zora arrives at the Everglades Cypress Lumber Company camp, she avers, "I saw at once this group of several hundred Negroes from all over the South was a rich field of folklore" (60), but they resist her inquiries. Her shiny gray Chevrolet

and $12.74 Macy's dress arouse their suspicions that she is a revenue officer or a detective of some kind. Unlike the diffident daughter of Eatonville, this Zora is able to spin a few "lies" of her own, and she quickly claims to be a bootlegger on the lam. She later shows that she appreciates good "woofing" (stylized talk) and passes the final test by singing a few verses of "John Henry." Through this rite, she wins acceptance in the community. "By the time that the song was over, before Joe Willard lifted me down from the table I knew that I was in the inner circle. . . . After that my car was everybody's car. James Presley, Slim and I teamed up and we had to do 'John Henry' wherever we appeared" (65).

One of the singers in this scene is Big Sweet, who proves in short order to be the most assertive character in the book. Although the text provides few details about her appearance, the woman's name—with its suggestions of physical power and sexual attractiveness, of strength and tenderness—aptly defines her persona. At the same time, the lack of a conventional proper name makes her seem larger than life.[54] The space associated with Big Sweet is not the porch but the jook—in Hurston's definition, a combination dance hall, gaming parlor, and pleasure house. It is the incubator of the blues. As Alice Walker would demonstrate anew in *The Color Purple*, the ethics of the jook, and of the blues, give women far more personal freedom and power than the women on the store porch enjoy. Free of the constraints of ladyhood, the bonds of traditional marriage, and the authority of the church, women improvise new identities for themselves.[55]

In *Dust Tracks on a Road*, Hurston describes her first encounter with Big Sweet. Significantly, Hurston hears Big Sweet before she sees her; and it is her talk that attracts Hurston's attention. Big Sweet is "specifying," "playing the dozens" with an out-matched male opponent. Before a large and appreciative audience, she breaks the news to him "in one of her mildest bulletins that his pa was a double-humpted camel and his ma a grass-gut cow." This performance gives Hurston a "measure of this Big Sweet," and her judgment is soon verified by the opinions of others on the job.[56] Though fearsome, Big Sweet is not feared as much as she is respected, because the

Hurston in the field with "Sassy
Susie." Beinecke Rare Book and
Manuscript Library, Yale University..

community draws a distinction between meanness and the defense of one's integrity. Hurston sees the wisdom of acquiring her friendship and hence protection. Big Sweet becomes the author's guardian and guide. She identifies informants, awards prizes in "lying" contests, and eventually saves Hurston's life.

Whereas the folktales are told by informants, the narrator recounts the story of Big Sweet. In keeping with the strategies employed in the earlier section, it is told through the between-story conversations. Formidable though she is, Big Sweet contributes only two folktales to *Mules and Men*: neither focuses on female identity. In the general narrative of her experiences in Polk County and in her descriptions of the specific situations in which stories are told, however, Hurston shows how Big Sweet asserts and maintains her identity. From these descriptions, readers can take their own measure of this woman.[57]

The dramatic performance of Big Sweet's "specifying" is not recounted in *Mules and Men*; her first words here are low-keyed. Indeed, they offer a weak contrast to the series of memorable tales of John the slave's outwitting his master that dominate the scene. Big Sweet's two tales, "Why the Mocking Bird Is Away on Friday" and "How the 'Gator Got Black," are told matter-of-factly, but the second is preceded by an exchange that reveals a bit of her mettle. Someone else has recited "How Brer 'Gator Got His Tongue Worn Out," which has reminded Big Sweet of the tale she knows. Before she gets a chance to begin her story, however, Big Sweet is interrupted and must reclaim her place in the discussion. "When Ah'm shellin' my corn, you keep out yo' nubbins" wins her readmission, and the tale is told.

Later, as the others joke and lie good-naturedly, Big Sweet interjects a personal and pointed warning to her lover. The scene that follows prefigures the oft-cited one in *Their Eyes* when Janie takes the floor against Joe. "And speakin' bout hams," Big Sweet begins apropos of nothing, but "meaningly," "if Joe Willard don't stay out of dat bunk he was in last night, Ah'm gointer sprinkle some salt down his back and sugar-cure *his* hams" (124). A leader of the group and very much a man of words, Willard tries initially to shrug off Big Sweet's challenge. "Aw, woman, quit tryin' to signify." But she is undeterred and announces she will signify as much as she pleases. Making an

appeal to male solidarity, Willard tries to draw the other men to his side. But they know they can't beat Big Sweet's signifying. Her declaration of independence cuts right to the heart of the matter. "Lemme tell *you* something, *any* time Ah shack up wid any man Ah gives myself de privilege to go wherever he might be, night or day. Ah got de law in my mouth" (124). These words are emblematic of her power, for they signal her ownership of self.

Big Sweet's behavior conforms to the pattern Abrahams outlines; she can *talk sweet* and *talk smart* as circumstances require. She uses "Little-Bit" as a term of endearment for Zora in *Mules and Men*, warns her that collecting songs from one of the men has provoked his lover's jealousy, and promises to defend her. A conversation between her and Hurston quoted in *Dust Tracks* further evidences her ability to *talk sweet*. Not understanding why Hurston wants to collect "lies," she pledges to aid her in doing so. Such conversations are held privately; the public smart talking she does earns Big Sweet respect.

A crucial incident recounted in *Mules and Men* pits Big Sweet against her arch-rival, Ella Wall, a woman whose feats are also chronicled by Leadbelly and other country blues singers. With characteristic sexual assertiveness, Ella Wall enters the camp "jook" and sends a message to Big Sweet's man. The two women exchange verbal insults, then physical threats, until the conflict is halted by the arrival of the white quarters boss. While Ella Wall is disarmed and thrown off the job, Big Sweet stands up to the white man and refuses to yield her weapon. In a telling compliment, Joe Willard expresses the admiration of the group; he also offers a self-serving response to the incident: "You wuz noble! You wuz uh whole woman and half uh man. You made dat cracker stand offa you" (152). To be sure, Willard confirms and honors the androgynous ideal Big Sweet embodies. But for understandable reasons, given his own culpability, he reads the incident in racial rather than personal terms. The courage he praises is the courage Big Sweet has shown in her struggle with the white man. Her fierce conduct in that struggle enhances her value as a woman. In its wake, her lover proudly escorts her home.

Zora Hurston knew that approval of Big Sweet was not shared by the world outside the lumber camp. The life of this hard living,

knife-toting woman was the stuff of myriad stereotypes. Hurston's narrator seems all too aware of this judgment when she reflects, "I thought of all I had to live for and turned cold at the thought of dying in a violent manner in a sordid saw-mill camp." A dramatic realization follows: "But for my very life I knew I couldn't leave Big Sweet if the fight came. She had been too faithful to me" (151). She vows to stand by her friend. Passages such as this have caused some critics to accuse Hurston of being condescending and self-serving in her presentation of the rural black community. She does seem to be playing to her audience here: "sordid" voices their opinion of the camp and its people; it also reimposes the good/bad woman dichotomy this section of the narrative otherwise suspends. Hurston's problem was to legitimize Big Sweet's conduct without apologizing or positing sociological explanations for it. Her solution was to identify the sources of its legitimacy within the culture itself. Just before the fight scene, Hurston interpolates "a little drama of religion." A traveling preacher arrives in the camp. His sermon, "Behold de Rib," is a variant of the biblical creation myth; its text is Genesis 2:21, and its message is female equality:

> So God put Adam into a deep sleep
> And took out a bone, ah hah!
> And it is said that it was a rib.
> Behold de rib!
> A bone out of a man's side.
> He put de man to sleep and made wo-man,
> And men and women been sleeping together ever since.
> Behold de rib!
> Brothers, if God
> Had taken dat bone out of man's head
> He would have meant for woman to rule, hah.
> If he had taken a bone out of his foot,
> He would have meant for us to dominize and rule.
> He could have made her out of back-bone
> And then she would have been behind us.
> But, no, God Amighty, he took de bone out of his side
> So dat places de woman beside us;
> Hah! God knowed his own mind.
> Behold de rib! (141)

Its rhythm and imagery place "Behold de Rib" squarely in the tradition of black American preaching, but its message is anomalous. Hurston had transcribed other sermons in her field notes, including the one that became the centerpiece of her novel *Jonah's Gourd Vine*. The purposeful selection of "Behold de Rib" allows her both to celebrate a verbal art she greatly admired and to register a protest against the tradition that shaped it, a tradition that for the most part neither welcomed women's participation nor fostered their equality.

Hurston draws no connection between the sermon and the agon between Big Sweet and Ella Wall. Here and throughout the book, her method is presentational, not analytical. Nevertheless, the reader's approbation of Big Sweet seems won in part by the juxtaposition of the two scenes. The care Hurston took to legitimize Big Sweet's behavior intimated the expected reaction to an assertive woman. Tellingly, the spiritual sanction for Big Sweet is located in only the most heterodox form of Christianity existent in the black community; it comes from the words of a much maligned figure in the oral tradition, the jackleg preacher, who is here relegated to ministering to pick-up congregations in lumber camps. The spiritual sanction is functional nonetheless. Unlike, for example, the conventional Christianity followed by Delia Jones in Hurston's early story "Sweat," this revisionist tenet allows a woman to assert her self without risking her soul's salvation. Big Sweet has no qualms about her behavior; as she puts it, "Ah got jus' as good uh chance at Heben as anybody else" (177).

Throughout the text, Big Sweet is empowered to speak and to act. But in the interim between Big Sweet's conflict with Ella Wall—when she fights to defend her honor and to keep a faithless man—and her final appearance in the narrative—when she fights to defend her honor and her faithful friend Zora—Hurston interpolates a series of tales that allude to an alternative or complementary spiritual tradition, hoodoo. Clearly, Big Sweet, who keeps a piece of gamblers' lucky hoodoo in her hair to help her win at cards, is conversant with this tradition, too.

To explore it more fully, the narrator Zora must journey farther South, this time to the Crescent City, New Orleans. Well tutored and

emboldened by her encounter with Big Sweet, she is now prepared to navigate spiritual mysteries. These in turn unlock the key to her personal power, the power of the word.

The final section of *Mules and Men* locates the sources of female empowerment firmly within the pre-Christian, Afrocentric belief system of hoodoo.[58] For Hurston, hoodoo was an intrinsic part of that "which the soul lives by"; it was a means by which African-Americans could exert control over their interior lives. Metaphysically decentered and clerically nonhierarchal, hoodoo offered some women a more expansive vision of themselves than did Christianity. Within hoodoo, women were the spiritual equals of men. They had like authority to speak and to act.[59] Both the first and last hoodoo practitioners introduced in *Mules and Men* are women, while the greatest teacher of all is the dead New Orleans priestess, Marie Leveau. Under the providential guidance of her spirit, Zora is completely transformed.

Hoodoo—with its curses and cures and its prescriptions to rent a house, make a man come home, and ease illnesses of the body and spirit—offered its adherents instruments of control. To represent that point, all the formulae prescribed and all the ceremonies conducted in *Mules and Men* yield the desired results. If *Mules* does not stint on representing the mundane, however, it seems more concerned finally with the sacred.

As historian Lawrence Levine abstracts the metaphysical underpinnings of nineteenth-century African-American sacred beliefs from which hoodoo is derived, the fundamental premise was that life was not random or accidental. Events were meaningful, and human beings could divine and understand their causes. Human beings could "read" the phenomena surrounding and affecting them because people were "part of, not alien to, the Natural Order of things, attached to the Oneness that bound together all matter, animate and inanimate, all spirits, visible or not." Personal misfortunes were not accidental or due to bad luck; once people understood the root cause of their trouble, they could end or reverse it.[60]

Psychologically, hoodoo empowered all of its adherents; it allowed them to perceive themselves as actors in the world, not the passive reactors the dominant society held them to be.[61] Conversely, hoodoo

put the masters' power in a new perspective. As a result of their belief, historian John Blassingame observes, "many of the slaves constructed a psychological defense against total dependence on and submission to their masters. Whatever his power, the master was a puny man compared to the supernatural."[62] Indeed, hoodoo could be used to exact justice from the master as well as revenge against fellow slaves.[63] Finally and most pertinent, power in hoodoo was de-centered; the absence of clerical authority militated against male dominance within the slave community. Consequently, hoodoo was particularly empowering for women. Unlike the slave preacher, the plantation conjurer could as easily be a woman as a man. As Hurston documents, these features remained operative in the early decades of the twentieth century.

The first scholar to undertake a formal investigation of hoodoo, Hurston originally published her research in an extended article, "Hoodoo in America," in the *Journal of American Folklore.* Writing in the dispassionate tones of the social scientist, she compared and contrasted the beliefs of blacks in the United States and the Caribbean, outlined the ways in which hoodoo took on the prevailing religious practices of its location, listed the means by which a man or woman could become a hoodoo doctor, and catalogued the "routines" associated with each practitioner.[64] Even here, however, Hurston could not foreswear the personal. The initiation rituals she recounted were all rendered in the first person; they are transcribed virtually verbatim in *Mules and Men.* What Hurston adds to this narrative in addition to a heightened emphasis on the personal are the contexts for the relatively small percentage of routines she includes and repeated narrative patterns that bind the two sections of the text.

"Part Two: Hoodoo" begins with temporal and geographical markers ("so I slept a night, and the next morning I headed my toe-nails toward Louisiana and New Orleans in particular") that echo earlier patterns; the reference to toe-nails alludes to conjure practices. The anthropological definition of hoodoo that took up several pages of the article is condensed to one paragraph. Far more important is the definition of hoodoo "the way we tell it," that is, through a folktale. The tale functions as a bridge between the two parts of the text; moreover,

its content, which links the spirit with the word, both spoken and written, restates a major theme of *Mules and Men*.

Beginning with a creation myth, the tale focuses on the human quest for the transcendent knowledge that hoodoo represents.[65] According to the tale, the first man who attained even a portion of the knowledge (which is necessarily linked to language, as in "God's power-compelling words") was Moses, and "it took him forty years to learn ten words." Moses, like Big Sweet, achieves an identity between word and deed; he made a book and a nation. In acknowledgment, God presents Moses with the rod that becomes the emblem of his power. The rod is also the figure of the snake that is omnipresent in hoodoo iconography; this association is appropriate because the power that does not come from God, Moses learns from Jethro, his Ethiopian father-in-law. Their mentoring relationship is reenacted between Sheba and Solomon. Sheba, the Ethiopian, has power (knowledge) unequal to man; she chooses to make Solomon wise and gives him her talking ring. Solomon then builds himself a room with a secret door and *writes* down the ring-talk in books.

Through this multilayered tale, Hurston establishes the African provenance of hoodoo, its antiquity, and its comparability with Judeo-Christian tradition. As she notes, the Bible is the greatest conjure book of all. Certainly, the Bible is used to legitimize hoodoo for the readers of *Mules and Men*.[66] More important yet, the folktale puts into play the complex connections between hoodoo and the word, that is, between power and language. Those possessing spiritual power gain access to the power of the word. While spiritual power is to some degree a gift, imaged here in the sexual metaphors of rod and ring, those who would possess it fully must seek it. In the tale, as in Hurston's fiction, learning words is a slow and arduous process, though those "in the spirit" may unexpectedly find their tongues unleashed. However wise the words then spoken, the one who gains credit for the wisdom is the one who writes them down.[67]

The gender transpositions between the tale and the surrounding narrative are significant. Zora, readers are encouraged to imagine, has at some point found a room with a secret door and written down the words before us. But, unlike Solomon, she is not claiming the

wisdom she is recording as her own. Moreover, it is not gleaned from any one source. Indeed, the diffusion of authority in hoodoo requires the representation of various practitioners. In this respect, its depiction extends the communal perspective sustained throughout *Mules and Men*. The creativity and wisdom of the people are never misrepresented as individual property. Still, the question of exploitation that this folktale implicitly raises is answered most profoundly in the last section of the narrative. Zora earns the right to write the words by first seeking the power through which she may invest them with meaning.

Taking great pains to distinguish the sacred beliefs from the "voodoo ritualistic orgies of Broadway and popular fiction," the narrator emphasizes throughout the secrecy with which adherents practice their faith (185). "Hoodoo is private"; it yields its secrets sparingly. To this extent, it is of a piece with all the knowledge revealed in *Mules and Men*. Superficially, Zora is in the same position in relation to the knowledge of her culture that she was in the beginning. But, if she still must struggle to find answers, if she searches for four months and comes up empty, Zora now knows the questions to ask.[68]

Her posture as supplicant is conveyed most compellingly in the representation of her experiences with Luke Turner, a New Orleans practitioner who claims to be the nephew of Marie Leveau. Zora reports that she had studied under five hoodoo doctors before finding Turner, and she introduces the narrative of their association in words informed by the rhythms of ritual. Indeed, from its first paragraph, the entire chapter seems written "in the spirit":

> Now I was in New Orleans and I *asked*. They told me Algiers, the part of New Orleans that is across the river to the west. I went there and lived for four months and *asked*. I found women reading cards and doing mail order business in names and insinuations of well known factors in conjure. Nothing worth putting on paper. But they all claimed some knowledge from Marie Leveau. From so much of hearing the name I *asked* everywhere for this Leveau and everybody told me differently. But from what they said I was eager to know to the end of the talk. It carried me back across the river into the Vieux Carre. All agreed that she had lived and died in the French quarter of New Orleans. So I went there to *ask*. (191, emphasis added)

The repetition of the verb "ask" not only structures the paragraph; "asking" becomes a metonym for the rite of initiation, which is the climax to which the chapter builds. The verb is repeated in succeeding paragraphs. Zora must, for example, make four trips to Luke Turner, asking about Marie Leveau before he responds to her inquiries. Eventually, he tells how Leveau would seek the spirit herself, then listen "to them that come to ask."

Only after Zora proves her trustworthiness does Turner begin to share the secret knowledge he has been taught by Leveau. Indeed, the narrative dramatizes this event to suggest that the spirit of Leveau accepts Zora as acolyte; permission comes in the course of Turner's performance of Leveau's curse-prayer. If the talk about secret knowledge is powerful enough to "carry" Zora across the physical river, then the knowledge itself transports Zora to worlds unknown. Or, to put it in secular terms, Zora confronts her "self" in its various dimensions.

As the description of the harrowing initiation makes clear, this Zora has physical strength and mental stamina that is many times greater than any of the Eatonville homefolk would have attributed to Lucy Hurston's daughter. After nine days of preparation, she arrives at Turner's home with the three snake skins and clean underwear required for the ritual. Naked and stretched out on the skin of the snake that had been Leveau's icon of power, she fasts for three days. "For sixty-nine hours I lay there. I had five psychic experiences and awoke at last with no feeling of hunger, only one of exaltation" (199).[69] On the experiences themselves, the text is silent.

Symbols are then drawn on Zora's back (the lightning symbol, her sign that the spirit would speak to her in storms) and on her face (the pair of eyes painted on her cheek, the sign that she could see in more ways than one). A banquet follows the rites of communion, and the initiation climaxes in a damp and dismal swamp with an animal sacrifice. This muck becomes ceremonial ground. A "chant of strange syllables rose. I asked Turner the words, but he replied that in good time I would know what to say. It was not to be taught" (202). The moment in which the petition is answered goes undescribed. But in that silence we can read Zora's possession of the word.

That possession is manifested throughout *Mules and Men*, but no-where more compellingly than in this chapter. Written "in the spirit," it inscribes the rhythm and passion of the ritual. It serves as well to allegorize the journey of the artist who travels both to the matrix of the culture and to the deepest regions of the self. Having completed this dual journey, the narrator is empowered to tell her story to the world.

Throughout the 1930s, Zora Hurston dispatched her stories to the world in rapid succession. "The Gilded Six-Bits," published by *Story* magazine in August 1933, so impressed publisher Bertram Lippincott that he wrote inquiring whether she was working on a novel. She was not, but within months she completed *Jonah's Gourd Vine*, which was published in May 1934.[70] A fictionalized treatment of her parents' lives, set in Notasulga and Eatonville, the novel brimmed with folk-lore texts that its author had collected: work songs, courtship rituals, prayers, and the mellifluous sermon that she had heard preached by the Reverend C. C. Lovelace in Eau Gallie, Florida, in 1929.

By the time *Jonah's Gourd Vine* appeared, Hurston had spent a se-mester on the faculty of Bethune-Cookman College in Daytona Beach, Florida. Hired to establish a school of dramatic arts "based on pure Negro expression," Hurston found herself almost immediately at odds with the school's president, the formidable Mary McLeod Bethune. Hurston resented equally the college's social obligations and low pay. Bethune, an exemplary race woman, founder of the Na-tional Council of Negro Women and soon-to-be adviser to President Roosevelt, did not tolerate challenges to her authority on her home turf. After producing another version of *From Sun to Sun*, Hurston left the faculty. Subsequent attempts to establish an academic career failed. A preliminary offer to teach at Fisk in 1934 was retracted. Unable to devise a plan of study acceptable to the Rosenwald Foun-dation, which had offered fellowship support, Hurston in effect withdrew from the graduate program in anthropology at Columbia in the spring of 1935. She spent the semester she was enrolled working on a novel, possibly an early draft of *Moses, Man of the Mountain*. In 1939, her experience with Mrs. Bethune would be repeated at North Carolina College for Negroes in Durham, where she clashed with its

founder and president, James Edward Shephard and, in her capacity as director of dramatic productions, failed to stage a play.[71]

Other venues were more conducive to Hurston's talents. Onstage and in the field, she continued to promote and study African-American vernacular art. She led a troupe of performers to Saint Louis in 1934 to participate in the National Folk Festival; she continued to produce folklore concerts. In June 1935, she joined folklorists Alan Lomax and Mary Elizabeth Barnicle, who were traveling through the South recording material for the Music Division of the Library of Congress.[72] The access to rural black communities Hurston gained for her white colleagues caused Lomax to credit her with being "almost entirely responsible for the success" of the first part of the expedition. By the time *Mules and Men* was published in October 1935, Hurston was employed as a dramatic coach for the WPA Federal Theatre Project in New York.

The following March, she was awarded a Guggenheim Fellowship "to make an exhaustive study of 'Obeah' practices" in the West Indies. She arrived in Kingston, Jamaica, on April 14, 1936, after making a brief stopover in Haiti. Over the next five months, she visited all of the parishes in Jamaica, spending an extended period with a community of Maroons, the descendants of people legendary for their heroic resistance to slavery. Another focus of her research was on African survivals in Jamaican religious practices, such as the "Nine Night," a ritual to appease the spirit of the dead. On September 22, Hurston departed for Haiti, where she found a surfeit of material. She began to learn Creole in order to facilitate her investigations. But, in the midst of these preparations, she felt compelled to turn again to fiction. By the third week of December, she had finished *Their Eyes Were Watching God*.[73]

Hurston's classic novel was published in September 1937. Retrospectively, Hurston offered a romantic account of the novel's conception; it was "dammed up in me, and I wrote it under internal pressure in seven weeks." Its genesis was a failed love affair: Hurston had again chosen her work over a relationship, and she left her lover, a Columbia University graduate student she identified only by his initials, to pursue her research in Haiti and Jamaica. "The plot was far

from the circumstances, but I tried to embalm all the tenderness of my passion for him in *Their Eyes Were Watching God*" (*Dust Tracks*, 188–89).[74] Rather than the romance plot, the plot to which Hurston seems to have turned, or actually returned, was that of *Mules and Men*. The protagonist, Janie Crawford, retraces the journey from store porch to jook to muck mapped in *Mules*. Like that book, *Their Eyes* consists of a series of verbal performances—personal narratives, speeches, folktales, sermons, and "between-story conversation and business"—some of which are borrowed directly from the earlier work. Similarly, too, Hurston adapts and revises traditional vernacular forms to give voice to women. Indeed, in *Their Eyes Were Watching God*, *Mules and Men*'s subtext of female empowerment becomes the primary theme.

During the twenty-odd years spanned by the plot, Janie grows from a diffident teenager to a woman in complete possession of herself. To achieve selfhood, she must resist the definitions of "what a woman should be" imposed on her by her grandmother Nanny and by the three men she marries. Like Nanny, two of her husbands, Joe Starks and Vergible (Tea Cake) Woods, are powerful manipulators of language. Through Janie's struggles with and against them, the novel clarifies the relation between voice and self-discovery that had been a central concern in Hurston's fiction since "Sweat." That Janie becomes an articulate heroine is confirmed by the novel's prologue when, as her friend Pheoby listens in rapt attention, Janie begins to tell her own story. Both her speech and her troubling silences in the narrative that follows may be better understood when the novel is compared to its predecessor, *Mules and Men*.

Among Hurston's many revisions, none seems more telling than the reworking of the mule metaphor. In *Their Eyes*, the black woman is figured as the mule of the world. The metaphor is drawn from a folktale, which Nanny tells in order to persuade Janie to marry Logan Killicks and to secure the protection of marriage and property Nanny as a slave had been denied:

> Honey, de white man is de ruler of everything as fur as Ah been able to find out. Maybe it's some place way off in de ocean where de black man is in power, but we don't know nothin' but what we see. So de white man throw down de load and tell de nigger man tuh pick it up.

He pick it up because he have to, but he don't tote it. He hand it to his womenfolks. De nigger woman is de mule uh de world as fur as Ah can see. (14)

In *Mules and Men*, the same tale, "Why the Sister in Black Works Hardest," is told by a male informant as part of a discussion on the relation of blacks to work. Race, not gender, is the topic. Similarly, "mules" in the book's title refers to the exploitation of black people's labor, not to the condition of black women. Only by reading backward from the novel to the earlier narrative does one perceive how the title *Mules and Men* situates black men both in relation to work, and therefore implicitly to white men, and in relation to black women. Black men, though oppressed and treated as mules by whites, create alternative spaces where they succeed more often than not in asserting their selfhood. In *Their Eyes*, the focus shifts to the ways in which black men suppress black women, treating them as mules, while women respond by constantly negotiating spaces in which to assert their selfhood.

The title *Mules and Men* encapsulates Hurston's conception of black folklore. Rather than record tales about mules, Hurston drew on a longstanding identification of black people with mules and demonstrated how this negative identification could be transformed into a positive one within the group. "The phrase meant not only that black people were treated as mules, but that they were defiantly human—mules *and* men."[75]

In contrast to the earlier volume, the figure of the mule recurs throughout the more tightly constructed novel. It is also engendered. As Sherley Anne Williams observes, the mule becomes "a metaphor for the roles that Janie repudiates in her quest for self-fulfillment" (xii).[76] Unlike *Mules*, which posits an ironic reversal of the racist image of black people as mule-like, the movement of *Their Eyes* is to reject and transcend the racist and sexist image of black women.

Thus Janie's decision to flee her first loveless marriage is spurred by Logan Killicks's announcement that he will buy Janie a mule of her own so that she can plow alongside him. Recognizing that Killicks's plan threatens to reduce her to the status Nanny abhorred, Janie decides to escape with Joe Starks. Citified and stylishly dressed,

"with his hat set at an angle that didn't belong in these parts," Joe flatters Janie and talks to her in rhymes. With his fine clothes and big ambitions, he seems totally unlike Killicks, a rough-hewn farmer who, Janie complains, "don't take nothin' to count but sow-belly and cornbread" (29). Starks offers Janie "a high chair for her to sit in and overlook the world" (58). If Killicks promises to actualize Nanny's fears for Janie, Starks actualizes Nanny's dreams. The threat that bourgeois marriage represents to Janie's selfhood is less obvious, however, and the novel's rendering of the mule metaphor is consequently more abstract.

The novel counterposes Janie's growing dissatisfaction with her role as "Mrs. Mayor Starks" to the "mule talk" on the store porch, an extended sequence of tales about Matt Bonner's yellow mule. In these tales, both the abused animal and its oppressive owner are targets of the town's ridicule. That the tales mask an underlying identification by the townspeople with the mule is manifested during the mock funeral held for the beast. Parodying folk sermons in which divine justice would invert the relationship between slaves and their masters, the eulogist imagines that "the dear departed brother would look down into hell and see the devil plowing Matt Bonner all day long in a hell-hot sun and laying the raw-hide to his back" (57).[77]

Janie's identification with the mule is more personal. Interspersed among the comic "crayon enlargements of life" are passages describing Janie's deepening frustration with Joe's prohibitions and requirements: he refuses to allow her to participate in the "lying sessions" and compels her to cover her hair while she clerks in the post office and the store, work that she despises. Janie's muttered protest on behalf of the mule links the themes of the "mule talk" and the novel:

> They oughta be shamed uh theyselves! Teasin' dat poor brute beast lak they is! Done been worked tuh death; done has his disposition ruint wid mistreatment, and now they got tuh finish devilin' 'im tuh death. Wisht Ah had mah way wid 'em all. (53)

This passage foreshadows the eventual dissolution of the Starkses' marriage. But its immediate effect is to prompt Joe to buy the mule and allow it to die in peace. That action inspires Janie's first public

utterance. Joe cannot easily object, because Janie speaks in praise of him. Her fulsome comparisons—she likens Joe's act to Lincoln's freeing of the slaves—cause one auditor to proclaim: "Yo' wife is uh born orator, Starks. Us never knowed dat befo'. She put jus' de right words tuh our thoughts" (55). The judgment must surprise Joe, as it does the reader, for to this point the novel has given little evidence of Janie's oratorical skills. Indeed, her short speech, coming as it does in a chapter replete with elaborate verbal performances, strikes a rather modest note. But that is thematically appropriate, because from the beginning the novel emphasizes the obstacles Janie as a woman faces in her struggle to gain a voice in a culture that places such a premium on speaking. In this regard, the novel extends the cultural critique set forth in *Mules and Men*.

This continuity is suggested by the parallel opening scenes of the two books. Janie, like Zora, returns to Eatonville, a community to which she no longer belongs. Similarly, too, her return is far more mysterious than her departure. But the novel represents the community rather than the protagonist ambivalently. The scene opens with a description of the transformation central to Hurston's conception of African-American expressive culture:

> It was the time for sitting on porches beside the road. It was the time to hear things and talk. These sitters had been tongueless, earless, eyeless conveniences all day long. Mules and brutes had occupied their skins. But now, the sun and the bossman were gone, so the skins felt powerful and human. They became lords of sounds and lesser things. They passed nations through their mouths. They sat in judgment. (1)

Nowhere in Hurston's oeuvre is the transformation from mules to men expressed more lyrically. But this description does not valorize the performances that transformation enables. Instead, the passage deftly balances celebration and critique. Empowering themselves against great odds to speak, the porch sitters wield that power against one of their own. Their judgments are rooted in the hierarchal values that the novel will repudiate. Their speech is itself further described as inherently paradoxical: "burning statements," "killing tools," and "mass cruelty" resolve themselves into "a mood come alive. Words

walking without masters; walking together like harmony in a song" (2). Janie's status in the scene best explains the narrator's ambiguous response to this speech.

Unlike Zora in *Mules*, Janie is the silent object of the men's gaze ("the men noticed her firm buttocks like she had grape fruits in her hip pockets . . .") and the women's envy and ridicule—which are likewise directed at Janie's sexuality and age. The novel makes it clear from the start that the store porch is for Janie an alienating space; she is excluded from its rituals. Janie is free to speak only at home in the loving company of her closest female friend. "Full of that oldest of human longing—self revelation" and urged on by Pheoby's "hungry listening," Janie prepares to tell her tale.

Quickly, she reveals herself to be, in Henry Louis Gates's phrase, "a master of metaphorical narration"; she figures her life "like a great tree in leaf . . . dawn and doom was in the branches" (8).[78] But no sooner than she recounts her vision of marriage, in one of the most beautiful prose poems in the text, than Janie is effectively silenced. Another voice, one initially "lacking in command," interposes itself between Janie and her vision of the pear tree in bloom. The voice is Nanny's, and her remembered voice seizes control of Janie's narrative just as she seized control of the events Janie narrates.

Their Eyes is, as Elizabeth Meese observes, "a novel about orality—of speakers and modes of speech."[79] Nanny's power derives in substantial measure from the forcefulness of her speech. Apart from her voice, she is powerless. "Nanny's head and face looked like the standing roots of some old tree that had been torn away by storm. Foundation of ancient power that no longer mattered" (12). Physically ravaged by age, socially oppressed, and impoverished, Nanny dominates Janie by her superior manipulation of their culture's expressive codes. She is an accomplished storyteller, skilled slave narrator, and powerful preacher, whose metaphors fuse the biblical and the domestic in arresting ways.

To Nanny, her granddaughter's nascent sexuality is alarming. Stoic in the face of her own death ("one mornin' soon, now, de angel wid de sword is gointuh stop by here"), she wants just to live long enough to see Janie "safe in life" (14, 15). Having been unable to protect her-

+ Fauset

self and her daughter from sexual exploitation, Nanny determines to safeguard Janie. Marriage is the only haven. When Janie protests that she does not know anyone to marry, Nanny responds that "de Lawd will provide." Above all, her response reflects her deep Christian belief, but it is also a variant of Fauset's philosophy that the post-slavery woman is finally free to be virtuous.[80]

Marriage had not been an option for the grandmother, who as a slave was impregnated by her master; her mistress had forced her to flee with her newborn infant. When freedom came, Nanny resolved to "take a broom and a cook-pot and throw up a highway through the wilderness" for her child (15). But her daughter was raped by a black schoolteacher, convincing Nanny that male treachery knows no racial bounds. Though unable to fulfill her dreams of what a woman should be for herself and her daughter—as she explains, the inability to ful-fill one's dreams was one of the "hold-backs of slavery"—she has remembered them. For Nanny, the dream is indeed the truth: "Ah wanted to preach a great sermon about colored women sittin' on high, but they wasn't no pulpit for me" (15). She has saved the text for Janie.

Even without a pulpit, Nanny is a powerful preacher. Her half-sung, half-sobbed "chant prayer" runs on for several pages. In it, she envisions Janie on the pedestal reserved for southern white women, far above the drudgery that has characterized Nanny's own life—the drudgery that has made the black woman "de mule uh de world." She explains her plan for Janie to marry Logan Killicks, an old man whose sixty acres and a mule constitute his eligibility. The impact of Nanny's words is overwhelming. "The vision of Logan Killicks was desecrating the pear tree, but Janie didn't know how to tell Nanny that" (13). When at the end of her prayer, Nanny entreats, "Put me down easy, Janie, Ah'm a cracked plate," Janie has no choice but to accede to her wishes.

Indeed, Janie does not dare disobey Nanny's commands until the old woman is safely dead. When Janie escapes with Joe Starks, she fails to recognize how much his values resemble her grandmother's. Both believe, as Houston Baker observes of Nanny, that "property en-ables expression."[81] While Nanny has dreamed of an elevated pulpit,

Joe determines to be a "big voice" and "ruler of things." His first act upon arriving in Eatonville is to buy two hundred acres of land; in a single stroke, he affords Janie a degree of "protection" that far exceeds Nanny's dreams. Even before he has consolidated his power as landlord, storekeeper, postmaster, and mayor, he claims the platform his growing status ensures. Joe Starks becomes a great speech maker.

Biblical references are as much a part of Joe's public speeches as they are of Nanny's private ones. There is a profound difference, however. Unlike Nanny's rhetoric, whose blend of biblical allusion and domestic metaphor bespeaks the internalization of religious principle, Joe's appropriation of religious references is a mask for self-aggrandizement. For good reason, his favorite expletive is "I god."

The lamplighting ceremony offers an example. Starks's purchase of a streetlight for the town occasions the kind of "impromptu ceremony always ready for every hour of life" that Hurston had described in "Characteristics of Negro Expression." Starks is the speaker of the hour. He convenes the town for an event that is "something for us all tuh remember tuh our dyin' day." Comparing himself implicitly to the "Sun-maker," he lights the "first street lamp in uh colored town":

> "And when Ah touch de match tuh dat lamp-wick let de light penetrate inside of yuh, and let it shine, let it shine, let it shine. Brother Davis, lead us in a word uh prayer." (43)

The ceremony concludes as the townspeople sing the hymn "Jesus, the Light of the World." What is satirized here is not so much the conflation of religious rhetoric and secular purpose—a common characteristic of African-American discourse—as the self-deification of Joe Starks.

Starks's hubris maims all of his relationships. Though the townspeople admire his accomplishments, they find him "compellent." As one observes, "He loves obedience out of everybody under de sound of his voice" (46). "Everybody" naturally includes Janie. Joe uses his wife, as he does the big white house and other accoutrements of wealth, to mark the difference between himself and the townspeople. "She must look on herself as the bell-cow, the other women were the gang" (39). The great speech maker forbids Janie to speak in public:

"mah wife don't know nothin' 'bout no speech-makin'. Ah never married her for nothin' lak dat. She's uh woman and her place is in de home" (40–41).

As she had with Nanny, Janie tries to resist. After the lamplighting ceremony, she complains that being Mrs. Mayor is a "strain." She feels as if she's marking time while Joe is always talking and doing, and she hopes it will all be over soon. He responds that his being a big voice makes a big woman out of her (43). Janie recognizes both the hollowness of Joe's voice and the presumption of his claim to speak for her. She understands as well how public speech is sanctioned for men.

During the extended sequence of storytelling that constitutes much of chapter 6, Sam Watson and Lige Moss carry on a "contest in hyperbole." Sam accuses Lige of contending that "God talked His inside business" with him. Sam's point is to satirize Lige's intellectual pretensions. The text challenges the intellectual and spiritual pretensions of all the men on the store porch, as they engage in a lying session as viciously sexist as the one represented in *Mules and Men*. Indeed, the speech Hurston invents for Joe Starks echoes the between-story conversation in the earlier text. Starks proclaims, "Somebody got to think for women and chillun and chickens and cows. I god, they sho don't think none theirselves" (67). When Janie finally gets up the courage to "thrust herself into the conversation," something she has never done before, she attacks the rationale behind Joe's chauvinism:

> Sometimes God gits familiar wid us womenfolks too and talks His inside business. He told me how surprised He was 'bout y'all turning out so smart after Him makin' yuh different; and how surprised y'all is goin' tuh be if you ever find out you don't know half as much 'bout us as you think you do. It's so easy to make yo'self out God Almighty when you ain't got nothin' tuh strain against but women and chickens. (70–71)

Joe Starks does not find Janie's performance amusing. As she realizes, he requires her silence and the submission it signals. Moreover, like Nanny, Joe uses physical violence to compel obedience. Janie "learn[s] to hush."

In so doing, she contents herself to practice a kind of passive re-sistance against Joe's tyranny until he pushes her to the point when she must "talk smart" to this man who so consistently threatens her selfhood. Her specifying is provoked by Joe's increasingly cruel taunts—taunts that recall the town's badgering of Matt Bonner's mule—but Janie finds the strength to claim her voice and her hu-manity. She retaliates: "Humph! Talkin' 'bout *me* lookin' old! When you pull down yo' britches, you look lak de change uh life" (75). In common usage, the phrase "change of life" denotes female meno-pause. As Mary Helen Washington comments: "The experience of having one's body become an object to be looked at is considered so demeaning that when it happens to a man, it figuratively transforms him into a woman."[82] By unmanning him, Janie's words wound Joe mortally.

Talking back, however belatedly, is nevertheless liberating for Janie. Janie confronts Joe with more painful truths, even as he lies on his deathbed. Her words reveal how well she comprehends the effect of his domination: "Mah own mind had tuh be squeezed and crowded out tuh make room for yours in me" (82). Her attack on her dying husband is not an act of gratuitous cruelty; it is an essential step toward self-reclamation. Moreover, in terms of the narrative, the deathbed episode posits a dramatic break with Janie's past. She is henceforth a different woman. Hurston reinforces this point meta-phorically. Just after Joe dies, Janie stands before a mirror and recalls that years before, "she had told her girl self to wait for her in the looking glass. . . . The young girl was gone, but a handsome woman had taken her place" (83). Janie has integrated her inside and outside selves. Now that she can see herself whole, she reflects on her past and realizes that her grandmother, though acting out of love, has wronged her deeply. At base, Nanny's sermon has been about *things*, when Janie wanted to journey to the horizon in search of *people*. Janie is able at last to reject her grandmother's way and to resume her origi-nal quest. That quest culminates in her marriage to Tea Cake, with whom she builds a relationship radically different from those she has known before. Having discarded Nanny's text, she is free to impro-vise one of her own.

Tea Cake is a troubadour, a traveling bluesman whose life is dedicated to aesthetic and joyful pursuits. More than any other character in the novel, Tea Cake exemplifies the aesthetic principles Hurston set forth in "Characteristics of Negro Expression." Everything he does is acted out. Tea Cake makes a performance out of leaving a room. He plays an imaginary guitar after he pawns his real one and begs Janie's forgiveness by singing her a song. His speech is dipped in blues. He might get "his habits on," that is, drink and gamble, but he assures Janie that she has "de keys to de kingdom."

A manipulator of cultural codes and bearer of traditions, Tea Cake is both a man of words and a man of action. He is a sweet-talker, a fighter, and a gambler. The space associated with him is the jook. Both his attributes and his name recall Big Sweet, and like her he becomes the protagonist's guide and protector. Of course, "Papa Tea Cake" becomes Janie's lover as well. Important as this romance plot becomes, Tea Cake's role as a cultural guide remains crucial.[83] Joe Starks has "classed [Janie] off." Denied the right to participate in the rituals of her culture, Janie has become estranged from them. Notably, she is alone in the store when Tea Cake first enters; the townspeople have all gone to a baseball game. To a substantial degree, Janie has grown to resemble those "colored folks" who Nanny described as "branches without roots" (15). Tea Cake offers Janie the chance to know herself through her culture and thus to "utilize [herself] all over" (107).

Through Vergible (Tea Cake) Woods, Hurston also explores an alternative definition of manhood, one that does not rely on external manifestations of power, money, and position. Tea Cake has none of these. He is so immune to the influence of white American society that he does not even desire them. Tea Cake, a veritable man of nature, or natural man, seems at ease being who and what he is. That assurance, along with his cultural knowledge, helps him foster the growth of Janie's self-acceptance. Unlike Joe, he has no desire to be a "big voice"; he wants a woman to talk to, not at. Tea Cake and Janie engage in small talk and invent variations of traditional courtship rituals.[84] They play checkers, fish by moonlight, and display their affection freely. An unselfish lover, Tea Cake delights in Janie's pleasure. Alluding to Hunter's "Down-Hearted Blues," he tells her:

"You'se got de world in uh jug and make out you don't know it. But Ah'm glad tuh be de one tuh tell yuh" (99). Understandably, Janie soon concludes that Tea Cake "could be a bee to a blossom—a pear tree blossom in the spring" (101). Over the protests of her neighbors, she marries this man several years younger than she, whose only worldly possession is a guitar.

Though their courtship is certainly idyllic, Tea Cake is not a completely idealized character. In his initial meeting with Janie, he alludes to the blues quoted at the top of this chapter. He boasts: "Ah don't need no pocket-full uh money to ride de train lak uh woman. When Ah takes uh notion Ah rides anyhow—money or no money" (93). The statement is revealing, for as Zora Hurston well knew, Tea Cake as a son of the folk culture is heir to its prejudices as well as to its wisdom. She knew besides that female autonomy cannot be granted by men; it must be demanded by women. Janie gains her autonomy only when she insists upon it. An important turning point occurs shortly after their marriage. Tea Cake has taken Janie's money and returns hours later to explain that he has used it to throw a party for his friends. His reason for not including Janie is that she is too much the lady to mingle with "railroad hands and dey womenfolks." Janie's response is swift and sure: "Looka heah, Tea Cake, if you ever go off from me and have a good time lak dat and then come back heah tellin' me how nice Ah is, Ah specks tuh kill yuh dead" (119). Unlike Logan, who threatens to beat her when she "talks smart," or Joe Starks, who slinks off and dies, Tea Cake negotiates with her. "So you aims tuh partake wid everything," he asks, and she responds affirmatively.

They embark on a nomadic existence that takes them to the rich farmland of the Florida Everglades. On the "muck," Janie joins Tea Cake in the fields and works harder than she does at any other point in the novel. This work is freely chosen and inspired by love; hence Janie is happy to do it. Moreover, the work strengthens the bond not only between Janie and her husband, but between her and the group. Notably, the group consists of blacks from all over the South and the Caribbean as well; it is a Pan-African community, reminiscent of the "Ditch" in McKay's *Banjo*. But Hurston's model is clearly the Ever-

glades Cypress Lumber Camp, where she had met Big Sweet. If in Polk County, the water tastes like cherry wine, on the muck "the jooks clanged and clamored. Blues made and used right on the spot" (125).

Janie and Tea Cake's cabin becomes "the unauthorized center of the job," the focal point of the community like the store in Eatonville. Here, in sharp contrast, Janie "could listen and laugh and even talk some herself from listening to the rest" (129). She and Tea Cake achieve a remarkably egalitarian marriage; they both work in the fields, and they both do household chores. They fight through the petty jealousies that bedevil all romantic unions. For a sweet season, they sustain the intensity of their love.

Ultimately, however, Janie and Tea Cake bear out the Polk County dictum "Everlasting love is a lie." Repeating the pattern of the earlier ones, Janie's last marriage is destroyed by her husband's internalization of hierarchal values. Although Tea Cake remains impervious to the lure of money, he cannot resist a challenge to his ego. That the challenge does not come from Janie, but from Mrs. Turner, the character who is most identified with the white world, is telling. Mrs. Turner is the light-skinned restaurant proprietor who, while making her living from the black migrant workers on the muck, clearly "took black folk as a personal affront to herself" (136). Her attitudes are reminiscent of characters like Angela Murray, Mrs. Hayes-Rore, and Irene Redfield. Judging Janie by her looks, Mrs. Turner thinks she has found an ally. She has not; yet Janie is mainly silent in the face of Mrs. Turner's all-too-conventional wisdom.

To an extent, Janie reacts to Mrs. Turner with the same jejune passivity she has shown in the similar confrontation with her grandmother; she seems able to reject Mrs. Turner's designated suitor only because she is already married. Tea Cake's reversion to stereotypically chauvinist behavior is more dramatic; he beats Janie. Then he brags about it in language that echoes Joe Starks: "Janie is wherever AH wants tuh be. Dat's de kind uh wife she is and Ah love her for it" (141). Janie's silence persists, and no voice in the text rises to condemn Tea Cake's violence.

However, the scene's configuration makes the connection between that violence and the capitalist, racist, and elitist values Mrs. Turner represents. Those values have previously been represented by Nanny, the victim of the system in which those values are enshrined and the conveyor of those values to Janie, and by Joe Starks, who attempts to escape domination by devising and controlling his own version of the system. Mrs. Turner's presence on the muck demonstrates the impossibility of even the most marginalized black people's escaping the dominant society's influence. Her attempt to replicate the social hierarchy of the larger society causes Janie and Tea Cake to revert to the stereotyped gender roles that society endorses. Necessarily, it disrupts their marriage, which has granted them the freedom to transgress those roles. Subsequently, Mrs. Turner's actions destroy the egalitarian community the workers on the muck have built, a border community that, like Eatonville, exists with the sufferance of the dominant society. The hurricane that shortly thereafter occurs is the sign of these disrupted unions.

But is it all her agency?

It may also be read as a sign of Janie's spiritual transformation. When the characters reenter the frame tale, Janie tells Pheoby that she has been to the "horizon and back." She is eager to teach the lesson she has learned in her travels: "Two things everybody's got tuh do fuh theyselves: They got tuh go tuh God, and they got tuh find out about livin' fuh theyselves" (183). Though Janie's spiritual progression (unlike Zora's in *Mules*) is not explicitly charted, she is surely not referring to a physical destination alone when she tells her friend: "It's uh known fact, Pheoby, you got tuh *go* there tuh *know* there" (183).

That Janie's quest has been partly or wholly spiritual is reflected in the text's recurrent references to her expanding spiritual consciousness. One of the earliest and most important references is encoded in her often-cited vision of marriage:

> She was stretched on her back beneath the pear tree soaking in the alto chant of the visiting bees, the gold of the sun and the panting breath of the breeze when the inaudible voice of it all came to her. She saw a dust-bearing bee sink into the sanctum of a bloom; the thousand sister-calyxes arch to meet the love embrace and the ecstatic shiver of the tree from root to tiniest branch creaming in every blossom and frothing with delight. So this was a marriage! She had been summoned to behold a revelation. Then Janie felt a pain remorseless sweet that left her limp and languid. (10–11)

This scene of sexual awakening is also, as Michael Awkward contends, a scene of spiritual awakening in which nature becomes Janie's "instructor."[85] "Inaudible voice," "sanctum," "summoned," "behold," and "revelation" inscribe the spiritual import of the scene, as does Janie's subsequent reference to "seeking confirmation of the voice and the vision." But the spiritual does not supersede the sensual; Janie's vision is at once spiritual and erotic.

In "The Uses of the Erotic," Audre Lorde sets forth definitions that illuminate Janie's perspective. In Lorde's view, the erotic is an empowering resource for women, though Western patriarchy has corrupted and distorted its meaning. Calling for women to reclaim its power, Lorde defines the erotic as "a measure between the beginnings of our sense of self and the chaos of our strongest feelings [and] an internal sense of satisfaction to which, once we have experienced it, we know we can aspire. For having experienced the fullness of this depth of feeling and recognizing its power, in honor and self-respect we can require no less of ourselves."[86]

Janie's vision, which, like Lorde's definition, is at once spiritual and erotic, encapsulates this moment of self-recognition. Consequently, it becomes the standard by which Janie judges all her subsequent experiences. Though she sometimes deludes herself and mistakes the merely sensual for the erotic, Janie never gives up her quest for fulfillment.

In part, it is Janie's inability to name "the chaos of her feelings" that renders her vulnerable to her more eloquent grandmother and the men who would subjugate her vision to theirs. Her inability does not stem from her lack of education, despite her remark about not being like educated women who know how to contemplate ideas. The deficit is not in education but in language. No language is available to Janie, or, for that matter, to Zora Neale Hurston, in which to articulate the heterodox spirituality that is at the heart of the novel's vision. Hurston draws on hoodoo iconography as well as biblical allusion and blues stoicism to represent Janie's journey to spiritual wholeness.

While present throughout the novel, these elements come together most tellingly in the last third of the text, the section that is

most analogous to the second part of *Mules and Men*.[87] Indeed, I want to read the hurricane as an analogue to the initiation rituals Zora experiences; it is the sign that through a process abstracted from ritual, Janie, too, comes into possession of the word.

Just as the hoodoo rituals are prefaced by a folktale in *Mules*, the storytellers in *Their Eyes* sit outside Tea Cake and Janie's cabin as the storm approaches, "handling Big John de Conquer," i.e. telling tales about John de Conquer and his works. John de Conquer is a root with numerous uses in conjure, which Hurston throughout her writing associates with the legacy of John the Slave.[88] The tales referred to describe victories over death; they are told to a blues accompaniment. But the bravado that they express is swept away by the force of the storm. The characters are rendered mute and almost disembodied: "six eyes were questioning *God*" (151). Several paragraphs later, the novel's title, a variation of this statement, appears. Subsequently, the text defines "watching" as "trying to see beyond seeing" (162). The hurricane produces diverse transformations.

Instantly, the storm overturns the social hierarchy. The dispossessed Indians, not the propertied whites, are wise enough to seek higher ground. At least for the moment, divine power transcends temporal power, for as Janie puts it, "Ole Massa is doin' *His* work now" (150). That work dissolves one boundary after another—boundaries between young and old, rich and poor, natural and man-made, tame and wild, land and sea, living and dead: "the wind and water had given life to lots of things that folks think of as dead and given death to so much that had been living things. Water everywhere. Stray fish swimming in the yard" (151–52).[89]

The novel's most trenchant comment on racism is that amid all this upheaval the boundary between black and white holds firm—whites have preempted the safety of the bridge at Six Mile Bend and later insist on separating the corpses of the hurricane victims by race. But more startling and revelatory are the scenes such as this one that Tea Cake and Janie come upon: "they passed a dead man in a sitting position on a hummock, entirely surrounded by wild animals and snakes. Common danger made common friends. Nothing sought a conquest over the other" (156).

Such scenes have the force of visions. They call to mind the passages in *Mules* that recount Zora's apprenticeship with Luke Turner. Turner believes, for example, that Marie Leveau has passed power to him through a storm. As she prepared to die, a storm arose and tore her house away and set it in Lake Pontchartrain. The thunder and lightning grew until her followers' entreaties persuaded her to return to land, at which moment "the wind, the thunder and lightning, and the water all ceased" (204). Even more suggestively, when Zora completes her rites of initiation, Luke Turner gives her the name "the Rain-Bringer." Then "with ceremony Turner painted the lightning symbol down my back from my right shoulder to my left hip. This was to be my sign forever. The Great One was to speak to me in storms" (210).[90]

Whatever message Janie receives—and she is as silent on this score as Zora is about her five psychic experiences—after the storm, she speaks with a new assurance in her voice. Although Tea Cake takes charge of their escape (and miscalculates with every move) Janie remains imperturbable. She tells Tea Cake that she is unafraid to die. "If you kin see de light at daybreak, you don't keer if you die at dusk" (151). She forgives his errors in judgment. When he saves her from the rabid dog, she confers the accolade Big Sweet earns from her lover in *Mules*: "You was twice noble tuh save me" (158).

In the end, Janie is the character most comparable to Big Sweet, because her actions match the strength of her words. She meets the challenge that requires her to kill the man she loves in order to save herself. An apt pupil, she has learned the lessons Tea Cake has taught in both self-love and self-defense. Like Big Sweet, too, Janie is empowered by a heterodox spirituality that allows her to save rather than sacrifice her selfhood. Tea Cake has been her spiritual guide as well as her lover.[91] But Janie goes beyond her mentor, and beyond the specific beliefs of hoodoo, to shape a highly personal creed. She goes to God for and through herself.

In telling her tale to Pheoby, Janie responds to the cultural imperative that having completed the journey, she has to tell the story. She is conscious enough of societal realities to know that racism and sexism determine where the story might be comprehended. Conse-

quently, she chooses neither the courtroom nor the store porch. (While she is compelled to tell *a* story in the courtroom, the text reports rather than records it.) Instead, she tells her tale to her "kissin'-friend," on whom she can depend for a good thought and to whom she can give the "understanding" to go along with the story. Pheoby proves herself a worthy auditor when she responds to the tale's conclusion by proclaiming: "Lawd! Ah done growed ten feet higher from jus' listenin' tuh you, Janie" (182). If the transformative potential of Zora's tale in *Mules* is muted, the transformative effect of Janie's tale is made plain. Here and in its many allusions to its precursor, *Their Eyes Were Watching God* distills the vision of female empowerment set forth in *Mules and Men*.

Janie's physical and spiritual journey represents as well a triumphant resolution of the dilemma set forth by Marita Bonner in "On Being Young—A Woman—and Colored." Like Bonner's persona, Janie seeks to claim a racial and a gendered identity. After much hesitation, she does. Overcoming the self-hatred that is the residue of racism and loosening the constraints of sexism, Janie assumes authority in and for her own life. Moreover, by sharing her story with Pheoby, she demonstrates that the resources she summons for her journey are available to others.

Notwithstanding Janie's avowal that she "didn't read books" and presumably had no knowledge of what educated women did, *Their Eyes Were Watching God* constitutes Zora Neale Hurston's imaginative configuration of the ethnographic and literary ideas she had grappled with from the beginning of her career. Creating a literary counterpart of the blues, she had composed her novel according to the principles outlined in "Characteristics of Negro Expression." In *Their Eyes*, the drama of the impromptu ceremonies of everyday life provides a context for, and a correlative to, the drama the protagonist enacts. Adhering to the tenet of "the will to adorn," the novel deploys poetic metaphor both in its lyrical passages and in those moments when Janie "specifies" against Joe. In the former case, adorned language registers affirmation of African-American discursive traditions, while in the latter it protests against the oppressive structures imposed directly or indirectly by the dominant society.

Unfortunately, the novel did not find an audience as receptive as Pheoby; it did not find much of an audience at all. Reviews in the mainstream press were generally positive, if patronizing. Ralph Thompson, writing for the *New York Times*, saw in the novel "further evidence of a marked and honest talent," then singled out for praise what he called its "racial gayety." He was not impressed at all with the dialect. Herschel Brickell, his counterpart at the *New York Post*, was unreservedly enthusiastic for what he read as a "woman's story, and the story of a complete and happy woman, the kind we hear too little about in fiction."[92] Despite such notices, sales were slow.

If reviews in the white press did little good for the novel's commercial prospects, negative reviews from black male intellectuals did serious harm to its critical reputation. To a man, they faulted the novel for its alleged lack of racial militancy. Locke, for example, praised the book as "folklore fiction at its best," then wondered when Hurston would take up the challenge of "social document fiction." The most hostile response came from Richard Wright, who wrote in *New Masses* that the novel lacked a theme and any claim at all to seriousness. He located it instead in the tradition of minstrelsy and described its characters as caught "in that safe and narrow orbit in which America likes to see the Negro life: between laughter and tears."[93] Defining the novel in essence as one of feeling rather than ideas was, from Wright's masculinist perspective, another way of saying that *Their Eyes Were Watching God* was a woman's story.

Hurston moved on—though she did stop to reply to Wright in kind in her review of *Uncle Tom's Children*, his volume of short stories—but she never equalled the achievement of *Their Eyes Were Watching God*.[94] She kept on writing and traveling, even as both endeavors grew increasingly arduous. She completed *Tell My Horse*, the volume based on her Caribbean fieldwork, but it proved neither a critical nor commercial success. Her articles and reviews continued to appear in prominent publications, yet her pockets remained empty. In May 1938, she found employment with the Works Progress Administration (WPA). Attached to the Negro unit of the Florida Federal Writers Project, she resumed folklore research. The volume that was proposed, *The Florida Negro*, remained in manuscript; Hurston's substantial contributions to *The Florida Guide* were unattributed.

While employed by the WPA, Hurston met Albert Price, a playground worker, whom she married on 27 June 1939. She was forty-eight; he was twenty-three. That fall he stayed in Florida, while she went to teach in North Carolina. She filed for divorce in February, then after a reconciliation, they traveled together to Beaufort, South Carolina, where she studied religious trances in the sanctified church on a field expedition led by anthropologist Jane Belo. Whether or not Price was interested in Hurston's research, he knew enough about hoodoo to accuse her of working roots against him. Well in advance of their first anniversary, the couple had called it quits for good.[95]

Despite her personal travails, Hurston remained a productive writer. However, her writing shifted direction in ways that lost old admirers without winning new ones. Eatonville was no longer the setting for her fiction. Increasingly, she was drawn to broad spiritual and political issues. While African-American art and spirituality remained central concerns, she was interested in ancient history and global politics as well. Her ambitions for *Moses, Man of the Mountain*, the novel she published in 1939, had been grand: the novel was at once a retelling of the biblical legend, a meditation on the origin and function of myth, and an allegorical history of black Americans. As she well knew, these ambitions were at best only partially realized. In a letter to Edwin Grover, the white Rollins College professor to whom she dedicated the novel, she confided that she had "the feeling of disappointment about it." It had not achieved her ideal: she would "keep trying."[96]

The title *Dust Tracks on a Road* seems emblematic of the uncertainty Zora Hurston felt about her career at age fifty. What would remain of her work? Would her achievements be as ephemeral as dust tracks? In 1942, the vogue for Harlem and black art was a dim memory. It went unmentioned in her book. Less easy to ignore was the fact that *Their Eyes Were Watching God* had explored themes that engaged her Harlem Renaissance contemporaries; a new generation of black writers found these themes passé. *Native Son* had catapulted Wright to a height never attained by an African-American writer. When it was published in 1945, Wright's devastatingly eloquent *Black Boy* would reinvigorate the tradition of black autobiography, which dated to the slave narrative. His vision of black life, culture, and political struggle would remain ascendant for a generation.

Hurston's muddled perspective in *Dust Tracks* inspired no adherents. The fact that the book won the Anisfield-Wolf award (sponsored by *Saturday Review*) for its contribution to race relations says more about the state of race relations in the nation than about the clarity of Hurston's views. One source of the book's incoherence was the publisher's last-minute insistence on extensive revisions, notably the deletion of an extended critique of U.S. imperialism. *Dust Tracks* was by far Hurston's most heavily edited book, and the editorial changes were rarely for the better.[97] Yet, even a knowledgeable and sensitive editor would have been hard-pressed to extract a sustained perspective from Hurston's manuscript. The book's value derived instead from the beauty of the "linguistic moments" it represented. Some, such as the accounts of Lucy Hurston's death and of Big Sweet's specifying, were as fine as any in Hurston's writing. But most of the book's glints and gleams shone less brightly.

As dependent on patronage as when she began her career, Hurston had written much of her book in California, where she lived on the largesse of Katherine Mershon, another wealthy white woman. By the time *Dust Tracks* was published in November, Hurston was back in Florida, teaching creative writing part-time at Florida Normal College in Saint Augustine. She had spent the previous spring lecturing at southern black colleges and the summer collecting folklore in Florida. The wanderings that, as she wrote, commenced with her mother's death defined her life still: wanderings in geography, in time, and in spirit.

And yet, *Dust Tracks on a Road* was Zora Neale Hurston's sixth book in eight years. (A seventh, the novel *Seraph on the Suwanee*, was published in 1948.) During the meanest years of the depression, she had managed to write and to publish books, short stories, essays, and reviews virtually without interruption. Whether in college or graduate school, in the field, or working for the Federal Writers Project, she stole time to write. Often those with whom she shared her life— whether at school, on the job, or at home—had no knowledge of what her real work was. Nevertheless, she had somehow gotten it done. Whatever doubts she harbored about the lasting value of her work, she could look back on her life and sing with the blues singer:

Got on de train didn't have no fare
But I rode some
Yes I rode some.
Got on de train didn't have no fare
Conductor ask me what I'm doing there
But I rode some
Yes I rode some.

EPILOGUE

DESTINATIONS DEFERRED

On 27 March 1950, the *Miami Herald* carried a feature headlined "Famous Negro Author Working as a Maid Here Just 'to Live a Little.'" The headline introduced a series of paradoxes: the fact that a famous author was working as a maid, that domestic work represented a way to "live a little," that such an entity as a famous Negro author existed in Florida in 1950, and that fame—racially circumscribed though it was—could make so little difference in a black woman's life. The article recounted how an employer had been surprised to come across her "girl's" byline in a national magazine. "Conscience of the Court," a short story by Zora Neale Hurston, appeared in the *Saturday Evening Post* in March 1950. Its author, who had first done domestic work as a teenager, had traveled a long way to end up where she started.

"You can only use your mind for so long. Then you have to use your hands," a clearly abashed Hurston had explained to the journalist when he arrived to interview her. She was temporarily "written out." Although he had apparently never heard of Zora Neale Hurston, the reporter was convinced of her standing as a writer: she had published in the *Saturday Evening Post*. Charmed by her "infectious good spirits" and disarmed by her modesty, he was deaf to the contradictions in her story. She was written out, but she had recently sent a novel and three new stories to her agent. Or, she had taken this job to research the potential of establishing a magazine by and for do-

mestic workers. Then, she had declined offers of financial help from her friends in the literary community, who had heard of her financial straits. Besides, she planned to sail for Honduras in the fall to explore the interior of that "forgotten paradise." To black Americans, she offered this article of faith: "if you do well today all that you are permitted to do, tomorrow you will be entrusted with something better."

Had the journalist, James Lyons, read the preface to *Mules and Men*, he might have recognized this "feather-bed resistance" for what it was. He had asked his questions, "trying to know into somebody else's business," but she had "set something outside the door of my mind for him to play with and handle. He can read my writing but he sho' can't read my mind" (*Mules*, 3). Her "lies" masked the desperation of her situation; they did not protect her privacy. Instead, her lies proved so entertaining that the story was picked up by the national wire services.

Threads of truth were woven into the fabric of Hurston's lies. She had completed a new novel, but, like at least two earlier book manuscripts and the stories, it was not publishable. Her desire to explore the interior region of Honduras was rooted in reality. She had lived on the coast for almost a year while writing *Seraph on the Suwanee*. Her dream of discovering lost treasure in Central America was another matter. The commercial failure of the novel (a turgid melodrama of white Floridian life) helped keep this dream alive. By this time, Hurston had ample reason to prefer dreams to the realities of her life.

The most bitter reality was the scandal that had engulfed her in 1948. In September, Hurston was falsely accused of molesting a ten-year-old boy, the son of the Harlem landlady who had rented her a room the previous winter. Hurston was arrested and indicted, solely on the word of her young accuser. By mid-October, the press, notably the *Baltimore Afro-American*, was onto the story as the result of a tip from a black court employee. Shocked and devastated by these events, Hurston denied the charges, presented her passport as evidence that she was in Honduras when the alleged crime occurred, wondered whether racism was the impulse behind the court's acceptance of the emotionally disturbed child's accusations, and vowed "to

fight this horrible thing to the finish and clear my reputation." The case against her was finally dismissed in March 1949.[1]

Under the circumstances, Hurston's "infectious good spirits" so noticeable a year later bespoke her steadfast refusal to be "tragically colored." In retrospect, they deepen the tragic dimension of her life. Hurston's powers as a writer had long been on the wane. Some of the essays and stories she published during the 1940s, notably "High John de Conquer" and "Story in Harlem Slang," captured the flair and the force of her earlier writing; a few essays like "Crazy for this Democracy" wrapped sophisticated political critique in the glove of folk humor, but many pieces were little more than hack work. Age, ill health, and a spiritual crisis that she experienced, perhaps while doing fieldwork in Haiti, deepened her preoccupation with spiritual matters until they became an obsession. Her iconoclastic views on race matters calcified. The pithy adages that had adorned her fiction turned into platitudes like those she offered as her credo to the *Miami Herald* reporter. While Hurston's nostrums on self-help reflected a world view as illusionary as the quest for lost treasure, their circulation in the media made their effect pernicious. Hurston spent the last ten years of her life writing a biography of Herod the Great, which no one would read.

To some of Hurston's critics, her life seems a metaphor for the black woman writer. The idea resonates when one considers the situation of her peers. Their work had similarly faded from view. Indeed, most of the other women writers of the Harlem Renaissance had given up their literary careers by 1950. Many had gone on to lead impressively productive lives. Gwendolyn Bennett became an art teacher, director of an art center in Harlem, and, in retirement, an antiques dealer in rural Pennsylvania. After publishing a cluster of stories about a racially mixed, working-class Chicago neighborhood marked by economic conflict and cultural exchange, Marita Bonner stopped writing in 1941; subsequently, she raised three children and taught school. After retiring as a school librarian in 1945, Anne Spencer lived, wrote, cultivated her garden, and fought for civil rights in Lynchburg. Like Hurston, Georgia Douglas Johnson, who worked at a series of civil service jobs following her widowhood in 1925, con-

tinued to write; her final, self-published volume of poems, *Share My World*, appeared in 1962. The ever elusive Helene Johnson married, gave birth to a daughter, and withdrew from public life. Jessie Fauset moved with her husband to Montclair, New Jersey, in 1939; thereafter, apart from teaching, including a semester at Hampton Institute in 1949, she limited her activity to local cultural affairs. And, for almost two decades, Nella Larsen was employed as a nurse working the night shift at a Manhattan hospital.[2]

But more than the inattention paid to their writing, more even than the notable productivity of their lives links Hurston to her peers. What makes Hurston's life emblematic is the capacity for self-invention that allowed her to become an artist in the first place. That capacity is depicted in the fictional representations of Joanna Marshall and Clare Kendry and in lyric portraits such as Anne Spencer's "Lady, Lady." Their authors had also to invent themselves at a time when the terms "black," "woman," and "artist" were never complementary.

As her changes of name and identity demonstrate, Nella Larsen was continually reinventing herself. In her novels, she staged performances of identity for her protagonists, which reveal her awareness of the risks of asserting a self at odds with societal expectations, even as they expose her complicity with myths of race and gender. As she traveled from the parsonage in Philadelphia to the Pan-African conference in Paris and to Algiers, Jessie Fauset tried on the new ways of thinking that enabled her to become a writer. If, in her fiction, the values of her past prevail over these new ideas, the example she set by leaving and by writing is key. For a time, even that example appeared to be lost.

In the early 1960s, Hurston, Fauset, and Larsen died within four years of each other. Following a stroke, Hurston died of hypertensive heart disease on 28 January 1960 in the Saint Lucie County, Florida, welfare home. Fauset died of the same ailment in Philadelphia on 30 April 1961. A relative had taken her in after Herbert Harris's death two years earlier, when suffering from physical infirmities and senility, Fauset was no longer able to care for herself. Nella Larsen had been dead for several days when her body was found on 30 March 1964. Her coworkers had grown concerned when she failed to report

for her shift.[3] All three women died from illnesses associated with old age. For those few people who recalled their literary careers, their writing belonged to a bygone era. None of their books was in print. If their life journeys had ended, their writing—and that of their peers— had also been consigned to the past.

Then a new generation of black women writers came of age and went, in Alice Walker's evocative phrase, "in search of our mothers' gardens." They went in search, that is, of artistic models and a literary legacy. Individually and collectively, the biographies of the women of the Harlem Renaissance offer both models and cautionary tales. But if these literary foremothers were sometimes unable to *live* their dreams and convictions, they left a legacy in their art. Their literary legatees critique, revise, and extend the themes, forms, and metaphors that they employed in their poetry and fiction. Perhaps the most telling act of recuperation and revision is the determination of this new generation to bring to the surface those themes and plots that their precursors masked. The subtext has become the text. The lives and work of the women of the Harlem Renaissance constitute a chapter in a literary history that is in the process of being written and made.

NOTES

Prologue

1. Bennett to Harold Jackman, 23 February 1926; 17 May 1926, James Weldon Johnson Collection (JWJ), Yale University.
2. Bennett to James Weldon Johnson, 4 January 1938, JWJ.
3. For an extended biography, see Sandra Govan, "Gwendolyn Bennett: Portrait of an Artist Lost," dissertation, Emory University, 1980.

1. On Being Young—A Woman—and Colored

1. My title alludes to the essay by Marita Bonner discussed below and to the title of David Lewis's history of the Harlem Renaissance, *When Harlem Was in Vogue* (New York: Knopf, 1981); Lewis's title was itself an allusion to Langston Hughes's designation for the 1920s as the time "When the Negro Was in Vogue" in *The Big Sea* (New York: Knopf, 1940).
2. *The New Negro* (1925; rpt. New York: Atheneum, 1992), 4. The standard intellectual history of the period is Nathan Huggins, *Harlem Renaissance* (New York: Oxford University Press, 1971). Lewis's volume is unparalleled in its delineation of the period's social, political, and cultural life. Other general studies and anthologies include Arna Bontemps, ed., *The Harlem Renaissance Remembered* (New York: Dodd, Mead, 1971); Nathan Huggins, ed., *Voices from the Harlem Renaissance* (New York: Oxford University Press, 1976); Arthur P. Davis and Michael Peplow, eds., *The New Negro Renaissance* (New York: Holt, Rinehart & Winston, 1975); Victor Kramer, ed., *The Harlem Renaissance Re-examined* (New York: AMS Press, 1987); Amritjit Singh, William Shiver, and S. Brodwin, eds., *The Harlem Renaissance: Revaluations* (New York: Garland, 1989); and Cary D. Wintz, *Black Culture and the Harlem Renaissance* (Houston: Rice University Press, 1988). For revisionist analyses, see Houston Baker, *Modernism and the Harlem Renaissance* (Chicago: University of Chicago Press, 1987) and Hazel Carby, *Reconstructing Womanhood: The*

Emergence of the Afro-American Woman Novelist (New York: Oxford University Press, 1987).

3. Locke's analysis follows the model of Sigmund Freud, *Group Psychology and the Analysis of the Ego*, published in 1921. For discussions of earlier interpretations of "the New Negro," see Huggins, 52–72; Henry Louis Gates, "The Trope of the New Negro and the Reconstruction of the Image of the Black," *Representations* 24 (Fall 1988): 129–55, and Hazel Carby, 165.

4. These interpretations were somewhat at odds with the facts. To be sure, the numbers were dramatic. Over 400,000 blacks left the South between 1916 and 1918. Between 1915 and 1930, New York's black population grew over 250 percent, from 91,709 in 1910 to 327,706 in 1930. Although New York's black population was largest in absolute numbers, rate of growth in midwestern cities including Chicago, Detroit, and Cleveland was even higher (Wintz, 14). But many of the migrants did not come directly from rural areas; they had previously migrated to southern cities. A substantial number of the men were skilled laborers; they found jobs in the North not unlike those they held previously. Especially after the war, during which some women were able to obtain factory jobs, the majority of black women were domestic workers; although certain conditions of employment were different in the North—e.g., they were more likely to be "day workers" than live-in workers as they had been in the South—the character of the work was not dissimilar. For further analysis of this point, see Carole Marks, *Farewell—We're Good and Gone* (Bloomington: Indiana University Press, 1989), chap. 2. Despite the distinctive regional differences then, the journey from the South to the North was not quite analogous to a flight from "medieval America to modern." And, of course, although there was less racist terrorism in the North, blacks were hardly free of "racial problems."

5. Scholars have written extensively on Harlem's historic and symbolic significance. See, for example, Jervis Anderson, *This Was Harlem: A Cultural Portrait, 1900–1950* (New York: Farrar Straus Giroux, 1982); John Henrik Clarke, ed., *Harlem: A Community in Transition* (New York: Citadel Press, 1969); Harold Cruse, *The Crisis of the Negro Intellectual* (New York: Morrow, 1967); James de Jongh, *Vicious Modernism: Black Harlem and the Literary Imagination* (New York: Cambridge University Press, 1990); and Gilbert Osofsky, *Harlem: The Making of a Ghetto* (New York: Harper, 1971). Two pioneering studies of the community are James Weldon Johnson, *Black Manhattan* (New York: Knopf, 1930); Claude McKay, *Harlem: Negro Metropolis* (New York: Dutton, 1940).

6. The iconography of the first edition of *The New Negro* includes more representations of women than does the text, but it depicts them mainly in traditional roles. The most extreme example is the volume's frontispiece, "The Brown Madonna," by the German painter Winold Reiss. It depicts a youthful brown-skinned woman, hair curled into a pageboy, eyes looking downward, holding a plump curly-haired infant of indeterminate gender; the child's eyes, not the mother's, confront the viewer. Reiss also produced a series of portraits of Harlem Renaissance notables, including Locke, Jean

Toomer, Cullen, Paul Robeson (as "Emperor Jones"), Roland Hayes, Charles S. Johnson, James Weldon Johnson, Robert Russa Moton, and Du Bois. The women in the series were the educators Elise Johnson Mc-Dougald and Mary McLeod Bethune. Female figures were the focus of other sketches entitled "African Phantasie: Awakening," "Type Sketch: 'Ancestral,'" "From the Tropic Isles," "The Librarian," and "The School Teachers." The last three are notable for their depiction of dark-skinned women with distinctively Negroid features. Reiss's student Aaron Douglas drew abstract female figures in African-inspired motifs. Miguel Covarrubias drew the figure of a blues singer to illustrate poems by Langston Hughes.

7. "On Being Young—A Woman—and Colored," in *Frye Street & Environs: The Collected Works of Marita Bonner* (Boston: Beacon Press, 1987), 5. Subsequent references to this edition will be cited in the text.

8. The story of Bonner's notebooks is reminiscent of the publishing history of Alice Dunbar-Nelson's diary edited by Gloria Hull, *Give Us Each Day: The Diary of Alice Dunbar-Nelson* (New York: Norton, 1984). Hull recounts her discovery of the manuscript and her relationship with the diarist's niece who preserved it in "Researching Alice Dunbar-Nelson: A Personal and Literary Perspective," in *All the Women Are White, All the Blacks Are Men, But Some of Us Are Brave: Black Women's Studies*, ed. Gloria Hull, Patricia Scott, and Barbara Smith (Old Westbury: Feminist Press, 1982).

9. *When and Where I Enter: The Impact of Black Women on Race and Sex in America* (New York: Morrow, 1984), 183. Giddings asserts that "femininity, not feminism was the talk of the twenties." The idea that black women could be beautiful fit both the call to race pride and the dominant culture's emphasis on glamour.

10. 1926; rpt. in Nathan Huggins, ed., *Voices from the Harlem Renaissance* (New York: Oxford University Press, 1976), 306. Subsequent references to this edition will be cited in the text.

11. In addition to biographical and critical works on individual authors, feminist revisions of Harlem Renaissance studies include Maureen Honey, ed., *Shadowed Dreams: Women's Poetry of the Harlem Renaissance* (New Brunswick, NJ: Rutgers University Press, 1989); Gloria Hull, *Color, Sex, and Poetry: Three Women Writers of the Harlem Renaissance* (Bloomington: Indiana University Press, 1987); Lorraine Roses and Ruth Elizabeth Randolph, *Harlem Renaissance and Beyond: Literary Biographies of 100 Black Women Writers, 1900–1945* (Boston: G.K. Hall, 1990); Ann Allen Shockley, *Afro-American Women Writers, 1746–1933* (New York: New American Library, 1989); Cheryl A. Wall, "Poets and Versifiers, Singers and Signifiers: the Women of the Harlem Renaissance," in Kenneth Wheeler and Virginia Lussier, eds., *Women, the Arts, and the 1920s in Paris and New York* (New Brunswick: Transaction Press, 1982), 74–98; Mary Helen Washington, *Invented Lives: Narratives of Black Women 1860–1960* (New York: Anchor Books, 1987).

12. For a cogent summary of these debates, see Robert Stepto, "Sterling A. Brown: Outsider in the Harlem Renaissance?" in *The Harlem Renaissance: Revaluations*, ed. Amritjit Singh et al.

13. Nathan Huggins, *Voices from the Harlem Renaissance*, 3; Davis and Peplow, xxi; Kellner, *The Harlem Renaissance: A Historical Dictionary for the Era* (New York: Methuen, 1984), xxiv. Perhaps the most open-ended dates come from Houston Baker. In *Modernism and the Harlem Renaissance*, he perceives the awakening as a moment on a continuum that embraces Booker T. Washington and Charles Chesnutt on one end, and Richard Wright on the other. To my mind, Washington is at most a precursor of the Renaissance and one against which a number of authors write, while Wright represents a sharp break with the movement's prevailing trends. I find the notion of continuum very useful nonetheless.

14. Hull, *Color, Sex, and Poetry*, 30.

15. Sterling Brown, Arthur P. Davis, and Ulysses Lee, eds., *The Negro Caravan*. (1941; rpt. New York: Arno Press, 1969), 279; 142. The comments on Hurston's fiction are most positive. One notes that she "has written more fully than any other Negro of Southern rural life." Another judges that "sympathy and authenticity mark her work" (143). Significantly, all of the folktales in the anthology are taken from *Mules and Men*; a folk sermon from Hurston's novel *Jonah's Gourd Vine* is also reprinted in the "Folk Literature" section. The introductions do not draw attention to the fact that Hurston is among the best-represented authors in the volume.

16. *A Voice from the South* (1892; rpt. New York: Oxford University Press, 1988), 134. Cooper anticipated many of the themes Locke would use to promote the New Negro. For example: "Everything to this race is new and strange and inspiring. There is a quickening of its pulses and a glowing of its self-consciousness. Aha, I can rival that! I can aspire to that! I can honor my name and vindicate my race! Something like this, it strikes me, is the enthusiasm which stirs the genius of young Africa in America. . . ." (144–45). But she insisted that the regeneration of the race must begin with the black woman (28).

17. Gwendolyn Bennett, Jessie Fauset, Angelina Grimké, Zora Neale Hurston, Georgia Douglas Johnson, Helene Johnson, and Anne Spencer were the other female contributors. Fauset was the only other essayist. Hurston was represented by a short story, "Spunk," while the other women contributed poems. Total contributors to *The New Negro* numbered thirty-six, including Locke.

18. An important exception to this rule was the lesbian poet Mae Cowdery, whose work is notable for its exploration of erotic themes. For examples of these, see Honey, *Shadowed Dreams*, 129–39; Cowdery published a volume of poems, *We Lift Our Voices* (Philadelphia: Alpress Publishers, 1936).

19. *The Crisis* (April 1927): 49. The poem is reprinted in Maureen Honey, *Shadowed Dreams*, 60.

20. I think, for example, of Dunbar-Nelson's "I Sit and Sew" and Grimké's "Little Grey Dreams" and "Under the Days." For a detailed study of the lives and work of Johnson, Dunbar-Nelson, and Grimké, see Gloria Hull, *Color, Sex, and Poetry*.

21. J. Lee Greene, *Time's Unfading Garden: Anne Spencer's Life and Poetry* (Baton Rouge: Louisiana State University Press, 1977), 176.

22. In his biography cited above, J. Lee Greene details Spencer's successful efforts to organize a Lynchburg affiliate of the NAACP, to hire black teachers for the high school, and to organize the first public library to serve Lynchburg's black community.

23. Cullen, *Caroling Dusk: An Anthology of Verse by Negro Poets* (New York: Harper, 1967), 47.

24. Greene, 179.

25. Written by Bessie Smith. Recorded October 26, 1926, with Joe Smith, cornet; Buster Bailey, clarinet; Fletcher Henderson, piano; and Bessie Smith, vocals. Columbia 14179-D.

26. Ortiz Walton, *Music: Black, White & Blue* (New York: William Morrow, 1972), 28.

27. Carole Marks, 159.

28. Remarks by northern-born artist/intellectual Paul Robeson may illustrate the point. Speaking to an integrated audience in New Orleans in 1942, Robeson acknowledged that he "had never put a correct evaluation on the dignity and courage of my people of the deep South until I began to come south myself. . . . Deep down, I think, I had imagined Negroes of the South beaten, subservient, cowed." But his visits changed the view of the prominent actor, concert singer, and activist. He concluded, "I find that I must come south again and again, again and yet again. It is only here that I achieve absolute and utter identity with my people." "We Must Come South," in Robert Yancy Dent, ed., *Paul Robeson: Tributes and Selected Writings* (New York: Paul Robeson Archives, 1976), 64.

29. Written by Bessie Smith. Recorded on May 15, 1925, with Charlie Green, trombone; Buster Bailey, trumpet; Fred Longshaw, piano; James T. Wilson, miscellaneous sound effects; and Bessie Smith, vocals. Columbia 14079-D.

30. Marks cites all but the last of these in *Farewell—We're Good and Gone*, 123. One depiction of the negative impact of the migration on family life in *The New Negro* is "Vestiges," a series of sketches by Rudolph Fisher.

31. *The Book of American Negro Poetry*, 281.

32. Kenneth Clark, "A Conversation with James Baldwin," in Clark, ed., *Harlem: A Community in Transition*, 124.

33. In her entry for "mammy" in "Glossary of Harlem Slang," Zora Neale Hurston wrote "a term of insult. Never used in any other way by Negroes." Reprinted in *Spunk: The Selected Short Stories of Zora Neale Hurston* (Berkeley: Turtle Island Foundation, 1985), 94.

34. "How It Feels," in Alice Walker, ed., *I Love Myself When I Am Laughing . . . And Then Again When I Am Looking Mean and Impressive: A Zora Neale Hurston Reader* (New York: Feminist Press, 1979), 152. Subsequent references to this edition will be cited in the text.

35. In *Dust Tracks on a Road*, Hurston elaborates on the tensions operative in her relationships with her Eatonville neighbors. She considered herself

too curious, too imaginative, too unladylike, and too bold a child to be at ease with the dull, hardworking townspeople, who enforced their discipline with a palmetto switch. She escaped through books: "My soul was with the gods and my body in the village. People just would not act like gods. Stew beef, fried fat-back and morning grits were no ambrosia from Valhalla" (1942; Second Edition. Urbana: University of Illinois Press, 1984), 56. Hurston's views seem based in equal measure on her egotism, the town's provincialism, and her distaste for her family and neighbors' acceptance of racial and gender restrictions.

36. Gates, "Trope of a New Negro," 132.

37. Although I know of no specific reference to the term "New Negro," Hurston's impatience with the rhetoric of racial advancement is well documented. She enjoyed referring satirically to race leaders as "Negrotarians." In his description of her relationship to her colleagues on the journal *Fire!!*, Robert Hemenway notes that Hurston, "probably the quickest wit in a very witty lot . . . proclaimed herself 'Queen of the Niggerati'" (22–23, 44).

38. In a fascinating reading of Hurston's essay, Barbara Johnson glosses this passage thus: "The move into the jungle is a move into mask; the return to civilization is a return to veneer. Either way, what is at stake is an artificial, ornamental surface." Moreover, Johnson views Hurston's manipulation of color in this scene as a subversion of the binary oppositions (black/white, jungle/civilization) it addresses. See "Thresholds of Difference," 177.

39. Fisher, "The Caucasian Storms Harlem," in *Voices from the Harlem Renaissance*, 75, 80, 81.

40. *Harlem Renaissance*, 89–90.

41. James Weldon Johnson, *Black Manhattan* (New York: Knopf, 1930), 161.

42. In his critique of Harlem fiction, Sterling Brown described as "exotic primitives" those characters "whose dances—the Charleston, the 'black bottom,' the 'snake hips,' the 'walking the dog'—were tribal rituals; whose music with wa-wa trumpets and trombones and drum batteries doubled for tom-toms; whose chorus girls with bunches of bananas girding their shapely middles nurtured tourists' delusions of the 'Congo creeping through the black.'" He castigated as opportunists those black writers who, cashing in on the Negro vogue, treated "*joie de vivre* as a racial monopoly." See Brown, "A Century of Negro Portraiture in American Literature," 1966. Rpt. Abraham Chapman, ed., *Black Voices* (New York: New American Library, 1968) 564–89. No literary text offers a more scathing indictment of this cultural exploitation than Brown's own poem "Cabaret."

43. "'A Nutmeg Nestled Inside Its Covering of Mace': Audre Lorde's *Zami*," in Bella Brodzki and Celeste Schenck, eds., *Life/Lines: Theorizing Women's Autobiography* (Ithaca: Cornell University Press, 1988), 221. Another similarity worth considering is the way in which Hurston and Lorde image "home." Note for example Lorde's representation of Carriacou, the birthplace of her mother: "But underneath it all as I was growing up, *home* was still a sweet place somewhere else which they had not managed to capture yet on paper, nor to throttle and bind up between the pages of a schoolbook.

It was our own, my truly private paradise of blugoe and breadfruit hanging from the trees, of nutmeg and lime and sapadilla, of tonka beans and red and yellow Paradise Plums." See *Zami: A New Spelling of My Name* (Freedom, CA: Crossing Press, 1982), 14.

44. Chinosole, "Audre Lorde and Matrilineal Diaspora," in Joanne Braxton and Andree McLaughlin, eds., *Wild Women in the Whirlwind: Afra-American Culture and the Contemporary Literary Renaissance* (New Brunswick, NJ: Rutgers University Press, 1990), 379–94.

45. *I Love Myself*, 153. Not only was Hurston being paid for her own words; she was writing to pay for the words of a group of fellow artists. She wrote the article for *World Tomorrow*, a "progressive" white journal, to earn money to pay the bills still outstanding for *Fire!!*, the avant-garde black journal edited by Wallace Thurman, et al., in 1926.

See Priscilla Wald, "Becoming 'Colored': The Self-Authorized Language of Difference in Zora Neale Hurston," for a discussion of Hurston's rhetoric on race. *American Literary History* 2, 1 (1990): 79–100.

46. Written by Clarence Williams. Recorded on November 17, 1925, with Clarence Williams, piano, and Bessie Smith, vocals. Columbia 14109-D.

47. This notion of "home" is ancestral or spiritual; it does not denote the domestic sphere. For some of Hurston's contemporaries, notably Jessie Fauset, the ancestral home and the domestic hearth are one.

48. Analyzing the importance of Eatonville in what she terms "Hurston's mythology," Nellie McKay asserts: "In respect to race, the community Hurston claims might strike us as romantically idealized, but the specialness of its history is in the deprivileging of and liberation from the supremacy of American slave history over other aspects of the black American experience." ("Race, Gender, and Cultural Context," in Brodzki and Schenck, *Life/Lines: Theorizing Women's Autobiography*, 183).

49. In "Feminist Politics: What's Home Got to Do with It?" Martin and Mohanty analyze the autobiography of Minnie Bruce Pratt, a white, upper-class southerner, whose feminist politics and lesbianism force her to deconstruct the illusion that is her southern home. A signal difference between Hurston and Pratt is that Hurston, even in the awareness of its sexism and the destructive impact of the dominant society's racism, never rejects her Eatonville home. "Feminist Politics," in Teresa de Lauretis, ed., *Feminist Studies, Critical Studies* (Bloomington: Indiana University Press, 1986), 191–212.

2. Jessie Redmon Fauset

1. "Dark Algiers the White," *The Crisis* (April 1925): 255–58; (May 1925): 16–22. Page references will be made parenthetically in the text.

2. Fauset had hoped to visit Dakar, Senegal, on this trip as well. Letter to Langston Hughes, 20 April 1924, Langston Hughes Papers (LHP). In 1923, Hughes had sailed to West Africa on the crew of a freighter, which docked at

ports in Senegal, Nigeria, the Cameroons, the Belgian Congo, Angola, the Gold Coast, and the Ivory Coast. The same year Du Bois made his first journey to Africa, when he visited Liberia. Three years after Fauset's article appeared, McKay arrived in Casablanca; he lived in Morocco off and on until 1934.

3. Most egregious is the reference to "porters agile as monkeys [who] swarmed up narrow rope-ladders over the side of the ship," 255–56.

4. Hughes, 218; Lewis, 121.

5. According to Carolyn W. Sylvander in *Jessie Redmon Fauset, Black American Writer* (Troy, NY: Whitson, 1981), outgoing secretary Mary Childs Nerney proposed Fauset's name in 1916 (42). No black person had then held the post. See also Charles Flint Kellogg, *NAACP: A History of the National Association for the Advancement of Colored People, Vol. I* (Baltimore: Johns Hopkins University Press, 1967), chap. 5.

6. Arnold Rampersad, *I, Too, Sing America. The Life of Langston Hughes, Vol. I* (New York: Oxford University Press, 1986), 48; Cullen, *Caroling Dusk*, 74.

7. Sterling Brown set the tone for Fauset criticism when he labelled her "an apologist. She records a class in order to praise a race." See *Negro Poetry and Drama and the Negro in American Fiction* (1937; rpt. New York: Atheneum, 1968), 142. Robert Bone and Blyden Jackson, two of Fauset's harshest critics, follow Brown's lead. For Bone, her novels are "uniformly sophomoric, trivial and dull." He attributes these weaknesses to her privileged background as an "Old Philadelphian," concluding that she was "never able to transcend the narrow limits of this sheltered world" (101, 102). According to Jackson, "for all the nobility of her intentions, because she is herself so naively philistine, so breathless with adoration for good-looking people Nordic style (even when they are tinted with the tar brush), good-looking clothes, good-looking homes and country club ideas of *summa bona*, Jessie Fauset's defense of the Negro middle-class backfires into an indictment of her horrid copycatting of the wrong values" ("A Golden Mean for the Negro Novel," *CLA Journal* 3, Dec. 1959: 85). Feminist critics have paid relatively little attention to Fauset's writing. Mary Helen Washington excludes Fauset from consideration in *Invented Lives*. In *Reconstructing Womanhood*, Hazel Carby dismisses her work brusquely, after finding that "ultimately the conservatism of Fauset's ideology dominates her text" (167). Fauset biographer Carolyn Sylvander and critic Deborah McDowell are among the few scholars currently reconstructing the black female tradition to analyze Fauset's novels in detail.

8. *The Chinaberry Tree* (New York: Frederick A. Stokes, 1931), ix.

9. The Fauset family Bible gives Fredericksville, New Jersey, as Jessie's birthplace. Sylvander notes that Fauset's middle name was "Redmona." After Anna Fauset's death, Redmon Fauset married Belle Huff, a widow with three children of her own. Two sons, Arthur and Redmond, and a daughter, Marian, were born of this marriage. At her death, Jessie Fauset was living with her stepbrother, Earl Huff.

10. She wrote Alain Locke to ask whether he would mention in one of his essays for *The New Negro* that Arthur Huff Fauset was her brother: "I would

like it and I find it opens up an occasional doorway to him. Also it's nice for my father's memory from whom both of us receive such talent as we possess along this line." Letter, n.d., Alain Locke Papers/Moorland-Spingarn Research Center.

11. Interview with Arthur Huff Fauset.

12. *The Crisis* (Feb. 1922): 162.

13. Florida Smith Vincent, "There Are 20,000 Persons 'Passing' Says Noted Author," *The New York Evening Telegram*, rpt. in *The Pittsburgh Courier*, 11 May 1929.

14. Sylvander reconstructs the sequence of events that led to Fauset's matriculation at Cornell. She quotes a letter from Bryn Mawr president M. Carey Thomas in which Thomas mentions making herself responsible for Miss Jessie Fawcett's [*sic*] $60 tuition bill (28). One may infer that Thomas preferred paying Fauset's bill at Cornell to having her on campus at Bryn Mawr.

15. "Chiefly classical" was the description Fauset used in a letter to Du Bois, 26 December 1903, Herbert Aptheker, *The Correspondence of W. E. B. Du Bois* (Amherst: University of Massachusetts Press, 1973), 66. The course list is taken from Sylvander, 29. Fauset described herself as the "only colored girl" in a letter to Du Bois, 16 February 1905, *The Correspondence*, 95.

16. Letter to W. E. B. Du Bois, 26 December 1903; letter to Du Bois, 16 February 1905, Aptheker, *Correspondence*, 66, 94–95.

17. Paula Giddings, *When and Where I Enter*, 105; In its annual education number, *The Crisis* heralded the achievement of Sadie Tanner Mossell, Ph.D., University of Pennsylvania; Eva B. Dykes, Ph.D. Radcliffe; and Georgiana Simpson, Ph.D., University of Chicago. Dykes and Simpson taught at Dunbar High School (July 1921): 105, 106.

18. For details of the Smith case, see Sylvander, 39–42.

19. "Tracing Shadows," *The Crisis* (Sept. 1915): 247–51.

20. Fauset's appointment was announced in the "Men of the Month" column of *The Crisis* (Nov. 1919): 341. See Sylvander, 53.

21. *The Crisis* (Nov. 1910): 10.

22. Hughes is quoted in Steven Tracy, *Langston Hughes & the Blues* (Urbana: University of Illinois Press, 1988), 39–40. Rampersad quotes Spingarn in *The Art and Imagination of W. E. B. Du Bois* (Cambridge: Harvard University Press, 1976), 138. Saunders Redding, "Portrait of W. E. Burghardt Du Bois," *American Scholar* 18 (Winter 1948–1949): 93. The NAACP Archives referred to are located in the Library of Congress.

23. *The Crisis* (January 1919): 111; *The Crisis*, (February 1919): 173. Articles on the black participation in the war and the Paris Peace Conference, which Du Bois attended, proliferated throughout the year. Another prominent topic was the Pan-African Congress, which Du Bois organized.

24. Sept. 1919: 235.

25. *The Crisis* (April 1919): 277.

26. *Darkwater: Voices from within the Veil* (1920; rpt. New York: Schocken Books, 1969), 164–65.

27. "The Emancipator of Brazil," *The Crisis* (March 1921): 208–209; "Saint-George, Chevalier of France," *The Crisis* (May 1921): 9–12; "Looking Backward," *The Crisis* (January 1922): 125–26.

28. "Impressions of the Second Pan-African Congress," *The Crisis* (Nov. 1921): 12–18, 15. Subsequent references will be cited in the text.

29. Du Bois, who remained a dedicated Pan-Africanist all his life—he died in Ghana in 1963 at the age of ninety-five—overcame this African-American hubris. For an account of the evolution of his Pan-Africanism, see Sterling Stuckey, *Slave Culture: Nationalist Theory and the Foundations of Black America* (New York: Oxford University Press, 1987), 245–302.

30. "What Europe Thought of the Pan-African Congress," *The Crisis* (Dec. 1921): 66.

31. "The Thirteenth Biennial of the N.A.C.W.," *The Crisis* (Oct. 1922): 260.

32. For example, in the same issue of *The Crisis*, Fauset reviewed *Negro Folk Rhymes* by Thomas Talley. She wrote that the book was "extensive" and "fair" and averred that the "salient characteristics of the Negro are traceable in these songs." Among these she numbered "his sense of humor, his dryness, his tendency to make fun of himself, and above all his love of the sudden climax." But if they constituted "valuable and enlightening" sociological documents, "from the standpoint of beauty, these songs fail to satisfy" (68). I agree with Sylvander that for Fauset dialect is the barrier to beauty (109).

33. "The Symbolism of Bert Williams," *The Crisis* (May 1922): 12–15. A slightly revised version of this essay, "The Gift of Laughter," was published in *The New Negro*.

34. For more information, see Elinor Desverney Sinnette, "*The Brownies' Book*: A Pioneer Publication for Children," *Freedomways* (Winter 1965): 133–42.

35. "New Literature of the Negro," *The Crisis* (June 1920): 79; "No End of Books," *The Crisis* (March 1922): 208.

36. *The Crisis* (June 1922): 66–69.

37. *The Crisis* (March 1926): 238–39.

38. René Maran, *Batouala*, trans. Adele Szold Seltzer (New York: Thomas Seltzer, 1922), 105.

39. Jessie Fauset to Joel Spingarn, 25 Jan. 1922, Joel Spingarn Collection/NYPL.

40. "Pastures New," *The Crisis* (Sept. 1920): 224–26. In her review, Fauset had reflected on the difficulties of translation: "French poetry does not lend itself easily to our harsher, less flexible mold. So it is almost impossible to bring over to the reader in English, the verse of Haiti and have him perceive its charm" (225). Fauset's translation was published in James Weldon Johnson's *Book of American Negro Poetry* second edition (New York: Harcourt Brace and World, 1931), 208.

41. *The Crisis* (Jan. 1920): 128.

42. *The Crisis* (July 1922): 124.

43. *A Long Way from Home* (1937; rpt. New York: Harcourt, Brace & World, 1970), 112.

44. Letters to Jean Toomer, 17 February 1922; 22 August 1923, Jean Toomer Collection, Fisk University Archives. "Song of the Son" appeared in April 1922; "Banking Coal" appeared in *The Crisis* (June 1922): 65. Fauset to A. Spingarn, 20 January 1923, Arthur B. Spingarn Papers, MSRC.

45. Countee Cullen, "The League of Youth," *The Crisis* (August 1923): 167–68. Fauset to Cullen, 1 May 1923; 20 July 1923; n.d. [Oct. 1925?], Countee Cullen Papers.

46. "The Awakening," 15. Bontemps's poem "Hope" was published in *The Crisis* (Aug. 1924): 126.

47. Fauset recounts this incident in "Our Book Shelf," which contains her review of *The Weary Blues*. *The Crisis* (March 1926): 239.

48. Fauset to Hughes, n.d., LHP; *The Big Sea*, 94.

49. Fauset to Langston Hughes, 28 May 1923, LHP; Rampersad offers the best account of Fauset's role as a mentor in *The Life, Vol. I*, chaps. 2–5, *passim*.

50. This judgment was plainly social rather than literary. Critical opinion of the volume has climbed steadily upward. Rampersad deems it Hughes's "most brilliant book of poems and one of the more astonishing books of verse ever published in the United States—comparable in the black world to *Leaves of Grass* in the white" (*Life of Langston Hughes, Vol I*, 141).

51. Marion Starkey, "Jessie Fauset," *Southern Workman* (May 1932): 218.

52. *The Crisis* (June 1922): 67.

53. McDowell, "Neglected Dimension," in *Conjuring: Black Women, Fiction, and Tradition*, ed. Marjorie Pryse and Hortense Spillers (Bloomington: Indiana University Press, 1985), 87.

54. *There Is Confusion*, 97. With this sentiment, Fauset identifies Joanna with the views of New Negro intellectuals Alain Locke, Charles Johnson, and James Weldon Johnson.

55. "The Younger Literary Movement," *The Crisis* (Feb. 1924): 162; *New York Post*, April 9, 1924; "The Spirit of Phyllis [*sic*] Wheatley," *Opportunity* (June 1924): 181.

56. Charles S. Johnson, "The Debut of the Younger School of Negro Writers," *Opportunity* (May 1924): 143–44; Carl Van Doren, "The Younger Generation of Negro Writers," *Opportunity* (May 1924): 144–45. See also Arna Bontemps, "The Awakening: A Memoir," in Bontemps, ed., *The Harlem Renaissance Remembered*, 11–12; Patrick Gilpin, "Charles S. Johnson: Entrepreneur of the Harlem Renaissance," in Bontemps, ed., 224–25; Lewis, 89–95.

57. Fauset to Locke, 9 January 1933, ALLP/HU. Fauset never forgot Locke's mistreatment. In 1949, she wrote Langston Hughes to protest Arna Bontemps's biographical note describing her in *The Poetry of the Negro, 1746–1949*: "I've suffered a good deal from colored men writers from Locke down to Bontemps—you know. Only you and [Hugh] Gloster have been fair" (9 June 1949, Langston Hughes Papers).

58. William Wordsworth, "Yarrow Revisited," *The Poems of William Wordsworth, Vol. II* (London: Methuen & Co., 1908), 167; "The Enigma of the Sorbonne," *The Crisis* (March 1925): 216–19.

59. *Paris Tribune*, 1 February 1925, quoted in Shari Benstock, *Women of the Left Bank: Paris, 1900–1940* (Austin: University of Texas Press, 1986), 13.

60. Quoted in Lewis, 124.

61. Letter to Mr. and Mrs. Arthur Spingarn, 10 February 1925, Arthur B. Spingarn Papers/MSRC.

62. Letter to Arthur Spingarn, 26 January 1926, Arthur Spingarn Papers/ MSRC.

63. "'Wings for God's Chillun': The Story of Burghardt Du Bois," *The World Tomorrow* (Aug. 1929): 336. The article was published anonymously; Sylvander identifies Fauset as the author, 64–67.

64. Deborah King, "Multiple Jeopardy, Multiple Consciousness: The Context of a Black Feminist Ideology," *Signs* 14, 1 (Autumn 1988): 42–72.

65. Savage (1892–1962) studied sculpting at the Cooper Union from 1921–1924. In 1923, she won a fellowship to the Fontainebleau School of Fine Arts in France, but she was rejected when the U.S. sponsors learned she was black. Her case became a political cause, and Du Bois became one of its champions. She acknowledged his support with a sculpture that became one of her best-known pieces. In 1926, Savage won a fellowship to attend the Royal Academy of Fine Arts in Rome, which she had to decline because of inadequate funds. Not until 1929, the year *Plum Bun* was published, did Savage succeed in her effort to study abroad. With fellowships from the Rosenwald and Carnegie foundations, she went to Paris in 1929, 1930, and 1931. She went on to have a distinguished career as a sculptor and teacher.

66. One might compare this description to the one that introduces Hurston's short story "The Gilded Six-Bits": "It was a Negro yard around a Negro house in a Negro settlement that looked to the payroll of the G and G Fertilizer works for its support" (in *Spunk: The Selected Short Stories of Zora Neale Hurston*, 54). Both passages suggest, ironically, the improbability of anything significant occurring on these sites. But, again, the former stresses commonality, the latter difference.

67. Fauset and her husband moved to Montclair, New Jersey, in 1939. Apart from a short teaching stint at Hampton Institute in 1949, she resided in New Jersey until shortly before her death in 1961.

68. Jean Toomer's *Cane* makes this point memorably, when at the end of "Kabnis," the blind, mute, ex-slave Father John speaks; the protagonist cannot decipher his words. Hurston's Nanny is, by contrast, an eloquent witness to slavery.

69. For an analysis of Fauset's use of melodrama, see Hiroko Sato, "Under the Harlem Shadow: A Study of Jessie Fauset and Nella Larsen," in Arna Bontemps, ed., *The Harlem Renaissance Remembered*, 66–81.

70. *Comedy: American Style* (1933; rpt. College Park, MD: McGrath Publishing Co., 1969), 205. Subsequent references to this edition will be cited in the text.

71. Letter to Alain Locke, 9 January 1933, ALP, MSRC.

3. Nella Larsen

1. In an inside joke, the story's protagonist signs a letter with *her* maiden name. "The Wrong Man" was identified and reprinted by Charles Larson

in *Intimation of Things Distant: The Collected Fiction of Nella Larsen* (New York: Anchor Books, 1992). Page references to this edition will be cited in the text.

2. Consider, by contrast, Claude McKay's sentimental representation in "Harlem Shadows": "Ah, stern harsh world, that in the wretched way / Of poverty, dishonor and disgrace, / Has pushed the timid little feet of clay, / The sacred brown feet of my fallen race."

3. Larsen's second story, "Freedom," was published in *Young's Magazine* in April 1926; it is also reprinted in *Intimations*. Barely more than a sketch, "Freedom" features a male protagonist determined to be free of his mistress; he takes off and spends a year traveling the world. Upon his return he learns that the woman he abandoned has died in childbirth. He continues to commune with her spirit—almost in the manner of Edgar Allen Poe's necrophilic heroes—before leaping out of a window to his death. In its images of claustrophobia as well as in certain plot details, it anticipates elements of Larsen's novels, but the melodrama overwhelms the story's theme of the elusiveness and illusion of freedom.

4. The "mystery woman" epithet was attributed to Larsen by Mary Helen Washington, "Mystery Woman of the Harlem Renaissance," *MS* (Dec. 1980): 44–50.

5. For a full discussion of the tragic mulatto convention in novels by black women, see Barbara Christian, *Black Women Novelists: The Development of a Tradition* (Westport, CT: Greenwood Press, 1980), 35–61.

6. Larsen shaved two years off her birth date. Thadious Davis gives this date in *Nella Larsen, Novelist of the Harlem Renaissance: A Woman's Life Unveiled* (Baton Rouge: Louisiana State Univ. Press, 1994), 3.

7. This information is taken from a profile of Nella Larsen in the Harmon Foundation Files, Library of Congress, and from Adelaide Cromwell Hill, introduction to *Quicksand* (New York: Collier Books Edition, 1971), 9–17; Washington cites the quotation, 47.

8. Davis, *Nella Larsen, Novelist of the Harlem Renaissance*, 21–50.

9. See Davis, *Nella Larsen, Novelist of the Harlem Renaissance*, 51–66. Davis notes that Larsen had changed the spelling of her first name during her year at Fisk.

10. Department of State passport records refute Larsen's repeated claim of having traveled to Denmark. See Charles Larson, p. xx. Davis writes that "no documents have surfaced that would indicate Larsen studied in Copenhagen, and no records support her claim of having lived in Denmark as a teenager" (67).

11. Davis, *Dictionary of Literary Biography*, 183.

12. Harmon Foundation Profile, Library of Congress.

13. Information regarding Larsen's marriage and activities in New York is gleaned from the following sources: Thelma Berlack, *New York Amsterdam News*, 23 May 1928; Thadious Davis, "Nella Larsen's Harlem Aesthetic," in *The Harlem Renaissance: Revaluations*, ed. Amritjit Singh, William Shiver, and Stanley Brodwin, 245–56; and Ann Allen Shockley, *Afro-American Women Writers, 1746–1933*, 432–40.

14. Letter to Carl Van Vechten, n.d. [probably 1925], Carl Van Vechten Papers, New York Public Library.

15. "Three Scandinavian Games," *The Brownies' Book*, (June 1920): 191–92 and "Danish Fun," (July 1920): 219. Marion Starkey, "Jessie Fauset," *Southern Workman* 62 (1932): 218.

16. Letter to Carl Van Vechten, n.d. [probably 1925], Carl Van Vechten Papers, NYPL.

17. Larsen refers to three short stories, "Freedom," "Tea," and "Mahogany" in her application to the Harmon Foundation; the latter two have not yet been located.

18. Davis, "Nella Larsen's Harlem Aesthetic," 247.

19. "Negro Writers Come into Their Own," unpublished interview, Alfred A. Knopf Papers, Harry Ransom Humanities Research Center, University of Texas, Austin.

20. Letter to Carl Van Vechten, 1 July 1926, Carl Van Vechten Papers, Yale University.

21. Letter to Dorothy Peterson, n.d. [1927?], James Weldon Johnson Collection, Yale.

22. Letter to Carl Van Vechten, n.d. [1926?], Carl Van Vechten Papers, NYPL; Letter to Van Vechten, 7 December 1926, Carl Van Vechten Papers, Yale.

23. Letters to Carl Van Vechten, 18 February 1928; 1 July 1926, Carl Van Vechten Papers, Yale. It is worth noting that Knopf was also Van Vechten's publisher.

24. *Quicksand* (1928; rpt. New Brunswick, New Jersey: Rutgers University Press, 1986), 14. Subsequent references to this edition will appear in the text.

25. In "The Aesthetics of Race and Gender in Nella Larsen's *Quicksand*," Anne Hostetler analyzes the relationship of the detailed descriptions of Helga's dress and furnishings to the thematic representations of race and gender as binary oppositions. "Through her love of color Helga attempts to create a spectrum rather than an opposition, a palette that will unify her life rather than leave it divided" (35).

26. Sexism as an issue in the novel was first explored at length by Hortense Thornton in "Sexism as Quagmire: Nella Larsen's *Quicksand*," *CLA Journal* 16 (1973): 285–301.

27. Nathan Huggins notes Larsen's rejection of black primitivism in *Harlem Renaissance* (New York: Oxford University Press, 1971), 160–61. See also Addison Gayle, *The Way of the New World: The Black Novel in America* (New York: Anchor Press, 1975), 130–35.

28. A classic statement of female Otherness is found in Simone de Beauvoir, *The Second Sex* (1949; rpt. New York: Bantam, 1961): viii–xxix.

29. Hostetler, 36.

30. Thornton, 299.

31. In addition to the false information she gave to interviewers, Larsen heightened the impression within the text with specific references to public landmarks, hotels, theaters, and shops in Copenhagen; to Danish words; and to an earlier trip Helga had made to Copenhagen when she was a girl.

32. Phyllis Rose, *Jazz Cleopatra: Josephine Baker in Her Time* (New York: Doubleday, 1989), 25.

33. Quoted in Rose, 31.

34. Josephine Baker and Jo Buillon, *Josephine* (1977. Rpt. New York: Paragon House, 1988), 44.

35. Quoted in Lynn Haney, *Naked at the Feast: A Biography of Josephine Baker* (New York: Dodd Mead, 1981), 47.

36. *Josephine*, 49–50. Paul Colin quoted in Rose, 6.

37. Colin went on to draw Baker hundreds of times. Many of these caricatures and portraits were published in a portfolio of lithographs, *Le Tumulte Noir*, in 1927.

38. Haney, 66.

39. Larsen's sole reference to Josephine Baker appears in this snippet of conversational dialogue from her second novel, *Passing*: "Josephine Baker? . . . No, I've never seen her. . . . Well, she might have been in *Shuffle Along* when I saw it, but if she was, I don't remember her. . . . Oh, but you're wrong! . . . I do think Ethel Waters is awfully good. . . ." (219). None of the statements is attributed to a specific character. It is tempting to take the reference as another of Larsen's inside jokes.

40. Cullen quoted in Rose, 53.

41. Baker and Buillon, 52; Rose, 9.

42. Quoted in Haney, 136.

43. Baker and Buillon, 66; Haney, 88.

44. The following description of the production is taken from Josephine Baker, *Josephine*; Lynn Haney, *Naked at the Feast*; and Phyllis Rose, *Jazz Cleopatra*.

45. Quoted in *Josephine*, 55.

46. Rose, 19.

47. Parisians who thought "Danse Sauvage," the climax of *La Revue Nègre*, was "African" dance were wrong. Baker knew better than they, but perhaps she did not know that the historical antecedents of African-American dance were African. Commentators traced the Charleston variously to the Juba dance, performed by slaves in the nineteenth-century United States; to Haiti, where it was called by the name of La Martinique; and to the rituals of the Ashanti. According to Harold Courlander, the Charleston had some characteristics of traditional Negro dance but was itself "a synthetic creation, a newly devised conglomerate tailored for widespread popular appeal" [quoted in Lynne F. Emery, *Black Dance in the United States from 1619 to 1980* (Palo Alto: National Press Books, 1972), 227.]

48. *Josephine*, 55. Her contemporary, singer Adelaide Hall, considered Baker first and foremost a comedienne (interview in the film *Chasing a Rainbow: The Life of Josephine Baker*). In her discussion of Baker's "simultaneously ingratiating and subversive" comic mask, Phyllis Rose argues that Baker employed comedy as a survival mechanism offstage as well. Baker "did to others, in the guise of humor, what she would not give them the chance to do to her—mocking, dismissing, rejecting. . . . The cross-eyed, goofy, stereotypically blackface grin would become a kind of signature, even when—most effec-

tively when—she was glamorously dressed, so that it seemed a parodic comment on her own beauty, on conventions of beauty, on the culture that had made her famous" (Rose, 15, 16).

49. Bone, *The Negro Novel in America*, rev. ed. (New Haven: Yale University Press, 1966), 103. For discussions of the imagery of rooms in women's fiction, see, for example, Annis Pratt, *Archetypal Patterns in Women's Fiction* (Bloomington: Indiana University Press, 1981), 41–70, and Sandra Gilbert and Susan Gubar, *The Madwoman in the Attic: The Woman Writer and the Nineteenth Century Literary Imagination* (New Haven: Yale University Press, 1979), 83–92.

50. The novel illustrates the pattern in women's fiction whereby the confinement of pregnancy replicates the confinement of society for women. See Gilbert and Gubar, 88.

51. Jean Toomer, *Cane* (1923; rpt. New York: Liveright, 1975), 96.

52. "A Mulatto Girl," *The New York Times*, 8 April 1928; Margery Latimer, *The World Telegram*, 22 July 1928; and Roark Bradford, "Mixed Blood," *New York Herald Tribune*, 13 May 1928.

53. "Two Novels," *The Crisis* 35 (June 1928), 202. Among the critics who compare Fauset and Larsen are Sterling Brown, *The Negro in American Fiction* (1937; rpt. New York: Atheneum, 1968), 14–43; Hugh Gloster, *Negro Voices in American Fiction* (New York: Russell & Russell, 1948), 117, 135, 141–146; and Bone, 95–107. Recent commentators, more alert to the differences between these authors, include Hazel Carby, *Reconstructing Womanhood: The Emergence of the Afro-American Woman Novelist* (New York: Oxford, 1987), 163–174; Arthur P. Davis, *From the Dark Tower: Afro-American Writers, 1900–1960* (Washington, DC: Howard University Press, 1974), 90–98; Gayle, 130–149; and Amritjit Singh, *The Novels of the Harlem Renaissance* (University Park: Pennsylvania State University Press, 1976), 98 and *passim*.

54. Du Bois, 202. A publishing coincidence afforded Du Bois a second opportunity to compare the work of Larsen and McKay. *Passing* was reviewed alongside McKay's *Banjo* and *The Crisis* 36 (July 1929): 234, 248.

55. "The Ebony Flute," *Opportunity* (May 1928): 153. Bennett was an ideal reviewer for *Quicksand*. A poet and painter, Bennett had taught at Howard University and studied art in Paris during the twenties.

56. Harmon Foundation Files, Library of Congress.

57. Thelma Berlack, *The Amsterdam News*, 23 May 1928.

58. Mary Remals, *The World Telegram*, 13 April 1929.

59. Harmon Foundation Files, Library of Congress.

60. Spectatorship is a key concept in feminist film theory. Introduced by Laura Mulvey in an article, "Visual Pleasure and Narrative Cinema," (1975), the concept has been much debated, revised, and refined. To sample the debate, see Patricia Erens, ed., *Issues in Feminist Film Criticism* (Bloomington: Indiana University Press, 1990). My discussion owes less to this debate than to a close reading of *Passing*. The discourse of the novel, particularly its shifting references to the gaze, anticipates several aspects of the concept contemporary theorists define. Moreover, it suggests the ways in which a consideration of race problematizes their theories.

61. *Passing*, (1929; rpt. New Brunswick, NJ: Rutgers University Press, 1986), 143–44, emphasis added. Subsequent references to this edition will be cited in the text.

62. Most commentators have read *Passing* as a tragic mulatto story, but three recent critics offer sharply divergent views. Mary Mabel Youman argues that Irene is the one who actually "passes" because she gives up her racial heritage for middle-class security. See "Nella Larsen's *Passing*: A Study in Irony," *CLA Journal* 18 (1974): 235–41. In "Nella Larsen's *Passing*: A Problem in Interpretation," *Black American Literature Forum* 14 (1980): 142–46, Claudia Tate argues that *Passing* is an intriguing romance in which Irene Redfield is the heroine and the unreliable center of consciousness. According to Deborah McDowell, "though superficially, Irene's is an account of Clare's passing for white and related issues of racial identity and loyalty, underneath the safety of that surface is the more dangerous story—though not named explicitly—of Irene's awakening sexual desire for Clare" (xxvi).

63. In this regard, Clare fits Hazel Carby's description of the mulatto, which, "as narrative figure, has two primary functions: as a vehicle for an exploration of the relationship between the races and, at the same time, an expression of the relationship between the races." Carby argues that "the mulatto should be understood and analyzed as a narrative device of mediation" (*Reconstructing Womanhood*, 89). Unlike the mulatto in late-nineteenth-century African-American literature, Larsen employs this figure to comment on the risks of what was becoming less, not more, socially proscribed.

64. Hoyt Fuller, introduction to *Passing* (New York: Collier Books, 1971), 18.

65. Quoted by Judith Butler in *Gender Trouble: Feminism and the Subversion of Identity* (New York: Routledge, 1990), 47.

66. "Female Grotesques: Carnival and Theory," in Teresa de Lauretis, ed., *Feminist Studies, Critical Studies*, 213.

67. In a letter to Van Vechten, Larsen wrote of *Nigger Heaven*: "It is a fine tale, this story of the deterioration and subsequent ruin of a weakling who blames all his troubles on that old scapegoat, the race problem. Dangerous too. But with what exquisite balance you have avoided the propagandistic pitfall. But of course, you would. Like your Lasca Sartoris, who so superbly breasts the blood of racial prejudices (black and white)."

Amid the high praise that suffused the letter was a hint of a more ambiguous response. Asserting that she still preferred an earlier Van Vechten novel, *Firecrackers*, she admitted that the reason might be that *Nigger Heaven* was "too close, too true, as if you had undressed the lot of us and turned on a strong light. Too, I feel a kind of despair. Why, oh why, couldn't we have done something as big as this for ourselves?" 11 August 1926, Carl Van Vechten Papers, NYPL.

68. "On Being Young—A Woman—and Colored," 5.

69. McDowell cites this quotation to support her compelling reading of the theme of homoerotic desire in the novel; see the introduction to the Rutgers edition of *Quicksand and Passing*.

70. Tate insists that the evidence is inadequate to determine Irene's guilt or innocence.

71. Mark J. Madigan provides an interesting contextual note in "Miscegenation and 'the Dicta of Race and Class': The Rhinelander Case and Nella Larsen's *Passing*," *Modern Fiction Studies* 36 (Winter 1990): 523–528. Madigan expands on Irene's brief reference to this celebrated twenties court case in which a wealthy young white man, Leonard Kip Rhinelander, sued to annul his marriage to his wife, Alice, on the grounds that she had claimed to have Cuban parentage, when she was in fact an American Negro. Madigan reports that the "year-long event [was] marked by several bizarre developments, including rumors of bribery and extortion, the public reading of Leonard's love-letters, the partial disrobing of the defendant so that jurors could examine her skin, and testimony from such well-known persons as Irving Berlin and Al Jolson" (525). In this case, litigated before and after *Passing* was published, Larsen had a ready reference to the ways in which the element of race rendered the private public.

72. Huggins, 236.

73. *Forum* (April 1930): xli. "Mrs. Adis" is collected in Sheila Kaye-Smith, *Joanna Gooden Married and Other Stories* (New York: Harper & Brothers, 1926), 190–204.

74. *Forum* (April 1930): xli–xlii.

75. Several explanations have been suggested for Larsen's lapse. David Lewis cites Bruce Nugent's surmise that the story was one Larsen had overheard at Van Vechten's and appropriated without realizing it (*When Harlem Was in Vogue*, 250). In *Invisible Darkness* Charles Larson attributes it to fate, "a curse upon her for having a photographic memory" (Iowa City: University of Iowa Press, 1993, 208). Thadious Davis asserts that "the similarities of the two stories in language, description, setting, atmosphere, characterization, action, plot, and theme, all are too exact to be merely parallel lines" (*Nella Larsen*, 350–51).

From 1916 to 1923, the Lafayette Theater featured white plays adapted for black casts, among them Broadway hits like *Madame X* and *Within the Law*, dramatizations of novels like *Dr. Jekyll and Mr. Hyde*, and Shakespearean drama. *The Harlem Renaissance: A Historical Dictionary*, ed. Bruce Kellner (New York: Methuen, 1987), 214.

76. Letter from Harold Jackman to Countee Cullen, 27 April 1930, Countee Cullen Papers, Amistad Research Center.

77. "Breaking Chains and Encouraging Life," *MS* (April 1980): 35.

78. Letter to Carl Van Vechten, 11 May 1930, Carl Van Vechten Papers, Yale.

79. Adelaide Cromwell Hill, introduction to *Quicksand* (New York: Collier Books, 1971), 14.

80. Letter to Carl Van Vechten, 1 November 1930, Carl Van Vechten Papers, Yale.

81. Letter to Dorothy Peterson, 29 July 1933, James Weldon Johnson Collection, Yale.

82. *Baltimore Afro-American*, 7 October 1933. In a letter written to Dorothy Peterson, Larsen expressed her belief Imes had married Gilbert the same week the divorce was granted; she believed moreover that Gilbert was preg-

nant. No records confirm a marriage or child. Letter to Dorothy Peterson, 6 September 1933, James Weldon Johnson Collection, Yale. Elmer Imes continued to teach at Fisk until shortly before his death in 1941; he also remained in contact with the Van Vechtens, who visited him in the hospital in that year.

83. Letter from Dorothy Peterson to Grace Nail Johnson, 8 March 1932, James Weldon Johnson Collection, Yale; Walter White, *A Man Called White* (New York: Viking Press, 1948), 157.

84. Thadious Davis, *Dictionary of Literary Biography*, 190.

85. A more recent example of this tendency occurs in Hoyt Fuller's introduction to *Passing*. In a footnote he writes: "At one point in the twenties, Miss Larsen left her husband, Dr. Elmer Imes, and went off to live in Europe. Reportedly, she considered ending her marriage and becoming the wife of an Englishman. However, she finally returned to America and to Dr. Imes" (12). In a letter to Van Vechten, dated 25 January 1931, Larsen mentions an Englishman who was her "escort" abroad in 1931, long after she learned of Imes's affair. Fuller makes no mention of Imes's extramarital activities.

4. Zora Neale Hurston's Traveling Blues

1. *Dust Tracks on a Road*, (1942; rpt. New York: HarperCollins, 1991), 133. Further references to this edition will be cited in the text.

2. "'Survival Motion': A Study of the Black Writer and the Black Revolution in America," in Mercer Cook and Stephen Henderson, eds., *The Militant Black Writer in the United States* (Madison: University of Wisconsin Press, 1969), 121–24.

3. Frank L. Hayes, "Campaigns Here for Negro Art in Natural State," *Chicago Daily News*, 16 November 1934.

4. Alice Walker writes in "Zora Neale Hurston: A Cautionary Tale and a Partisan View": "In my mind, Zora Neale Hurston, Billie Holiday, and Bessie Smith form a sort of unholy trinity. Zora *belongs* in the tradition of black women singers, rather than among the literati." *In Search of Our Mothers' Gardens: Womanist Prose* (New York: Harcourt Brace Jovanovich, 1983), 91.

5. Robert Hemenway, *Zora Neale Hurston: A Literary Biography* (Urbana: University of Illinois Press, 1977), 12.

6. In an early revisionist assessment of Hurston's career, June Jordan asserted that "affirmation of Black values and lifestyle with the American context is, indeed, an act of protest." "On Richard Wright and Zora Neale Hurston: Notes toward a Balancing of Love and Hatred," *Black World* (Aug. 1974): 5.

7. *Tell My Horse*, (1938; rpt. Berkeley, CA: Turtle Island Foundation, 1981), 20.

8. See Karla Holloway, *The Character of the Word: The Texts of Zora Neale Hurston* (Westport, CT: Greenwood Press, 1987).

9. The 1900 U.S. Census enumerates the members of the Hurston family as follows: parents John (b. 1861) and Lucy (b. 1865) and children Hezekiah

(b. 1882), John (b. 1885), Richard (b. 1887), Sarah (b. 1889), Zora L. (b. 1891), Joel (b. 1893), Benjamin (b. 1895), and Everette (b. 1898).

10. Both Hemenway and Lillie Howard (*Zora Neale Hurston*, Boston: G.K. Hall, 1980), report conversations with Everette Hurston, Sr., in which he maintained that Zora was born in 1891.

11. In his essay "Zora Neale Hurston: A Negro Way of Saying," Henry Louis Gates deems Hurston's account of her conversation with her dying mother "one of the most moving passages in American literature." *New York Times Book Review*, 21 April 1985: 1, 43, 45. The essay is reprinted as an afterword to the Hurston volumes reprinted by Harper/Collins.

12. If, as the best evidence suggests, Lucy Potts Hurston died on 18 September 1904, Zora would have been thirteen, the age at which she writes she left Eatonville in "How It Feels to be Colored Me."

13. For Hurston's account, see *Dust Tracks on a Road*, chap. 9; Barbara Speisman, professor of English at Florida A & M University, has located Sarah Mack's Baltimore address in an old city directory.

14. Though less well educated, the remaining Hurston brothers were successful in their pursuits: John owned and operated a grocery store in Jacksonville, Florida; Richard was a chef; and Everette would eventually become a postal worker in Brooklyn, New York. For more on the Hurston family, see N. Y. Nathiri, compiler, *Zora! A Woman and Her Community* (Orlando: Sentinel Communications, 1991), 59–75.

15. Hemenway, *Zora Neale Hurston*, 22–23.

16. *Dust Tracks*, 167–68; the reference to Locke is taken from David L. Lewis, *When Harlem Was in Vogue*, 96. "Night" appeared in *Negro World*, 1 April 1922; "Journey's End" on 8 April 1922; and "Passion" on 15 April 1922. Tony Martin revealed the publication of Hurston's work in *Negro World* in his *Literary Garveyism* (Dover, MA: Majority Press, 1983), 74–75.

17. Letter to Alain Locke, 11 October 1927, AALP/MSRC.

18. *Fire!!* 1 (November 1926): 40–45; reprinted in *I Love Myself*, 197–207. Page references will cite the latter volume.

19. *Dust Tracks*, 168–70. Much has been written about the Hurston-Hurst relationship, beginning with Hurston's extended description of it in the *Saturday Review* (9 October 1937). After Hurston's death, Fannie Hurst published an essay, "Zora Neale Hurston: A Personality Sketch," *Yale University Gazette* 35 (1961). Both accounts make much of the fact that Hurst employed Hurston as a secretary; Hurst emphasizes that she was a most unsatisfactory secretary and thereafter became her chauffeur. According to new information Robert Hemenway has unearthed, Hurston was actually in Hurst's regular employ for less than a month. Clearly, the idea of the two, both writers, with strikingly similar names, appealed to the imagination of both. Likewise, they both chose to downplay the fact that Hurston worked as Hurst's servant.

20. Hemenway, *Zora Neale Hurston*, 168.

21. Letter to Lawrence Jordan, 24 March 1927, SCRBC.

22. Hemenway, *Zora Neale Hurston*, 168.

23. *Mules and Men*, 65–66; interview with Mazie O. Tyson.

24. *Dust Tracks*, 128–29. See also Langston Hughes, *The Big Sea*, 238–40 and Wallace Thurman, *Infants of the Spring* (New York: The Macauley Co., 1932), 229–30; in this novel the character Sweetie May Carr, who "knew her white folks," is clearly based on Hurston. Discussions of the Hurston/Mason relationship may be found in Hemenway, *Zora Neale Hurston*, 104–14; Huggins, *Harlem Renaissance*, 129–33; Lewis, *When Harlem Was in Vogue*, 151–53; and Rampersad, *I, Too, Sing America: The Life of Langston Hughes, Vol. I* (New York: Oxford University Press, 1986), 150–81.

25. Quoted in *Dust Tracks*, 129. The Mason-Hurston correspondence is collected in the Alain L. Locke Papers, Moorland-Spingarn Research Center (MSRC), Howard University.

26. The ledger is enclosed in a letter from Hurston to Charlotte Mason, 23 July 1931. The Hurston-Mason correspondence is collected in the Alain Locke Papers. Moorland-Spingarn Research Center (MSRC), Howard University.

27. Contract between Charlotte L. Mason and Zora Neale Hurston, 8 December 1927, Alain Locke Papers/MSRC.

28. Letters to Franz Boas, 27 December 1928; 21 April 1929; 8 June 1930. Letters from Boas to Hurston regarding Mrs. Mason, 3 May 1930; 13 June 1930. Franz Boas Papers, American Philosophical Society.

29. Hemenway, 105–06; Rampersad, *Langston Hughes, Vol. I*, 150–53.

30. Zora Neale Hurston to Langston Hughes, 12 April 1928, James Weldon Johnson Collection, Yale.

31. For reconstructions of the *Mule Bone* episode, see Hemenway, *Zora Neale Hurston: A Literary Biography*, 136–158; and Rampersad, 182–201.

32. Hurston to Mason, 10 March 1931, ALLP/MSRC. Hurston had published much of what became the conjure section of *Mules and Men* in the scholarly article "Hoodoo in America."

33. Hemenway, *Zora Neale Hurston*, 95–99. Letter from Cudjo Lewis to Charlotte Mason, 12 May 1932, ALLP/MSRC.

34. Locke to Mason, 9 June 1931, Alain Locke Papers/MSRC.

35. Hurston to Mason, 25 November 1930; 18 April 1931; 4 June 1931, Alain Locke Papers/MSRC.

36. Mason to Hurston, 20 January 1931, ALLP/MSRC.

37. Program of *From Sun to Sun*, Rollins College Archives.

38. From "Concert," appendix to *Dust Tracks on a Road* in *Folklore, Memoirs and Other Writings* (New York: Library of America, 1995), 805. Hurston coined the term "neo-spiritual" in the essay "Spirituals and Neo-Spirituals," published in *Negro*, the anthology edited by Nancy Cunard in 1934.

39. Paul Gilroy examines these issues in both historical and contemporary terms in "'Jewels Brought from Bondage': Black Music and the Politics of Authenticity," a chapter in *The Black Atlantic: Modernity and Double Consciousness* (Cambridge: Harvard University Press, 1993), 72–110.

40. "From Sun to Sun: A Program of Original Negro Folklore," The New School, 29 March 1932. The concerts followed a similar format, although the

titles of the numbers changed from production to production. Hurston comments on the Bahamian Fire Dance in "Concert," 805.

41. Robert Stepto defines the African-American immersion narrative as "an expression of a ritualized journey into a symbolic South, in which the protagonist seeks those aspects of tribal literacy that ameliorate, if not obliterate, the conditions imposed by solitude." The narrative ends "almost paradoxically, with the questing figure located in or near the narrative's most oppressive social structure but free in the sense that he has gained or regained sufficient tribal literacy to assume the mantle of an articulate kinsman" (*From Behind the Veil: A Study of Afro-American Narrative*, Second Edition [Urbana: University of Illinois Press, 1991], 167.)

42. *Mules and Men* (1935; rpt. New York: Harper Collins, 1990), 1. Subsequent references to this edition will be cited in the text.

43. *Workings of the Spirit* (Chicago: University of Chicago Press, 1991), 85.

44. Frank L. Hayes, "Campaigns Here for Negro Art in Natural State," *Chicago Daily News*, 16 November 1934.

45. Critics have responded to this ambivalence in various ways. In *Zora Neale Hurston* Robert Hemenway refers to the narrator as "a self-effacing reporter created . . . to dramatize the process of collecting and make the reader feel part of the scene" (164). Willis argues in *Specifying: Black Women Writing the American Experience* (Madison: University of Wisconsin Press, 1987) that Hurston's project in *Mules*, as elsewhere, was "to mediate two deeply polarized worlds, North/South, black/white, rural/urban, folk tradition/intellectual scholarship" (27). The narrator is the mediating agent. Both critics view the narrator as an essentially static figure. In "Thresholds of Difference: Structures of Address in Zora Neale Hurston," Barbara Johnson argues in contrast that the narrator is constantly shifting her ground and "deconstructing" the terms of reference. See Henry Louis Gates, ed., *"Race," Writing and Difference* (Chicago: University of Chicago Press, 1986), 317–28. In my reading, the persona of the narrator gains force throughout the narrative, though in keeping with Hurston's aesthetic, the development is not linear.

46. Hurston was concerned lest the "unscientific matter that must be there for the sake of the average reader" would prevent Boas from writing an introduction to the book. It did not. Letter to Franz Boas, 20 August 1934, American Philosophical Society.

47. Turner, introducing the 1970 edition of *Mules* (New York: Harper & Row), enumerates its scholarly shortcomings. It lacked an exhaustive description of the traditions, mores, and living habits of a folk; prescriptions for their future behavior; suggestions for further studies; and a comparative context for the tales (8). Hemenway highlights the interplay of text and context in his analysis in *Zora Neale Hurston*. In his introduction to *Mules* (Bloomington: Indiana University Press, 1978), Hemenway defends Hurston by pointing to her contention that the "conversations and incidents are true." He concludes that "Hurston's invention seems to have been limited to condensation and arrangement; she did not invent any folklore for the book" (xxiv–xxv). John Roberts is less certain about the "authenticity of the tran-

scriptions." But, referring to the book's narrative structure, he observes: "it provided her with a unique opportunity to present storytelling context. In the process, she demonstrated a folkloristic sophistication and sensitivity to folklore processes shared by few of her contemporaries." See Roberts, review of *Mules and Men* and *Their Eyes Were Watching God, Journal of American Folklore* 93 (1980): 463–466.

48. "Characteristics of Negro Expression," 49.

49. I would speculate that Hurston achieved this understanding through her academic training and fieldwork but also through her creation of the theatrical productions, variously entitled *From Sun to Sun, All de Livelong Day*, and *Singing Steel*, in which she first presented the material she collected.

For a detailed linguistic analysis of "adorned" expression in Hurston's fiction, see Karla Holloway, *The Character of the Word*, chap. 5.

50 Richard Bauman, *Story, Performance, and Event: Contextual Studies of Oral Language* (Cambridge: Cambridge University Press, 1986), 3.

51. "Characteristics," 64.

52. Roger Abrahams, "Negotiating Respect: Patterns of Presentation among Black Women," *Journal of American Folklore* 88 (1975): 58–80. An ongoing debate in folklore studies questions the kind of distinction between performance and presentation, public and private speech acts, that Abrahams's terms evoke. See, for example, Claire R. Ferrer, "Women and Folklore: Images and Genres," in Ferrer, ed., *Women and Folklore* (Austin, TX: American Folklore Society, 1975), vii–xvii. I find the terms useful nevertheless, because they highlight an issue that Hurston's text both raises and resolves.

53. Barbara Johnson, "Thresholds of Difference," 325.

54. That Big Sweet is so much larger than life makes the correspondence between her androgynous persona and the Fon deity, MawuLisa, especially striking. The deity combines Mawu (female) and Lisa (male) valences. Mawu, the moon, is cool and gentle; Lisa, the sun, is strong, tough, and fiery. In *Flash of the Spirit: African and Afro-American Art and Philosophy*, Robert Farris Thompson, the union of Mawu and Lisa represents a Fon ideal (New York: Vintage Books Edition, 1984, 176). In the secular realm, Hurston is proposing Big Sweet as an African-American ideal.

55. As several critics have noted, Walker's novel revises key plot structures, characterizations, and metaphors of *Their Eyes Were Watching God*. See, for example, Henry Louis Gates, *The Signifying Monkey: A Theory of Afro-American Literary Criticism* (New York: Oxford University Press, 1988), chap. 7; Mae Henderson, "*The Color Purple*: Revisions and Redefinitions," *Sage* 2 (Spring 1985): 14–19; and Diane Sadoff, "Black Matrilineage: The Case of Alice Walker and Zora Neale Hurston," *Signs* 11 (Autumn 1985): 4–26. It is noteworthy that in her revision of the relationship between Tea Cake and Janie, refigured in that between Shug and Celie, Walker restores the female bonding celebrated in the mother text, *Mules and Men*. Even the name Shug (short for Sugar) suggests an intertextual connection. Notably, Walker's first published reference to Hurston's writing, her incorporation of the curse-prayer in the short story "The Revenge of Hannah Kemhuff," was to *Mules and Men*.

56. See *Dust Tracks on a Road*, 136.

57. In the following analysis, I measure Big Sweet somewhat differently than I did in "Zora Neale Hurston: Changing Her Own Words," in Fritz Fleischman, ed., *American Novelists Revisited: Essays in Feminist Criticism* (Boston: G.K. Hall, 1982), 375–79.

58. According to the *Standard Dictionary of Folklore, Mythology and Legend*, most students hold that the word "hoodoo" is derived from the Haitian *vodun*, which in turn comes from the identical Dahomean (Fon) word that means "deity."

Albert Raboteau explains that while initially the cult and the magical system of voodoo formed an integral whole, voodoo as an institutionalized cult of ritual worship gradually disintegrated in the United States. What survived was hoodoo, a much less cohesive system of magic, divination, and herbalism. "'Hoodoo' became the name for a whole area of folklore, the realm of signs, powers, and conjuring." See Albert Raboteau, *Slave Religion: The "Invisible Institution" in the Antebellum South* (New York: Oxford University Press, 1978), 75–80.

In *The Myth of the Negro Past*, Melville Herskovits cited Hurston's account of hoodoo in New Orleans as evidence that "the former well-integrated system of ritual and belief has degenerated considerably, and taken the protective cloak of spiritualism." Nevertheless, he argued, "many direct correspondences will be found to exist among [the practices Hurston reported], Haitian *vodun* practices, and Dahomean cult rituals." See *The Myth of the Negro Past* (1941; rpt. Boston: Beacon Press, 1958), 245–46.

59. The freedom and creativity hoodoo made available to black women is reflected in many recent novels. In *Sula*, for example, Ajax's mother is an "evil conjure woman" and the only interesting woman he had ever met in his life.

60. See Lawrence W. Levine, ed., *Black Culture and Black Consciousness: Afro-American Folk Thought from Slavery to Freedom* (Oxford University Press, 1977), 58–59.

61. The value of this power has been called into question often enough, particularly its value vis-a-vis the political, i.e., "real," power of the white slave owners and their heirs. Levine's statement of the case seems very much in keeping with the premises of Hurston's text. "The whites were neither omnipotent or omniscient; there were things they did not know, forces they could not control, areas in which slaves could act with more knowledge and authority than their masters, ways in which the powers of the whites could be muted if not thwarted entirely" (73–74). These are precisely the areas explored in *Mules and Men*.

62. John Blassingame, *The Slave Community* (New York: Oxford University Press, 1973), 158.

63. One of the conjure stories Hurston records, although set in the post–Civil War era, illustrates this belief. Dave, who "was known to dabble in hoodoo," works for a wealthy planter who murders Dave's daughter. With no legal recourse available, Dave avenges his daughter's death by conjuring the planter's family (*Mules*, 240–42).

64. *Journal of American Folklore* 44 (1931): 317–418.

65. By introducing the myth, the text enacts a principle Mircea Eliade articulates in *The Myth and Reality*: "A rite cannot be performed unless its 'origin' is known, that is, the myth that tells how it was performed for the first time" (New York: Harper, 1963), 17. As I argue below, the text follows ritualistic patterns in several respects.

66. The tale contains as well the kernel from which Hurston would develop her 1939 novel, *Moses, Man of the Mountain*, in which Moses is at once the Old Testament lawgiver and Afro-American conjure man.

67. Marjorie Pryse makes the point forcefully when she compares the effect of *Mules and Men* on the black women's literary tradition to that of the Bible on seventeenth-century American colonial literature. "[*Mules and Men*] gave her the authority to tell stories because in the act of writing down the old 'lies,' Hurston created a bridge between the 'primitive' authority of folk life and the literary power of written texts. The point is that she *wrote them down*, thereby breaking the mystique of connection between literary authority and patriarchal power." See "Zora Neale Hurston, Alice Walker, and the 'Ancient Power' of Black Women," in *Conjuring: Black Women, Fiction, and Literary Tradition*, ed. Pryse and Hortense Spillers (Bloomington: Indiana University Press, 1985), 11–12.

68. The narrator knows when she must provide answers as well. When her first inquiry about hoodoo in Florida is met with a vigorous denial of any knowledge of "dat ole fogeyism," Zora responds: "'Don't fool yourself,' I answered with assurance. 'People can do things to you. I done seen things happen.'" The emphatic tone, intensified by the Black English grammar, contrasts sharply with the narrator's demure politeness in the opening chapter. In no time the professed unbeliever being addressed here directs Zora to the local hoodoo doctor.

69. For a discussion of the significance of the numbers, see Ellease Southerland, "The Influence of Voodoo on the Fiction of Zora Neale Hurston," in Roseann Bell, Bettye Parker, and Beverly Guy-Sheftall, eds., *Sturdy Black Bridges* (New York: Anchor Books, 1979), 172–75.

70. In *Dust Tracks on a Road*, she credits Robert Wunsch, an instructor at Rollins College in Winter Park, Florida, with sending her work to *Story*; the novel was dedicated to him. Along with Professor Edwin Grover, to whom she dedicated *Moses, Man of the Mountain*, Wunsch facilitated the production of *From Sun to Sun*, a folklore concert performed by a cast from Eatonville held at Rollins on 11 February 1933.

71. On plans for Bethune Cookman, see Hurston to Carl Van Vechten, 22 Jan. 1934, (JWJ); on position at Fisk, see letters from Hurston to James Weldon Johnson, 7 October 1934, (JWJ); Hurston to Thomas E. Jones, 12 Oct. 1934, (Fisk); and from Thomas E. Jones to Zora Hurston, 18 December 1934, (Fisk). On her year at North Carolina College, see Hemenway, 253–56.

72. See the Library of Congress Folk Archive Finding Aid (LCFAFA, No. 11) for a list of recordings made on this trip.

73. See *Dust Tracks*, 212–13, and Hemenway, 227–31.

74. *Dust Tracks*, 212, 260.

75. Hemenway, 222. Hurston's title drew the ire of at least one contemporary critic. Harold Preece wrote scathingly in *The Crisis*: "For when a Negro author describes her race with such a servile term as 'Mules and Men,' critical members of the race must necessarily evaluate the author as a literary climber." "The Negro Folk Cult," reprinted in Alan Dundes, ed., *Mother-Wit from the Laughing Barrel* (Jackson: University Press of Mississippi, 1990), 37. In a note, Dundes refers to "considerable evidence" that southern blacks tended to identify with the mule. Like slaves, mules were bought and sold by plantation owners; they were also overworked. At the same time, blacks admired characteristics such as stubbornness and strength, proverbially attributed to the mule.

76. Sherley Anne Williams, Foreword. *Their Eyes Were Watching God.* (Urbana: University of Illinois Press, 1978), xii.

77. In his discussion of the vision of heaven in the slaves' religion, Eugene Genovese notes that the other side of this concern is the vision of hell—the afterlife appropriate to the oppressor. "This sense of a revenge to come always carried with it the thrust of a political quiescence accompanied by vicarious thrills. . . . By sharpening a sense of class justice it prepared the way for explosive hostility, should circumstances present an opportunity for aggressive action." See *Roll, Jordan, Roll: The World the Slaves Made* (New York: Vintage, 1976), 251. To a degree, Janie's identification with Matt Bonner's mule serves an analogous narrative function in *Their Eyes*.

78. Gates, *Signifying Monkey*, 172.

79. *Crossing the Double-Cross: The Practice of Feminist Criticism* (Chapel Hill: University of North Carolina Press, 1986), 46.

80. Lorraine Bethel observes that the novel's initial description of Nanny, in which her head is bound in a wreath of palma christi leaves, "establishes her as a representative of the religious experience that stands at the center of Afro-American folk tradition. . . . While Janie represents the Black female folk aesthetic contained in the blues, her grandmother symbolizes the Black religious folk tradition embodied by the spirituals." See "'This Infinity of Conscious Pain': Zora Neale Hurston and the Black Female Literary Tradition," in Gloria Hull, Patricia Scott, and Barbara Smith, eds., *But Some of Us Are Brave* (Old Westbury, NY: Feminist Press, 1982), 181.

81. Houston Baker, *Blues, Ideology, and Afro-American Literature: A Vernacular Theory* (Chicago: University of Chicago Press, 1984), 57.

82. Mary Helen Washington, *Invented Lives*, 241.

83. In *Writing beyond the Ending*, Rachel Du Plessis argues that twentieth-century female writers have invented or deployed narrative strategies explicitly to delegitimate romance plots. She observes that in *Their Eyes* the romance plot becomes communitarian. "Through Tea Cake, Janie becomes one with the black folk community . . ." (Bloomington: Indiana University Press, 1985), 157.

84. For example, Janie initiates a courtship ritual when she asks Tea Cake whether he is buying passenger trains or battleships, and he asks her to state

a preference (153–54). Another example occurs earlier in *Their Eyes*, during the time Janie is imprisoned in the store (64–65).

85. See Awkward's chapter, "'The Inaudible Voice of it All': Silence, Voice, and Action in *Their Eyes Were Watching God*," in *Inspiriting Influences* (New York: Columbia University Press, 1989).

86. Audre Lorde, *Sister Outsider* (Trumansburg, NY: Crossing Press, 1984), 54.

87. In "The Influence of Voodoo on the Fiction of Zora Neale Hurston," Ellease Southerland traces a system of numerology among other patterns of imagery derived from voodoo in *Their Eyes Were Watching God*.

88. Both here and in a 1945 essay she wrote on the topic, "High John de Conquer," Hurston identifies the root with the protagonist of the John and Marster story cycle. It symbolizes "hitting a straight lick with a crooked stick. Winning the jackpot with no other stake but a laugh. . . . It is the power of love and laughter to win by their subtle power." Hurston contended that those who still believe in this power "do John reverence by getting the root of the plant in which he has taken up his secret dwelling, and 'dressing' it with perfume, and keeping it on their person, or in their houses in a secret place." Reprinted in *Mother Wit from the Laughing Barrel*, 541–548.

89. I am indebted to Eve Oishi, a student in my graduate seminar on Black Women Writers, for this observation.

90. Hurston explains in *Dust Tracks* that she lived through a five-day hurricane in 1929 while doing fieldwork in Nassau (195). It is noteworthy, too, that Hurston took time off from her investigations of spiritual traditions in Haiti to write *Their Eyes*. She eventually published her research in *Tell My Horse*. In the chapter on "Voodoo and Voodoo Gods," she described her initiations by Haitian houngans. As Gwendolyn Mikell asserts, Hurston's accounts of ceremonies and cosmology is "conveyed to us in the logic of one who practices and believes." See "When Horses Talk," *Phylon* 43 (1982): 226.

91. Passages that seem to deify Tea Cake might be reconsidered in this context. For example: "He seemed to be crushing scent out of the world with his footsteps. Crushing aromatic herbs with every step he took. Spices hung around him. He was a glance from God" (101–102). This might be read against the description of the altar in Marie Leveau's home, where the hide of the snake who rests upon the altar is "stuffed with spices and things of power . . ." (*Mules*, 203). If Tea Cake does end up resembling the tall, dark, mysterious stranger of romantic fiction as Washington argues, it seems clear that Hurston's aims for the character were quite unconventional.

92. *New York Times*, 6 October 1937; *New York Post*, 14 September 1937.

93. Alain Locke, "Literature by and about the Negro," *Opportunity* 1 (June 1938). Richard Wright, "Between Laughter and Tears," *New Masses* 5 (October 1937): 22, 25.

94. See "Stories of Conflict," *Saturday Review*, 2 April 1938, 32.

95. Hurston and Price were divorced on 9 November 1943. For more on their relationship, see Hemenway, 273–75.

96. Letter to Edwin O. Grover, 12 October 1939, ZNH Collection, University of Florida.

97. See Claudine Raynaud, "'Rubbing a Paragraph with a Soft Cloth?' Muted Voices and Editorial Constraints in *Dust Tracks on a Road*," for a careful analysis of the several versions of Hurston's manuscript. In *De/Colonizing the Subject: the Politics of Gender in Women's Autobiography*, ed. Sidonie Smith and Julie Watson (Minneapolis: University of Minnesota Press, 1992).

Epilogue

1. For the fullest account of the scandal, see Hemenway, 319–323.

2. For further information, see Sandra Y. Govan, "Gwendolyn Bennett: Portrait of an Artist Lost"; Joyce Flynn, introduction to *Frye Street & Environs: The Collected Works of Marita Bonner*; J. Lee Greene, *Time's Unfading Garden: Anne Spencer's Life and Poetry*; Gloria Hull, "Georgia Douglas Johnson," in *Color, Sex, and Poetry*; Carolyn Sylvander, *Jessie Redmon Fauset*; and Thadious Davis, *Nella Larsen*. In correspondence (9 January 1988) with the author, Helene Johnson, who gave a poetry reading in New York City in February 1987, at the age of 81, wrote that she had married William Hubbell; she was not forthcoming with much additional personal information.

3. Hill, 15. Davis, *Nella Larsen*, 444–52. Certificate of Death, no. 156-64-107204, State of New York, gives the cause of death as "acute congestive heart failure due to hypertensive and arteriosclerotic cardiovascular disease."

Selected Bibliography
of Writings by
Women of the Harlem Renaissance

Bennett, Gwendolyn. "The Ebony Flute" [monthly column]. *Opportunity* (Sept. 1926–May 1928).
——. "Hatred." *Opportunity* (June 1926): 190.
——. "Heritage." *Opportunity* (Dec. 1923): 371.
——. "Quatrains." *Caroling Dusk.* Ed. Countee Cullen. New York: Harper, 1927.
——. "To a Dark Girl." *The Book of American Negro Poetry.*
——. "Tokens." *Ebony and Topaz.*
——. "To Usward." *The Crisis* (May 1924): 19.
——. "Wedding Day." *Fire!!* (November 1926): 26–28.
Bonner, Marita. *Frye Street and Environs: The Collected Works of Marita Bonner.* Boston. Beacon Press, 1987.
Burrill, Mary ("Mamie"). *They That Sit in Darkness* [play]. *Birth Control Review* (Sept. 1919). Reprinted in Hatch and Shine, *Black Theatre U.S.A.* 1974.
Cowdery, Mae. *We Lift Our Voices and Other Poems.* Philadelphia: Alpress, 1936.
Dunbar-Nelson, Alice. *The Works of Alice Dunbar-Nelson.* 2 vols. Ed. Gloria T. Hull. New York: Oxford University Press, 1988.
Fauset, Jessie Redmon
 A. *Novels*
   The Chinaberry Tree. New York: Frederick A. Stokes, 1932.
   Comedy: American Style. New York: Frederick A. Stokes, 1933.
   Plum Bun. New York: Frederick A. Stokes, 1929.
   There Is Confusion. New York: Boni & Liveright, 1924.
 B. *Stories*
   "Double Trouble." *The Crisis* (Aug. 1923): 155–59; (Sept. 1923): 205–209.
   "Emmy." *The Crisis* (Dec. 1912): 79–87; (Jan. 1913): 134–42.
   "Mary Elizabeth." *The Crisis* (Dec. 1919): 51–56.
   "The Sleeper Wakes." *The Crisis* (Aug. 1920): 168–73; (Sept. 1920): 226–29; (Oct. 1920): 267–74.

"There Was One Time." *The Crisis* (April 1917): 272–77; (May 1917): 11–15.

C. *Poems*

"Again It Is September." *The Crisis* (Sept. 1917): 248.

"Courage, He Said." *Double Blossoms: Helen Keller Anthology.* Ed. Edna Porter. New York: Copeland, 1931, 39.

"Dance Souvenance." *The Crisis* (May 1920): 42.

"Dilworth Road Revisited." *The Crisis* (Aug. 1922): 167.

"Here's April." *The Crisis* (April 1924): 277.

"La Vie C'est La Vie." *The Crisis* (July 1922): 124.

"Oriflamme." *The Crisis* (Jan 1920): 128.

"Rain Fugue." *The Crisis* (Aug. 1924): 144.

"Rencontre." *The Crisis* (Jan. 1924): 122.

"The Return." *The Crisis* (Jan. 1919): 118.

"Ronceau." *The Crisis* (April 1912): 252.

"Song for a Lost Comrade." *The Crisis* (Nov. 1922): 22.

"Stars in Alabama." *The Crisis* (Jan. 1928): 14.

D. *Essays and Reviews*

"As to Books." *The Crisis* (June 1922): 66–68.

"'Batouala' Is Translated." *The Crisis* (Sept. 1922): 218–19.

"Brawley's Social History of the American Negro." *The Crisis* (April 1922): 260.

"Dark Algiers the White." *The Crisis* (April 1925): 16–20.

"The Enigma of the Sorbonne." *The Crisis* (March 1925): 216–19.

"The Eucalyptus Tree: A Reverie of Rome, the Catacombs, Christianity, and the Moving Beauty of Italy." *The Crisis* (Jan. 1926): 116–17.

"The Gift of Laughter." *The New Negro.* Ed. Alain Locke. New York: 1925.

"Henry Ossawa Tanner." *The Crisis* (April 1924): 255–58.

"Impressions of the Second Pan-African Congress." *The Crisis* (Nov. 1921): 12–18.

"In Talladega," *The Crisis* (Feb. 1928): 47–48.

[Review of *Le Petit Roi de Chimerie* by René Maran], *The Crisis* (Nov. 1921): 12–18.

"Looking Backward." *The Crisis* (Jan. 1922): 125–26.

"The Montessori Method." *The Crisis* (July 1912): 136–38.

"My House and a Glimpse of My Life Therein." *The Crisis* (July 1914): 143–45.

"Nationalism and Egypt." *The Crisis* (April 1920): 310–16.

"The New Books." *The Crisis* (Feb. 1924): 174–77.

"New Literature of the Negro." *The Crisis* (June 1920): 78–83.

"No End of Books." *The Crisis* (March 1922): 208–10.

"Nostalgia." *The Crisis* (Aug. 1921): 154–58.

"Notes on the New Books." With Alain Locke. *The Crisis* (Feb. 1923): 161–65.

"On the Book Shelf." *The Crisis* (June 1921): 60–64.

"Our Book Shelf." *The Crisis* (March 1926): 238–40.

"Out of the West." *The Crisis* (Nov. 1923): 11–18.

"Pastures New." *The Crisis* (Sept. 1920): 224–26.

"Rank Imposes Obligation: A Biographical Essay on Martin R. Delany." *The Crisis* (Nov. 1926): 9–13.

"Saint-George, Chevalier of France," *The Crisis* (May 1921): 9–12.

"Sunday Afternoon." *The Crisis* (Feb. 1922): 162–64.

"The Symbolism of Bert Williams." *The Crisis* (May 1922): 12–15.

"The Thirteenth Biennial of the N.A.C.W." *The Crisis* (Oct. 1922): 257–60.

"This Way to the Flew Market." *The Crisis* (Feb. 1925): 161–63.

"Tracing Shadows." *The Crisis* (Sept. 1915): 247–51.

"What Europe Thought of the Pan-African Congress." *The Crisis* (Dec. 1921): 60–67

"When Christmas Comes." *The Crisis* (Dec. 1922): 61–63.

"'Wings for God's Chillun': The Story of Burghardt Du Bois." *The World Tomorrow* (August 1929): 333–36. Published Anonymously.

"The 'Y' Conference at Talladega." *The Crisis* (Sept. 1923): 213–16.

"Yarrow Revisited." *The Crisis* (Jan. 1925): 107–109.

E. *Translations*

"Kirongozi." By G. D. Perier. *The Crisis* (March 1924): 208–209.

"The Pool." By Amédée Brun. *The Crisis* (Sept. 1921): 205.

"La Question des Noirs aux Etats-Unis." By Frank L. Schoell. *The Crisis* (June 1924): 83–86.

"The Sun of Brittany." *The Crisis* (Nov. 1927): 303.

"To a Foreign Maid." By Oswald Durand. *The Crisis* (Feb. 1923): 158.

"The Treasure of the Poor." By Jean Richepin. *The Crisis* (Dec. 1917): 63.

Grimké, Angelina Weld. "The Black Finger." *Opportunity* (Nov. 1923): 343.

———. "Little Grey Dreams." *Opportunity* (Jan. 1924): 20.

———. *Rachel.* Boston: Cornhill Co., 1921.

Hurston, Zora Neale

A. *Novels*

Jonah's Gourd Vine. Philadelphia: J. B. Lippincott, 1934.

Moses, Man of the Mountain. Philadelphia: J. B. Lippincott, 1939.

Seraph on the Suwanee. New York: Charles Scribner's Sons. 1948.

Their Eyes Were Watching God. Philadelphia: J. B. Lippincott, 1937.

B. *Nonfiction Books*

Dust Tracks on a Road. Philadelphia: J. B. Lippincott, 1942.

Mules and Men. Philadelphia: J. B. Lippincott, 1935.

Tell My Horse. Philadelphia: J. B. Lippincott, 1938.

C. *Drama*

Color Struck: A Play. Fire!! 1 (Nov. 1926): 7–15.

The Fiery Chariot. 1933. Unpublished play in one act. Zora Neale Hurston Collection, Rare Books and Manuscripts, University of Florida Library.

The First One: A Play. In *Ebony and Topaz*, ed. Charles S. Johnson, pp. 53–57. New York: National Urban League, 1927.

Mule Bone: A Comedy of Negro Life. Play in three acts written with Langston Hughes, 1931. New York: HarperCollins, 1991.

D. *Short Fiction*

"Black Death." Unpublished. 1925. Charles S. Johnson Papers, Special Collections, Fisk University Library.

"The Bone of Contention," in eds. George Houston Bass and Henry Louis Gates, *Mule Bone: A Comedy of Negro Life*. New York: Harper-Collins, 1991. 25–39.

"The Book of Harlem." *Spunk: The Selected Short Stories of Zora Neale Hurston*. Berkeley: Turtle Island Foundation, 1985. 75–81.

"Cock Robin, Beale Street." *Southern Literary Messenger* 3 (July 1941): 321–23.

"Conscience of the Court." *Saturday Evening Post*. 18 March 1950: 22–23, 112–22.

"Drenched in Light." *Opportunity* 2 (Dec. 1924): 371–74. Reprinted with the title "Isis" in *Spunk: The Short Stories of Zora Neale Hurston*. Berkeley: Turtle Island Foundation, 1985. 9–18.

"The Fire and the Cloud." *Challenge* 1 (Sept. 1934): 10–14.

"The Gilded Six-Bits." *Story* 3 (Aug. 1933): 60–70.

"John Redding Goes to Sea." *Stylus* 1 (May 1921): 11–22. Reprinted in *Opportunity* 4 (Jan. 1926): 16–21.

"Magnolia Flower." *Spokesman* (July 1925): 26–29.

"Muttsey." *Opportunity* 4 (Aug. 1926): 246–50.

"Spunk." *Opportunity* 3 (June 1925), 171–73. Reprinted in *The New Negro*. Edited by Alain Locke. New York: Albert & Charles Boni, 1925.

"Sweat." *Fire!!* 1 (Nov. 1926): 40–45. Reprinted in *I Love Myself*. Edited by Alice Walker. New York: Feminist Press, 1979. 197–20.

"Story in Harlem Slang." *American Mercury* 55 (July 1942): 84–96.

E. *Nonfiction Articles and Essays*

"Art and Such." 1938. In *Reading Black, Reading Feminist: A Critical Anthology*. Ed. Henry Louis Gates. New York: Meridian, 1990. 21–26.

"Back to the Middle Ages or How to Become a Peasant in the United States." Unpublished. n.d. (probably written in 1947). 18 pp. Rare Book and Manuscript Library, Columbia University.

"Characteristics of Negro Expression." In *Negro: An Anthology*, edited by Nancy Cunard, 39–46. London: Wishart, 1934.

"Conversions and Visions." In *Negro: An Anthology*, 47–49.

"Crazy for this Democracy." *Negro Digest* 4 (Dec. 1945): 45–48.

"Cudjo's Own Story of the Last African Slaver." *Journal of Negro History* 12 (Oct. 1927): 648–63.

"Dance Songs and Tales from the Bahamas." *Journal of American Folklore* 43 (July–Sept. 1930): 294–312.

"The Eatonville Anthology." *Messenger* 8 (Sept., Oct., Nov. 1926): 261–62, 297, 319, 332.

"The Florida Negro." Manuscript prepared by Hurston and others for the Federal Writers Project. 1938. Florida Historical Society Papers, University of South Florida Library.
"Turpentine," 3 pp.
"Folklore," 14 pp.
"The Ocee Riot," 5 pp.
"Eatonville When You Look at It," 2 pp.
"The Sanctified Church," 6 pp.
"New Children's Games," 9 pp.
"Negro Mythical Places," 5 pp.
"High John de Conquer." *American Mercury* 57 (Oct. 1943): 450–58.
"Hoodoo in America." *Journal of American Folklore* 44 (Oct.–Dec. 1931): 317–418.
"How It Feels to Be Colored Me." *World Tomorrow* 11 (May 1928): 215–16.
"The Hue and Cry about Howard University." *Messenger* 7 (Sept. 1925): 315–19, 338.
"I Saw Negro Votes Peddled." *American Legion Magazine* 49 (Nov. 1950): 12–13, 54–57, 59–60.
"The Last Slave Ship." *American Mercury* 58 (Mar. 1944): 351–58.
"Lawrence of the River." *Saturday Evening Post*, 5 Sept. 1942: 18, 55–57.
"The Lost Keys of Glory." Unpublished. n.d. (probably written in 1947). 16 pp. Rare Book and Manuscript Library, Columbia University.
"Mother Catharine." In *Negro: An Anthology*, 54–57.
"Mourner's Bench, Communist Line: Why the Negro Won't Buy Communism." *American Legion Magazine* 50 (June 1951): 14–15, 55–60.
"My Most Humiliating Jim Crow Experience." *Negro Digest* 2 (June 1944): 25–26.
"A Negro Voter Sizes Up Taft." *Saturday Evening Post*, 8 Dec. 1951: 29, 150.
"Negroes without Self-Pity." *American Mercury* 57 (Nov. 1943): 601–603.
"The 'Pet Negro' System." American Mercury 56 (March 1943): 593–600.
"Possum or Pig." *Forum* 76 (Sept. 1926): 465.
"The Rise of the Begging Joints." *American Mercury* 60 (Mar. 1945): 288–94.
"The Sermon." In *Negro: An Anthology*, 50–54.
"Shouting." In *Negro: An Anthology*, 49–50.
"Spirituals and Neo-Spirituals." In *Negro: An Anthology*, 359–61.
"Stories of Conflict." Review of *Uncle Tom's Children. Saturday Review*, 2 April 1938: 42.
[The Trial of Ruby McCollum]. In William Bradford Huie, *Ruby McCollum: Woman in the Suwanne Jail*. New York: Dutton, 1956. 89–101.
"Uncle Monday." In *Negro: An Anthology*, 57–61.
"What White Publishers Won't Print." *Negro Digest* 8 (Apr. 1950): 85–89.

Johnson, Georgia Douglas. *An Autumn Love Cycle.* With an introduction by Alain Locke. New York: Harold Vinal, Ltd., 1928.

———. *Bronze: A Book of Verse.* With an introduction by W. E. B. Du Bois. Boston: B. J. Brimmer, 1922.

———. *The Heart of a Woman and Other Poems.* With an introduction by William Stanley Braithwaite. Boston: Cornhill Co., 1918.

———. *Plumes: Folk Tragedy.* New York: French, 1927.

———. *Share My World: A Book of Poems.* Self-published. Washington, D.C., 1962.

Johnson, Helene. "Bottled." *Caroling Dusk*, ed. Countee Cullen. New York: Harper, 1927.

———. "Fulfillment." *Opportunity* (June 1926): 194.

———. "Magalu." *Caroling Dusk.*

———. "Poem." *Caroling Dusk.*

———. "Sonnet to a Negro in Harlem." *Caroling Dusk.*

———. "Summer Matures." *Caroling Dusk.*

———. "What Do I Care for Morning." *Caroling Dusk.*

Larsen, Nella. "Danish Fun." *The Brownies' Book* (July 1920): 219.

———. "Freedom." *Young's Magazine*, April 1926. 241–43. Published under the pseudonym Allen Semi.

———. *Passing.* New York: Alfred A. Knopf, 1929.

———. "Playtime: Three Scandinavian Games." *The Brownies' Book* (June 1920): 191–92.

———. *Quicksand.* New York: Alfred A. Knopf, 1928.

———. "Sanctuary." *Forum* 83 (Jan. 1930): 15–18.

———. "The Wrong Man." *Young's Magazine*, January 1926. 243–46. Published under the pseudonym, Allen Semi.

Newsome, Mary Effie Lee. *Gladiola Gardens: Poems of Outdoors and Indoors for Second Grade Readers.* Illustrated by Lois Maillou Jones. Washington, D.C.: Associated Publishers, 1940.

West, Dorothy. *The Living Is Easy.* Boston: Houghton Mifflin, 1948.

———. "The Typewriter." *Opportunity* (July 1926): 220–23, 234.

INDEX

CHERYL A. WALL is Associate Professor of English at Rutgers University. She edited *Changing Our Own Words: Essays on Criticism, Theory, and Writing by Black Women.*